ESSAYS ON
SCHUBERT

By the same author

★

SCHUBERT'S VARIATIONS
CHOPIN: An Index of his Works in Chronological Order
SCHUBERT: A Critical Biography

Schwind's 'Schubert-Abend bei Josef von Spaun'

ESSAYS
ON SCHUBERT

BY

MAURICE J. E. BROWN

MACMILLAN
London · Melbourne · Toronto

ST MARTIN'S PRESS
New York
1966

MACMILLAN AND COMPANY LIMITED
Little Essex Street London WC2
also Bombay Calcutta Madras Melbourne

THE MACMILLAN COMPANY OF CANADA LIMITED
70 Bond Street Toronto 2

ST MARTIN'S PRESS INC
175 Fifth Avenue New York NY 10010

Library of Congress catalog card number 65-22791

PRINTED IN GREAT BRITAIN

To

IGNAZ WEINMANN

CONTENTS

LIST OF ILLUSTRATIONS

PREFACE

Two of these fourteen essays on Schubert are not entirely new: the first part of 'Schubert and the Kärntnerthor Theater' appeared in the *Musical Times* for May 1959 as 'Schubert's early association with the Kärntnerthor Theater', and 'The Story of the "Trauerwalzer" ' has been enlarged and revised from a short article entitled 'Schubert's Trauerwalzer', which appeared in the (unhappily) extinct *Monthly Musical Record* for July–August 1960. My thanks are due to the editors of both journals for permission to use these two articles.

For permission to reproduce the various manuscripts, portraits, and sketches I am indebted to the directorates of the following institutions and offer them my warmest thanks: The Trustees of the British Museum; Dr. Hedwig Mitringer, Gesellschaft der Musikfreunde, Vienna; Dr. Walter Koschatzky, Albertina, Vienna; Dr. Franz Glück, Director of the City Museums, Vienna ; Dr. William Lichtenwanger, Library of Congress, Washington; Dr. V. Féderov, Conservatoire de Musique, Paris. I wish to thank particularly five people who have not only given me permission to reproduce material in their possession, but have also generously provided me with information about that material: Dr. Wilhelm Raab, Burlington, U.S.A.; Dr. Virginia Cysarz, Mönichkirchen, Austria; Dr. Curt Sluzewski, London; Mr. Alan Tyson, London; and Dr. Rudolf Floersheim, Aarau.

The illustrations numbered 1, 3, 6, 8, 9, 10, and 12 have never been published before; nor, to my knowledge, has the copy of the 'Trauerwalzer' written out by Schubert for Anselm Hütten-brenner been hitherto reproduced, although its companion piece, the copy he made for Ignaz Assmayr, is frequently quoted.

The catalogues given in the essays on the sonatas, the dance-music manuscripts, and the posthumously published songs are by no means mere summaries of information to be found in

O. E. Deutsch's *Thematic Catalogue* of Schubert's works; they supplement and amplify to a considerable extent the necessarily brief facts given by Deutsch. They also correct errors, for in the years since the *Thematic Catalogue* appeared (1951) the work of scholars, including that of Deutsch himself, has brought to light new information about the publication and manuscripts of Schubert's works.

Marlborough   M. J. E. B.
November 1964

I

The Music

DRAFTING THE MASTERPIECE

'IN truth, it seems to me as if, through the very incompleteness of the work, the scattered, half-finished indications, I became at once personally acquainted with your brother more closely than I should have done through a complete piece. It seems as if I saw him there, working in his room, and this joy I owe to your unexpectedly great kindness and generosity.'

These words of Mendelssohn's come from a letter written to Ferdinand Schubert on 22 March 1845. Ferdinand, grateful for Mendelssohn's championship of his brother's music, and particularly for the production and publication in Leipzig of the great C major Symphony, had sent him as a gift the manuscript of the Symphony in E, which Schubert had sketched and abandoned in August 1821. Mendelssohn's remarks aptly introduce the purpose of this essay. In glancing at the sketches that Schubert has left for a number of his masterpieces, perhaps we too may see him working in his room, so to speak, and become more closely acquainted with him.

There is this difference. The sketches to be considered here can be placed by the side of the finished masterpiece; they have been chosen for that purpose. The symphony sketches that Mendelssohn received had never been worked over by Schubert; they remain a fascinating relic, like a half-finished piece of sculpture that touched by another hand would lose its interest. When Schubert abandoned an instrumental movement, leaving it incomplete, and the Symphony in E is incomplete in all four of its movements, there was a very good reason for it: the movement was not, in his opinion, worth finishing. Several of Schubert's instrumental works, planned in four movements, are incomplete in a different fashion from the incompleteness of the Symphony in E; the String Quartet in C minor (1820), the Symphony in B minor (1822), and the Sonata in C major (1825) are examples. In these works certain movements are complete to the last detail, showing Schubert's satisfaction with them. The finished movements of the above three unfinished works are, in fact, supremely fine manifestations of his genius. It is the slow movement, or the scherzo, or the finale, which is started, shows hesitancy and indecision, and is abandoned. Some of the material left in this raw, half-finished condition may seem to us to have promise and high interest, but on the whole we probably feel that the composer was right in relinquishing his task, in refusing to go on and 'excite the membrane when the sense is cool'. On one of his manuscripts, the sketch for the song 'Nähe des Geliebten', he has cancelled his music and scribbled the words 'gilt nicht' — 'won't do'; that verdict must have been in his mind whenever he threw aside a movement that, however buoyantly it started, refused to remain airborne. In the case of a few movements, in particular those belonging to certain sonatas of 1817 and 1818, the incompleteness is more apparent than real; they are exceptions to the general rule; Schubert considered them complete. They are written as far as the recapitulation, and if the opportunity for performance or publication had presented itself, little would remain to be done except copying out.

The attraction of the autograph manuscript sketch is a strong one and made up of subtly mixed elements; there is something of the sacred relic about it, something of the keepsake, something of the artifact; that is to say, it arouses feelings compounded of veneration, affection, and curiosity. To the lover of the composer's music it represents a material link between him and the object of his affection; to the student a source of inquiry; to the editor a correlative text. But there are imponderable and perhaps unidentifiable emotions beyond these. Eric Blom once wrote:

There may be no resemblance between a composer's features and those of his music — we must in fact beware of seeking it — but once an auditive impression has been strengthened by a visual one, it is much more likely to remain. A composer's autograph has almost as strong an associative effect. One need be no graphologist to see in a signature or in a manuscript music-page something of a man's character and, it follows, the character of his work.[1]

[1] Preface to Georg Kinsky's *History of Music in Pictures*, English ed., London, 1930.

1. First page of Schubert's draft for the Pianoforte Trio in E flat major, D. 929

2. From the sketch for the Fantasia in F minor, D. 940

Blom is here concerned naturally with all manuscripts, fair copies as well as rough drafts. But Schubert's character, and also his creative mind, can be more keenly assessed if we examine his sketches as well as his finished autographs.

His personality is revealed, and it is not too fanciful, if we spend hours brooding over the actual manuscript to which he gave his whole being, to claim that the man himself emerges from the pages; Mendelssohn was right when he wrote: 'I became at once personally acquainted with your brother . . .'. And examination of Schubert's pages reinforces the words that Richard Capell once wrote: 'The mere look of a composer's pages is characteristic. The first glance at Schubert suggests a rippling movement, and by the side of the rippling a flowering. Or it is the opening of a window — the air is stirred.'[1]

Schubert's autograph sketches present a man to whom music was life — the overflowing fullness of the musical writing, with its detailed paraphernalia of grace-notes, accentuation, dynamics, and phrasing, was not penned by one who was doing a mere duty. Compare them with those of another composer — Chopin: he hated the task of writing his music and used every possible contraction and labour-saving device in the performing of it; he relinquished the duty to any friend who would undertake it. Schubert's penmanship suggests again and again exaltation and passion, excitement and pleasure; it becomes completely stilted and commonplace when he is merely filling in or copying out recapitulatory episodes — the difference is unmistakable.

But there is another aspect of his sketches, and it is this one with which we are concerned. They show his first impulses at work and how his shaping mind worked on them and brought them to their perfected end. This is the more profitable pursuit, for in that shaping, the proliferations of his first ideas, the growth of that inner logic, which is loosely called 'form', and which embodied his overwhelming need and desire for creative expression, we are helped to understand that universal, but often inarticulate, love and admiration felt for Schubert's music.

[1] *Schubert's Songs*, London, 1928; 2nd ed., 1957.

The idea of a consideration of Schubert's sketches and drafts for his finished masterpieces would until only a matter of forty years ago have seemed incredible. In the first edition of Grove's *Dictionary of Music and Musicians* there is an entry called 'Sketches, Sketch-books, Sketching', by W. S. Rockstro, a pupil of Mendelssohn's and a friend and collaborator of Grove's. The article is a well-written, if superficial, examination of the sketches of various composers — a good idea, but dropped from subsequent editions. Rockstro's remarks on Schubert are quoted here, not at all with a derisory intent, although they are in fact widely off the mark, but as indicating the opinion of musicians everywhere in the 1880's. As an outcome of its formulation in Rockstro's article the opinion was firmly established in England, and echoes of his opinions, and of his very words, are found in the Schubert literature for the next fifty years. Here is the relevant extract:

> Schubert's method of working differed entirely both from Mozart's and Beethoven's. He neither prepared a perfect mental copy, like the former; nor worked out his ideas, as did the latter, from a primordial germ; but wrote almost always on the spur of the moment, committing to paper, as fast as his pen could trace them, the ideas which presented themselves to his mind at the instant of composition — proceeding, in fact, as ordinary men do when they sit down to write a letter. This being the case — and there is ample proof of it — we are not surprised to find that he was no Sketcher, though we cannot but regard with astonishment the remarkable freedom of his Scores from evidence of afterthought. It is true, we do sometimes find important modifications of the first idea. [Rockstro here deals with the manuscripts of 'Erlkönig' and the great C major Symphony.] But, these cases are far from common. As a general rule, he committed his ideas to paper under the influence of uncontrollable inspiration, and then cast his work aside, to make room for newer manifestations of creative power. By far the greater number of his MSS. remain, untouched, exactly in the condition in which they first saw the light.[1]

Rockstro had based his opinion largely on the descriptions given to him by Grove, who had examined in Vienna numerous Schubert manuscripts, either in the offices of C. A. Spina, the

---

[1]Grove, *Dictionary*, 1st ed., vol. iii (London, 1883), p. 531.

then owner of Diabelli's music-publishing business, or in the rooms of Schubert's nephew Eduard Schneider. In every case they were fair copies, and it seems, apart from anything else, a little naïve of Rockstro to have assumed, without further thought, that these manuscripts were necessarily Schubert's first drafts; as a composer himself he might have realized that fair copies would be made for publishers and that such copies rarely if ever show after-thoughts and alterations. But the crux of the matter is in the fact that at the period when he penned his article the existence of Schubert's sketches was entirely unknown to the public at large; they were, indeed, only just becoming known to a small number of interested scholars and collectors, and any comprehensive idea of their extent and number still lay in the future — in the distant future too.

The reason for this general unawareness is not hard to find. A large part of Schubert's works were still unpublished in 1883. The piles of manuscripts handed on from Ferdinand Schubert had been turned over by many hands; those sold to Diabelli by his agents and employees, those still unsold by Ferdinand himself, and by his heir, his nephew Schneider. At various times catalogues, invariably incomplete, had been compiled — by Ferdinand, Aloys Fuchs, Anton Schindler, Kreissle — but they were chiefly concerned with the finished works, both instrumental and vocal, and sketches or unfinished compositions were understandably omitted. Occasionally the more fragmentary of Schubert's manuscripts had accidentally remained with various friends — Schober, Gahy, or Spaun — or even in the homes of people he had visited at Graz or Steyr. No wonder, since the full tally of his finished works was only hazily known, that the existence and enumeration of the many sketches and fragments was not even guessed at. The passage of such papers from hand to hand until their ultimate destination to-day can be given only in connection with the works to be looked at in this essay, but the general channels are indicated above.

To return to Rockstro's article: he deals fully with the sketched Symphony in E, for this manuscript seemed to prove his point.[1] It

[1] The manuscript was at that time in Grove's possession; it had been given to him by Mendelssohn's brother, Paul, in 1868.

is, in fact, no true sketch, and Schubert never used the scheme at any other time either before or after 1821. He did attempt, in this one case, to compose a symphony as, in Rockstro's words, ordinary men do when writing a letter. Each page is looked upon as a full symphony score, and in every bar from the first to the last something is written — the first violin part, the first flute part, scraps of string accompaniment, or harmonic filling-in chords on brass or woodwind.

In truth [concludes Rockstro] it exactly represents a canvas, fully prepared to receive the future painting; and may, therefore, be fairly accepted as evidence that Schubert was not addicted to the practice of sketching, a conclusion which is strengthened by the Score of the unfinished Symphony in B minor, No. 8, the first two Movements of which are completely finished, while, of the remainder, nine bars only were ever committed to writing.

It is in this final sentence that Rockstro, not knowing the facts, draws so completely false a conclusion. For we have, preserved as precious relics, the very sketches that Schubert, as was his usual practice, made for the B minor Symphony, and it is with these sketches that we make a start.

They are devised as a score for piano and are themselves incomplete, for the first few pages are lost and the music begins in the middle of the recapitulation section, at what is bar 250 in the full score. We have an immediate indication of the refining powers of his craftsmanship, since the point reached in bar 250 is the approach to the second subject. The long-held note on the horns, which melts, as it were, into the cadence on horns and bassoons, was originally a rather tedious, threefold repetition of this cadence. The second subject then follows, in D major, first on the cellos, then echoed by the first violins. But the falling phrases, which extend the melody to a chord of F sharp major, and which create the mood of complete withdrawal, were afterthoughts, absent from the first conception in the sketch. The subsequent passage was entirely recast, not so much in external matters as in tonality and balance. Although there are the same alternations between outbursts of the full orchestra and passages of imitation based on the second subject, as in the final form of the symphony movement, the extended phrases mentioned above have brought about a complete change of plan. In the sketch the second subject has ended in D major. The *fortissimo*, which follows after the bar's rest, has this form:

Example 1

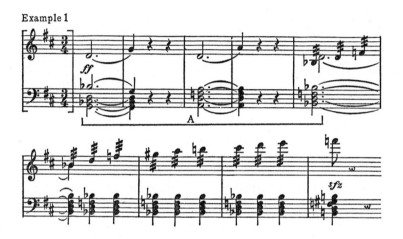

In the final version the second subject ends on a B minor cadence, and presents the *fortissimo* passage above with chords of E minor, B minor, and G major, but it preserves the ascending minor third (marked 'A'), which recalls the opening theme of the movement. The music continues as in the sketch, transposed a minor third down, until Schubert eventually picks up his original ideas and original key, with the climax in B major.

The sketched movement continues with the attractive passage of imitation based on the first two bars of the second subject, except that there it is merely marked for repetition, with no indication of its final orchestral dress, the first appearance for the strings, the second for the woodwind. There is, however, merely a hint of the marvellous coda, and that a plain, plagal cadence. The later visitation of an idea to superimpose on those bare chords the rising minor third of the opening theme is one of pure genius.

Example 2

Schubert's first idea was to end the movement with a B major chord, sustained *pianissimo* for three bars. His rejection of this major-key ending is entirely justified in view of the prevailing mood of the movement. Yet it would have both indicated and justified the choice of key for his slow movement. The remarkable and unprecedented choice of E major for a classical symphony in B minor loses some of its startling quality if the sketch is borne in mind.

The sketch for the second movement is fully preserved. It is, in all but a dozen or so details, identical with the Andante con moto as it exists in the final score, even to such necessities as harmonic schemes, accompaniment figures, counterpoints to the main themes, and occasional orchestral indications. But those dozen or so details, either latent in his mind as he penned the sketch or flashing into it as he completed the score, are every one worth looking at.

The first two occur at the start of the second section; this is introduced by the three simple, but supremely effective, notes for the first violins alone. In the sketch the clarinet solo in C sharp minor enters immediately they have finished. When Schubert reached the point in the recapitulation, however, he clearly felt that a short prelude, introducing the syncopated chord accompaniment, was preferable; when he composed the final version, this two-bar prelude was reintroduced into the exposition. The second point concerns the famous counterpoint on the first violins played beneath the oboe solo and provides the only example in which Schubert simplified the abundance of his first idea: it remains a moot point though as to whether we have not lost a little here:

Example 3

A few bars farther on the oboe continues the melody in D flat major with the syncopated string accompaniment fully indicated. But that wonderful touch of imitation on the cellos (bar 85 onwards), the first stirrings of life, as it were, after the tranced vision of the previous moments, appears neither here, in the sketch, nor later in the recapitulation; it belongs to the work on the final score. The two-bar phrase, consisting of short, falling arpeggios, appears once only, for the oboe. In the sketched recapitulation it is played twice, by clarinet, then flute. Only in the completed score do we find the threefold repetition, in both exposition and recapitulation. At the start of the coda there occurs a remarkable passage, which, we can see in retrospection, introduces a false note. It is a cerebral idea, a playing with cross-rhythms that does not come off. The *pizzicato* bass of the horns-and-bassoons chords is subjected to the following distortion:

Example 4

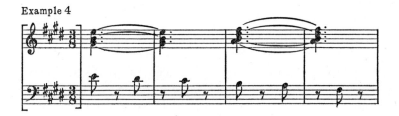

Schubert obliterated it completely when he came to the finished conception, and instead substituted a far finer and completely spontaneous prolongation, which does not smack in the least of the oil-lamp, but springs from the same overflowing poetry as the rest of the movement; the violin arpeggio continues its song with an exquisite extension:

Example 5

8va bassa

and the wind chords, with the *pizzicato* bass, balance the extension with an equally exquisite one of their own:

Example 6

The famous harmonic subtleties, introduced by the sustained notes on the first violins, are fully sketched; only the arpeggio enrichments of the cadences that close the coda were added by Schubert when he devised the finished movement.

The last pages of the sketches contain Schubert's outline of a Scherzo in B minor, with the mere beginning of a Trio in G major. The movement has been severely judged, and occasionally its inferiority has been put forward as the reason for the unfinished condition of the symphony: Schubert's realization of the weakness of his Scherzo, it is suggested, led him to throw up his task. This is unconvincing. The full score contains the first page of a fully scored version of the sketched Scherzo, and the true reason for its relinquishment at this point is beyond conjecture. One point may be made. If this Scherzo had been completed, a mere scoring of the sketch, and had shown none of those incredibly fine afterthoughts that, in Schubert, so frequently lift the ordinariness of his first ideas into the highest poetry, and if, on completion, the movement had not shown the inevitability and authority of the two preceding movements, it would have been a unique instance in all his major works, from 1819 onwards, of an inferior Scherzo. Schubert's third movements are invariably full of his most attractive ideas, even when they display, to borrow a term of Sir Donald Tovey's, a 'grotesquerie', as in the Scherzo of the Grand Duo in C major, op. 140. It is impossible to assess from these first jottings exactly what Schubert would finally have made of them. The theme, strongly conceived, is based on a favourite Schubert pattern; in straightforward terms one could say, perhaps, that he balances the upper half of the scale (subdominant) against the lower (tonic); a parallel instance can be found at the start of the D minor String Quartet:

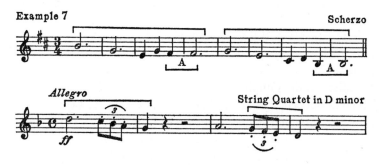

Example 7   Scherzo

Allegro   String Quartet in D minor

The weakness in the Scherzo theme, and the weakness pervades the whole rapid conception, lies in the *tum-tum* effect at the end of each phrase (marked 'A' in Example 7); it gives a stodginess, an unyielding quality, to the progress of the music, besides bringing it to a standstill every few bars. The first nine bars only are orchestrated, but the theme in this final version, although improved by a slight change, does not get rid of the basic rhythmic weakness. Unless Schubert intended to modify it in the course of the movement, it is not easy to see how even his alchemical powers could have transmuted this particular aspect of his Scherzo. This is not to go back on the view put forward above, that in ways now unforeseeable, by details of counterpoint and orchestral colours he would have succeeded in creating out of the unpromising material a worth-while movement.

Equally full and ample sketches exist for the Pianoforte Trio in E flat major, op. 100. The eleven pages contain preliminary work on the first three movements; sketches for the finale are not preserved with them. The first page is headed 'Trio' and carries the date 'Nov 1827' and the composer's signature. These manuscript sketches were for many years in the possession of Brahms, who bought them from Schubert's nephew Eduard Schneider; after Brahms's death they were acquired by the Vienna Gesellschaft der Musikfreunde. For the most part they show that Schubert's first conception needed only a final polish to become the music of the Trio as we know it, but in several cases the subsequent changes and reshapings are radical enough to provide greater interest than even the corresponding sketches for the 'Unfinished' Symphony.

The exposition of the opening theme was unchanged except for two small additions; the interpolation of an extra bar to serve as a prelude for the entry of a subsidiary theme reminds us of a similar expedient in the symphony sketches. But after the main theme has been announced, by bar 23, there is a remarkable instance of fresh thinking. The first sketch, from bar 24 onwards, was conceived in an entirely different tonality. The *fortissimo* passage, commencing with a sudden shift of key, was originally written in C flat major. The long trill on the strings, with chromatic scales on the piano, was based on D flat (becoming C sharp) and steered the music into F sharp minor; in this key the whole of the second subject was first written. It concludes with a violin cadence in B flat major, and at that point the piano continues thus:

Example 8

The passage is repeated by the strings in D minor and B flat major, the triplet runs in imitation following in the piano in E flat major. Eventually we reach the restatement of the main theme, in G minor, in this form:

Example 9

From there on the sketch traces the outline of the course of the movement as it stands in the final version up to the double bar.

What led to the modification and developments of these first primitive conceptions? The transpositions seem, at first glance, almost arbitrary — one scheme is as good as the other; bars 24–27 are raised a fifth from C flat major to G flat major; bars 28–66 are raised a fourth, the trill now sounding on G flat and F sharp, and the second subject occurring in B minor. The passage concludes in E flat major. But the changes are, of course, not arbitrary; they are part of an original and Schubertian use of tonality. However wayward his tonality may seem in his exposition sections, he is invariably orthodox in concluding the section according to standard classical rule — in the dominant key and, in this movement, in B flat major. His fondness for 'Neapolitan' relationships suggested B minor for the second subject, as a colourful and unconventional approach to the key of B flat major; it is now possible to see why he preceded the advent of the second subject by the long passage in G flat major (enharmonically identical with F sharp major, the dominant key of B minor). Moreover, the key of G flat is related to the main key of E flat in what one might call a Schubertian manner: the shift to keys a minor third apart — as are E flat and G flat — is one of his basic procedures. The underlying tonality of the exposition section can be seen to arise from its first crude beginnings to this finished pattern:

E flat major

G flat major = F sharp major

B minor

(G minor: C minor: F major)

B flat major

The evolution of the subsidiary theme in the second-subject group is no less interesting. The triplets in imitation at the end of Example 8 showed Schubert how to give much greater significance to the octaves at the start; in the final form they generate the attractive theme played on the piano (bars 67 et seq.).

Example 10

Even this only hints at the variety and charm of the melodies that grow from the germ that first occurred to Schubert.

The first part of the development section is preserved from the sketch; at the point where the music modulates to F major the sketch breaks off. A small but significant change was later made in the melody; both variants are given here:

Example 11

The slow movement exists as a complete and very full first draft, covering nine closely written sides of music paper. It is, in my opinion, the most fascinating and important of all Schubert's manifold sketches. To deal adequately with these embryo ideas and motifs would unfortunately entail an impossibly large number of musical quotations; one day, it is hoped, the sketched movement will be printed in full so that it can be placed side by side with the final version in op. 100. Only then can the interested observer fully appreciate the marvellous — no less marvellous if partly unconscious — power of Schubert's genius working on the fertile ideas that first came into his mind. All one can do here is to analyse the sketched movement in words and describe how it was modified and embellished to become the flowing perfection of the profound and impassioned Andante con moto in the final version. The sections of the finished movement are clearly defined, and a descriptive analysis is therefore possible, since they can be given a conveniently short title for the purpose of reference. Here is a form-analysis of the slow movement with the episodes called by these terms:

A   Bars   1–40:   'Main theme (C minor)'
B   Bars   41–66:   'Arpeggio theme (E flat)'
C   Bars   67–81:   'Fortissimo Chord theme (E flat)'
A' Bars   82–128: 'Main theme + development (C minor)'
B' Bars   129–57: 'Arpeggio theme (C major)'
C' Bars   158–95: 'Fortissimo Chord theme (A major)'
A" Bars   196–212: 'Main theme + coda, *un poco più lento* (C minor)'

It will be seen that Schubert's Andante con moto is in simple rondo form, but, remarkably enough, this simplicity and in-evitability of structure is an evolution from a more chaotic primary scheme. This is given here, using the terms of reference from the final version above:

A Bars   1–40:   'Main theme (C minor)'
C Bars 41–56:   'Fortissimo Chord theme (C major)'. Schubert has written here on the manuscript 'in Es' ('into E flat')
B Bars 57–72:   'Arpeggio theme (E flat)'
B' Bars 73–84: A passage based on the 'Arpeggio theme', in E flat minor, discarded altogether: the first five bars are actually crossed through
B Bars 85–95:   'Arpeggio theme (E flat major)'. This contains a familiar cross-reference sign used by Schubert — 'ϴ'; it is an indication that this passage is to be used elsewhere in the movement. The composer has also added the words 'mit mehr Coloratura' ('with more coloratura') an instruction to himself, which he carried out in the final version (bars 129–57: see above)
A' Bars 96–118: 'Main theme (C minor)'. This is marked by Schubert 'Variert' and this too was done for the final version (bars 82–128: see above)
A'' Bars 119–42: 'Main theme (F minor)'. This is marked by Schubert 'bleibt in c' ('to remain in C minor')
B Bars 143–58:   'Arpeggio theme (F major)'
D Bars 159–71:   A new treatment of the 'Arpeggio theme'. The writing of this episode indicates an excited mind at work: it is hurried and scrappy, and when it was finished Schubert crossed it through. The material was not used, although it contains this not unattractive variant:

Example 12

B″ Bars 160–71: The 'Arpeggio theme' (C major). This episode bears the cross-reference sign '*Θ*', and evidently the passage was to be used in connection with bars 85–95 above

A (?) Bars 172–200: The 'Fortissimo chord theme' is used as the basis for these bars, starting in A major; the theme is developed in spirited fashion and provided the substance of the climax reached just before the close

A Bars 201–27: 'Main theme (C major–C minor)' and coda. (There is no change of tempo as in the final version.) This is introduced by the low trills on the cello part, first on D flat, then on D natural, as in the finished work; the rising and falling scale figure with which the piano closes the movement is written in the sketch, but there is no hint there of the harmonic arabesques that give such beauty and such a haunting quality to the final appearance of the main theme

The analysis of the sketch shows it to be longer than the movement that arose from it. It is possible that familiarity with the slow movement adds something to the impression of inevitability in its progress; but renewed study of the preliminary sketch for it reawakens wonder at the way in which Schubert brought about this sense of purpose and spontaneity from the disorderly mass of his first ideas.

The remaining pages of the manuscript are devoted to the Scherzo and Trio. The sketched movement follows in outline the progress of the music as it stands in the printed version. Only the latter part of the Trio is more rudimentary in the sketch; Schubert's original plan lacked the continuation of the cello melody just before the opening bars are recapitulated. This final section of the Trio was written on a blank side left at the end of the slow movement; it indicates that the eleven pages represented the full sheaf of papers available at the moment, and that the lost sketches for the Finale were separate from those for the first three movements. That these sketches have survived is a fortunate chance. When his bigger instrumental works were finished, it is evident that Schubert destroyed any preliminary drafts.

The manuscript of the four impromptus, published as op. 142, is dated by Schubert December 1827. Only recently a sketch for the first one, in F minor, hitherto known only to the members of the family who owned it, has come to light. It is untitled and undated, but belongs to the same period as the sketches for the Pianoforte Trio in E flat. The sketch and the impromptu it later became were both composed while Schubert was staying as Schober's guest in the Tuchlauben, Vienna. After the composer's death Schober handed over all the manuscripts in his possession to Ferdinand Schubert, but a few sketches — undoubtedly overlooked — were left behind.[1] Among them was the page under discussion. As with the sketch for the Fantasia in F minor, it passed from Schober to his cousin Isabella Raab (*née* Doré or Dorie) and eventually came into the possession of Isabella's great-nephew Dr. Wilhelm Raab.[2]

The sketch of the impromptu fills the front page of the leaf and extends to two braced staves on the back page. There are forty bars altogether, and although the first thirty-eight are substantially the same as in the final version, they offer the same interest as others of his sketches. There is the same unerring instinct for refinement and subtlety of detail as in the shaping of the slow movement of the Pianoforte Trio in E flat. A glance at the opening of the sketch suggests that Schubert's original idea was to write an altogether lighter, swifter piece, more in keeping with the impromptu of its title:

Example 13

[1] See p. 86.
[2] I am indebted to Dr. Raab, Burlington, U. S. A., for permission to reproduce the sketch in facsimile and for much of the information about its history.

3. Sketch for the Impromptu in F minor, D. 935, no. 1

The removal of the up-beat, the addition of the wide-spread harmonies, and the change of tempo to Allegro moderato produced a more dignified and sombre essay.

The remainder of the back page is filled with sketches for bars 60–108 of the 'Hymnus an den Heiligen Geist' for male-voice quartet, T.T.B.B. They were intended for the first version of the offertory, D. 941, now lost.[1]

Schubert's last three sonatas, written in a single, sustained spell of burning, creative energy, were finished on 26 September 1828: that date appears at the end of the Finale of the last one, in B flat major. Exactly when he started the composition of the first is unknown; it could hardly have been earlier than the end of August, and in all probability it was after his removal to his brother's lodgings on 1 September 1828. The ability to lavish such unremitting energy on the composition of the three long, superb works, completed within little more than three weeks, is stupendous enough in itself, but it seems superhuman, beyond credence almost, when it is realized that side by side with these sonatas, sketches, often in great detail, of every movement were also composed. The simple statistics alone are staggering: the sketches fill 17 leaves (34 pages), the fair copies 47 leaves (94 pages). Both sketches and fair copies are extant, the former now in the possession of the City Library, Vienna, bequeathed to that library by Nicolaus Dumba. The material in these sketches has been made slightly more accessible to the student, since Mandyczewski printed the greater part of it in the *Revisionsbericht* of the *Gesamtausgabe*; 'slightly', because this 'Editors' Report' is so rare today as to be almost unobtainable; but it can, at least, be consulted in the bigger libraries of world capitals.

[1] For a fuller description of this leaf, see the *Neue Zeitschrift für Musik*, Mainz, March 1963.

c

The sketch for the Sonata in C minor contains eight pages. It is the most straightforward of the three drafts. The first movement is prepared only to the end of the exposition, but its outlines are followed perfectly in the final version; one gains the impression that the music was coming to Schubert so readily that, in this case, he abandoned the sketch at that point. The printing of the sketched movement in the *Revisionsbericht* is somewhat misleading, since all cancelled bars and phrases have been omitted, which gives an impression that the sketch is closer to the final version than is actually the case. The slow movement (no tempo indicated) is, in essentials, complete and as we have it in the published sonata, but in numerous details the changes and alterations made later are vitally important; all of them add a more spacious, leisurely flow to the course of the finished Adagio. One section may be quoted to illustrate this masterly reshaping of a first, rough-hewn idea. Towards the end of the Adagio there is a favourite moment when the music drops, so to speak, from a *fortissimo* in F minor, to a soft, lyrical episode in B flat major. Here is the music as we have it in Schubert's last version:

Example 14

The whole story of his working over this slow movement is told if we compare that passage with the form it took in its first jotting down in the sketch:

Example 15

The 'Menuetto' sketches are more fascinating. They prove to
the hilt the arguments put forward earlier in the case of the
sketches for the third movement of the 'Unfinished' Symphony;
the movement as it stands in this first draft is as inferior as that in
the symphony sketches, and no one could have foreseen the
attractiveness of the 'Menuetto' that evolved from it. Here is the
opening, dense and ungainly:

Example 16 *(a)*

In the final version Schubert gives grace and balance to this
passage by superimposing a springing theme above the basic
harmonies, and when, during the course of the Minuet, he does
use the chords of his first idea, he gives them a touch of whimsi-
cality and surprise by breaking the sequence twice with a bar's
rest.

The final page contains a mere jotting down of the basic
rhythmic scheme of the main subject of the Finale: it was later
embodied in different melodic contours; having decided on the
external features of his Finale movement he left it. The sketch
extends to sixty-nine bars; the Finale that arose from it, the
longest of all Schubert's movements, contains 717 bars.

Example 16 *(b)*

Menuetto: *Allegro*   Final version of minuet

The eight leaves devoted to sketches for the second sonata, in A major, are indeed Schubert's 'foul papers'. Besides drafts for all four movements they also contain the start of a fair copy of the first movement; it is incomplete, was abandoned as a fair copy, and continued as a sketch of the development section and coda. There is also material on one page for the third sonata, in B flat major. One leaf is missing. Mandyczewski, in the *Revisionsbericht*, omitted the 'fair copy' section altogether, and merely printed those parts of the sketch that show some differences from the final version.

The pages devoted to the A major Sonata, sorted into some kind of order, contain this material:

I. 1 leaf, 2 sides: material for the first movement, ending at the close of the exposition section, but containing no hint of the codetta phrase that forms the basis of the development section. Right at the end of the second side there are sketches for the coda of the first movement of the B flat Sonata.

2. 1 leaf, $1\frac{3}{4}$ sides filled: the slow movement, Andante. It is essentially the same as in the final version, except that the stormy middle section is shorter and more primitively designed in the sketch.

3. 1 leaf, $1\frac{1}{2}$ sides: Scherzo, 'Allegro vivace'; Trio, *un poco più lento*. The Finale, 'Allegretto: Rondo', commences on the last half-side.

4. 3 leaves, 6 sides filled: the remainder of the Finale is written on these pages. There is a remarkable instance of second thoughts. The second episode of the movement, extending from bar 32 to the beginning of the 'development' — for this Finale is more truly a rondo-sonata than a simple rondo — was radically altered. The material is different, and it is differently treated from the episode as we have it in the final version. Schubert discarded it completely. Derived as it is from the opening pages and preserving the same stylistic features, the rejected passage has an uncanny resemblance to the pages with which Schubert replaced it, for these, too, derive material and style from the opening section; the two passages might be compared, perhaps fancifully, to two different photographic studies of the same person.

5. The fair copy of the first movement: two leaves are preserved, one leaf, coming between them, is lost. (These pages, somewhat confusingly, have been placed at the start of the sketches in the folder provided by the City Library.) Schubert has headed his fair copy 'Sonate II'. The missing leaf contained the material between bars 65 and 130. The last side and a half contain the development-section sketches and at the end Schubert wrote 'etc.'. The remaining half-side he headed 'zum Schluss' ('for the end'): it contains a draft of the coda for the first movement.

But if these pages for the A major Sonata are 'foul', those for the last sonata, in B flat major, are yet more confused, and reveal pretty closely the climax of mental exhilaration and feverish energy in which the composer worked. The batch of five leaves is an assortment of different-sized papers, an unusual thing to find in the last years of Schubert's working life; there are two 'upright' oblong leaves, two 'long' oblong, sixteen-stave leaves, and one 'long' oblong, twelve-stave leaf. Moreover, examination of the music written on these pages reveals an unusual fact, that Schubert must have completed the Finale of the sonata before the first movement was finished. From all his other sketches it is easy to deduce the fact that the finale of an instrumental work was not

only last, but least in his scheme of work; in many instances there
are no sketches for the finale at all, and if they exist they constitute
a mere memorandum. But in the case of the B flat Sonata the end
of the development section of the first movement is written into
the staves left blank at the close of the Finale sketch, and, as we
have seen, the coda of this movement was written in staves left
blank in the sketches for the previous sonata. The five leaves
contain the following material:

1. 'Long' oblong, sixteen-stave leaf, headed '3. Sonate'. Both sides
are filled with a draft of the first movement up to the start of the
development section.

2. 'Upright' oblong, sixteen-stave leaf: the first side continues the
development up to what is approximately bar 170 of the final version.
The other side contains the conclusion and *presto coda* of the Finale.
The four empty staves at the bottom of this side were then used for the
close of the development section of the first movement.

3. 'Upright' oblong, sixteen-stave leaf: both sides are filled with the
finale sketch up to the point reached above.

4. 'Long' oblong, sixteen-stave leaf: both sides contain a full sketch
of the slow movement, Andante sostenuto.

5. 'Long' oblong, twelve-stave leaf: the first side and half the other
side contain sketches for the Scherzo; there are no tempo or expression
marks of any kind. The second half of the side contains the Trio. The
sketches follow the final version very closely.

The single leaf containing the Andante sostenuto — one of
Schubert's profoundest and most poetical essays — is frail, and
the ink is fading; one takes it in one's hand and wonders with awe
how such a page, scrawled so hurriedly and so faintly, can embody
an experience that belongs to the highest aspirations of man: truly
one of humanity's priceless documents.

From the point of view of craftsmanship the two topics of chief
interest lie in the exposition of the first movement and in the
evolution of the second theme, in A major, in the slow movement.
The first thing that strikes one is the way in which Schubert trans-
formed the prosaic, march-like steps of his sketched first movement into the expansive, proud progress of the movement as we
have it in the final version. This is achieved mainly by his treat-

ment of the trill on G flat in the left-hand part. This almost ominous interruption, which has the effect of a question-mark, appears once only in the sketch, jotted down on the bass line below the first cadence. Its germination in Schubert's mind during the course of the development section later flowered into its effective use in the opening bars, and again in the coda. The exposition is further amplified by a much more lyrical treatment of the second subject (in F sharp minor) and its subsequent linear developments.

The A major theme of the Andante sostenuto was greatly modified, and its embryonic appearance is almost commonplace. This is how it first occurred to Schubert:

Example 17

The continuation in the sketch, however, gives this unpromising theme a graceful and colourful treatment, passing into D minor and B major with true Schubertian skill and feeling. While one cannot but be thankful for the splendour of the final form of this germinal idea, a lingering regret for what was jettisoned must remain.

Two days after the completion of the fair copy of the B flat Sonata, on 28 September 1828, Schubert himself played from the three works at an evening gathering in Vienna. He died a few weeks later, having had no opportunity to submit the sonatas for publication. Had he been able to do so the sketches would doubt-less have been destroyed. The fact that they have been preserved enables us once again to see him at work and, as Mendelssohn wrote, we seem to become at once personally acquainted with him.

Brooding over Schubert's drafts for his masterpieces is, for any sensitive soul, a moving experience. To glance thus over his shoulder, as it were, is to have a share — infinitely small no doubt, but both instructive and ennobling — in the creative act itself.

THE GENESIS OF THE GREAT
C MAJOR SYMPHONY

Amongst the idlest of the parlour games in musicology is the one the Germans call *Reminiszenzjagd* — the hunting out of resemblances between themes and ideas in works by different composers. Direct plagiarism is not sought for; the point of the game is rather to draw attention to influence or derivation. That composers do receive stimulus and inspiration from the work of others is a fact on which we all agree; it is very uncertain, however, that such influence as is exerted by any one composer on those who follow him is to be established by instancing short, melodic resemblances or similar harmonic progressions occurring in their works. But people who indulge in the pastime rarely dip deeper than this. When these melodic or technical fragments do closely resemble each other, it is tempting to isolate them from their contexts and bring them startlingly together, and we are all of us liable to succumb to the temptation. Donald Tovey uttered some strongly critical remarks on the practice and derided its practitioners; but he himself was by no means immune, and if it suited his purpose he quoted any pair of resemblances that he had noted. The whole subject was dealt with, ably and wittily, by William McNaught some years ago.[1]

A more profitable aspect of the pastime, and a more justifiable one, traces reminiscences in the themes and styles that exist in different works by the same composer. This can often illuminate the work-processes and the aspirations of the man and the evolution of his music, as well as intensify the response of his listeners. Even then more is called for than the simple juxtaposition of extracts from this work and the other. Where Schubert is concerned, there are plenty of opportunities to point to musical

[1] *Musical Times*, London, Feb. 1948 and May 1950.

analogues from his compositions. The strongly personal element in his melodies and modulations was bound to produce such musical likenesses. Unless the placing together of these likenesses achieves some purpose, it becomes, as already mentioned, simply an idle pursuit. Self-borrowing, of course, is another matter. To draw attention to his use of the B flat Entr'acte in *Rosamunde* for the slow movement of the A minor String Quartet, or of the introduction to the 'Italian' Overture in D major, D. 590 in that of *Die Zauberharfe* Overture is essential in any discussion of the works in question, and it would seem odd if any commentator omitted to do so.

With these reservations in mind I propose to discuss the inception of Schubert's last symphony in the light of many of his foregoing works; among its various aspects there is this one to be considered: that unlike any other work of his it seems to be, in an almost fore-ordained fashion, hinted at, its motifs and procedures foreshadowed, by many occasions in his earlier works. I do not suggest that Schubert consciously wrote in his symphony a kind of Schubertian apotheosis; I suggest only that the apotheosis was achieved because he set out on his task with every faculty striving to produce the highest of which he was capable. To Schubert, the 'symphony' was the supreme musical form, and he was composing one for performance by the leading Viennese musical society. The hypernatural alertness with which he approached the composition has given us in this symphony the best of Schubert: grace, poetry, tenderness, melodic beauty, warmth of heart, fiery exuberance; but that attitude of mind also struck deeply into his subconscious creative powers, and the over-stimulated brain reached back and found successful practices from the past to use them in a more finished and more mature manner, in order to contribute to a symphony that would be the crown of his work.

No one denies the problematic aspect of his only other mature symphony, the 'Unfinished'. The reasons why he never completed that work will be sought for and discussed until doomsday. But one problem facing us with the great C major Symphony comes before, and not after, the composition of the work. For there is a problem if one takes the trouble to think about it. The possibility that the symphony had its origin at Gmunden and Gastein, and was first sketched there in 1825, I have discussed elsewhere, and I do not intend to touch upon that controversial matter again here.[1] But that 'March 1828' says all there is to say about the composition of the symphony cannot be accepted. This is the date on the first page of Schubert's manuscript, preserved in the archives of the Gesellschaft der Musikfreunde in Vienna, for which society it was composed. This copy is like many other of Schubert's copies of his bigger works, e.g., the sonatas in D major, op. 53, or G major, op. 78: it is impossible to say which sections of it are 'first drafts' and which 'fair copy'. Handwriting does not help us to decide, for no doubt Schubert, like the rest of us, would make fair copies as quickly as he could. Nor are the attempts of some commentators to distinguish between the colours of his ink very convincing, when one gets down to a study of the symphony manuscript. As the quill drained of its ink the writing grew fainter; redipped, the colour of the ink regained its original depth. It does not follow, therefore, that a page containing parts in a faint brown ink and others in a dark brown ink was written at different times. It is, perhaps, over-imaginative to try and assess from the pages of this manuscript the emotional excitement in Schubert's mind as he penned certain very famous passages in this work. But the writing of the two duet episodes between cello and oboe in the Andante con moto has a distinctive appearance — the notes are bolder, the phrases exquisitely written, as if the composer's exalted state of mind had communicated itself to his penmanship. The same strong feelings seem apparent also when one examines the pages containing the famous trombone entries in the codetta of the first movement.

Schubert's changes in the thematic structure of some of his main subjects in this symphony are well known; two important ones are dealt with by Mandyczewski in his report on the volume of symphonies in the *Gesamtausgabe* (Serie i). All these revisions in the melodies were made after the score was finished, and they entail a great number of alterations. This fact, together with the existence of numerous added bars and cancelled passages, which

[1] *Schubert: A Critical Biography*, appendix i, pp. 354–61.

we find throughout the four movements, suggest a revision that is more thoroughgoing than usual with Schubert. Afterthoughts they may be, but it is one thing to have afterthoughts where single, small episodes are concerned, and quite another to have them with regard to the main subjects of the movement, from which much subsidiary material will have been derived. The problem becomes acute if one considers the very first radical revision that Schubert made in the symphony. It occurs on the front page, in the opening bars. Schubert's adjustment is adroitly done, and has escaped notice. But his opening horn theme ran thus:

Example 18 (a)

Then he neatly drew extra bar-lines in bars 3 and 4 and inserted the familiar phrases, producing the eight-bar melody as we all know it.

Example 18 (b)

This was no error in copying, which, in any case, would hardly be likely to occur in the first bars of a full score. I think it possible that the fully fledged theme emerged in Schubert's mind only as the Andante introduction proceeded, and that he then went back and reshaped the initial theme. Even this is too glib a solution — for consider the very end of the first movement. Here is the final appearance of the horn theme, blazoned forth by the full orchestra:

Example 19

Apart from the slight, rhythmic change, in part necessitated by the *alla breve* tempo, this is exactly the same as the original penning of the opening theme! No one satisfactory conclusion can be drawn about this theme reshaping and its effect on the first movement; answers to the problem merely conflict. One might conclude that originally the symphony started with an Allegro ma non troppo, and the original conception of the horn theme used as a striking coda; or that the original Andante prelude was much shorter and devoted to little more than an exposition of the original theme; or that the whole movement, introduction as well, was recast after it was first written out, and that Schubert either did not wish, or did not trouble, to alter the first form of the theme in the coda. We enter the realm of guess-work as Sherlock Holmes would say: the problem remains.

At the start of the Allegro ma non troppo there occurs another alteration of the main theme; this was mentioned by Mandyczewski in the *Revisionsbericht* of the *Gesamtausgabe*, and is well known. The change is thoroughly justified, for the original form of the theme, though serving Schubert's purpose well enough, strikes us as very flat compared with the spring and verve in what it later became. Schubert's first idea for the introductory subject and the subsequent revision are quoted here:

Example 20 (a)

Before discussing this theme and its revision we could perhaps digress a little. It must be borne in mind that to Schubert his earlier symphonies, productions of his boyhood, were as good as non-existent. The great C major Symphony would be, to the public, his first symphony. The B minor Symphony, abandoned in the middle of its third movement, had been composed nearly six years previously — a lifetime before! — and forgotten. More than this, as far as he was concerned each symphony he composed in his younger days was consigned to oblivion as soon as it had been performed, either by the students' orchestra of the Stadt-konvikt school or by the little, private orchestra of which he was a member. As a result we are never aware of Schubert composing in a consciously different manner with each successive symphony. He never, so to speak, remembered, and so avoided what he had done in the previous symphony. He had no need to. Consequently his first six symphonies are strikingly alike in style, in technical manœuvrings, in mood, and in intention. They are distinctive only because the subject-matter of each one, melody and figuration and, to a certain extent, orchestration, are so markedly different from those in its neighbours, infused with individuality and freshness. In one sense, then, Schubert was writing the same symphony in all six of his early works, and also in the two un-finished symphonies of May 1818 and August 1821, which followed them. The 'Unfinished' Symphony is not only an astonishingly original departure from the classical traditions of Mozart and Haydn, it is also, in the same way, an astonishing departure from Schubert's own symphonic style. The C major Symphony is much more akin to the six early symphonies than it is to the 'Unfinished' Symphony. To return to the main theme of the Allegro ma non troppo of the C major Symphony: is it not, for example, an unconscious delving into the memories of his third symphony, in D major? The main theme of the first movement, announced on the clarinet, is as follows:

Example 21

These phrases are linked by semiquaver runs on the strings in a manner comparable to the linking of the string phrases in the C major Symphony by triplet runs on bassoon and horn. The effectiveness of this beginning to the quick movement of his third symphony, after a lingering cadence in D minor, may have returned to his mind when he came to the similar place in the C major Symphony. The development section of the Allegro ma non troppo in the C major Symphony uses the same mingling of ideas from the exposition as we find in that of the earlier symphony: the second subject of each movement (to use a conveniently brief label) dominates the start of the section, and then gives way to figuration and theme-particles from the first subject. The music of the third symphony, or, at least, the manner of it, haunted the composer during the course of the 1828, and, as we shall see later, its Finale returns, transfigured, in that of the later symphony.

Other early works contributed to the material of the first movement of the C major Symphony, most notably the two overtures mentioned above: the overture in the Italian style, in D major, was composed in 1817, probably at the same time as its companion overture in C major, the score of which is actually dated November 1817. Three years later Schubert re-used the attractive themes and modulations in its Adagio introduction for the Andante introduction to his overture for *Die Zauberharfe* (known today as the *Rosamunde* Overture). He also took some effective material from the coda of the D major overture and embodied it in the Vivace conclusion of the later overture. Both these orchestral works had been performed several times in Vienna, so that Schubert was aware of their actual sound and of their effectiveness in performance. Here is the coda passage from the *Zauberharfe* Overture, which, except for the key, is almost identical with that of the 'Italian' Overture:

The passage is then repeated, with the *fortissimo* arpeggios at * bursting out into E flat major. This telling orchestral device, with its urgent, thrusting movement, is without doubt the germ of those superb passages in the development section of the first movement of the C major Symphony.

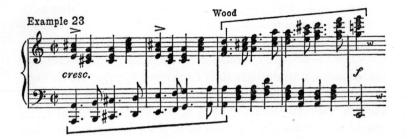

And it occurs, yet again, as the basis of the splendid coda to the movement:

Example 24

The Andante con moto of the C major Symphony is the only slow movement in Schubert's symphonies to begin with a few bars of accompaniment. All the others commence at once with the main theme. Even the two preludial bars in the slow movement of the 'Unfinished' Symphony are an integral part of the opening theme and are developed individually quite as significantly as the violin theme that they herald. But the first half-dozen bars of the Andante con moto, having served to introduce the oboe theme, have fulfilled their task and never appear again. The key, A minor, is unusual too. Only one other work in the dozen or so by Schubert whose main key is C major has a slow movement in A minor, and that is a very early string quartet, No. 2, composed when he was a lad of fifteen (D. 3). The markedly processional style, instigated at once by the *staccato* string chords, reminds us of the movement of 'Gute Nacht' that opens the song-cycle *Winterreise*. Schubert was evidently attracted by the march-like thrumming of these chords in a minor key, above which his melodies could hover, sustained and pointed by the unvarying beat below them. The Andante con moto of the Pianoforte Trio in E flat, op. 100, of November 1827, has exactly the same pulsating metre. The return of the oboe theme in the A minor slow movement is preceded by one of the most famous

D

passages in orchestral literature. The reiterated G on the horns punctuates *pianissimo* string chords; the chords are easy to analyse harmonically, since they consist of dominant sevenths in C major, F major, and D minor, each of which contains the note G as part of its structure. But Schubert's pattern is decidedly not easy to analyse, and the ambiguity and unbalance of the passage is genius at its most daring. The G of the horns finally resolves, not into any of the suggested keys, but on to a chord of B flat major, which is a characteristic Schubertian approach to his desired key of A minor — a 'Neapolitan' sixth cadence. This miraculous episode is a poeticized version of the conclusion of another song from the *Winterreise* cycle, the 'Der Wegweiser'. The words at the end of the song are also well known, since they have been applied to Schubert himself:

> Einer Weiser seh' ich stehen,
> Unverrücket vor meinem Blick,
> Eine Strasse muss ich gehen,
> Die noch keiner ging zurück.

> (I see a signpost standing,
> Immovable before my eyes,
> I must tread a path
> Which no one retraces.)

'Der Wegweiser' also, like 'Gute Nacht', uses the throbbing of minor chords to support its melody. (All these movements, incidentally, are in 2/4 time.) The melody to the above words sings itself to a conclusion on the note G. The piano reiterates the note for two bars, and then the melody is repeated, with an entirely different harmonization, while the G is repeatedly struck:

Example 25

The processional music of this song must have been in Schubert's mind during the composition of the symphonic A minor movement. Not only do the bars quoted above contribute to the famous horn passage, but several touches in the song accompaniment are recalled in the symphonic movement:

Example 26

The poignant phrase to which the final words, 'Die noch keiner ging zurück', is sung recurs transfigured in the symphony:

Example 27 (a)

Towards the end of the movement the incessant tread of the quaver-phrases is broken by a triplet figure in violins and oboes. It reminds us of a similar device, with exactly the same desire to relieve an incessant rhythmical pattern, at the end of the slow movement of the fourth symphony, the 'Tragic'; there the unvarying semiquaver movement on the strings gives way at length to a triplet movement in just the same way as in the slow movement of the C major Symphony.

Of all the four movements of the symphony the Scherzo has, perhaps, the most striking foreshadowing in an earlier movement of Schubert's. The promise of this greatest of all his scherzos was so astonishingly made in the Finale of the String Quartet in B flat, op. 168, that many commentators have drawn attention to it with wonder. The Finale of the string quartet is one of the composer's finest and most original movements in the earlier chamber-music forms; it dates from September 1814. Above sustained chords on the lower strings the first violin utters a rapid quaver theme that eventually takes this form:

Example 28

This evolves into two further, more elaborate, figures (bars 58–60 and 68–79) and finally emerges as a canon between treble and bass strings:

Example 29

We have here the inspiration of the main Scherzo theme in the symphony and its later *fugato* use:

Example 30

But between the Finale of 1814 and the Scherzo of 1828 there is an important link. It is to be found in the Scherzo that Schubert sketched, in pianoforte score, and almost completed for the symphony he designed in May 1818. He takes over the pattering figures of the Finale of the string quartet and combines them with an arching theme in the bass: it is a true pointer to the G major theme of the 1828 Scherzo. Here is Schubert's sketch for the 1818 Scherzo at bar 17:

Example 31

The subsequent development of these ideas preserves the same sense and style of the later Scherzo, and even introduces the figure — crotchet and four quavers — that is to give such charm to the symphonic movement.

The melody that streams into the C major Scherzo, first given to the flute, is one of its loveliest moments:

Example 32

It was, as Grove pointed out, first used in embryo in the Scherzo of the Octet and forms there a splendidly lyrical interlude; the repetition a semitone higher is an unexpected and thrilling stroke on Schubert's part:

Example 33

He repeats the procedure exactly in the symphonic Scherzo (see Example 32), modulating from C flat major to C major and repeating the melody on violins and oboe. It is clear from Schubert's manuscript that he did not originally intend to repeat the four-bar theme played by the flute. After it was written, however, he marked the bars (89–92) for repeat (*bis*) and then continued by giving the violins and oboe the theme in C major. This may possibly be a harking back to the treatment he had so successfully used in the Scherzo of the Octet.

The Trio to the symphonic Scherzo, in A major, is introduced by a series of repeated E's on brass and woodwind. It is a simple and quite effective transition, and Schubert had used a similar device twice before, in both cases at precisely the same point in earlier symphonies: in the sixth symphony, of 1817–18, a sustained E on the woodwind leads from a Scherzo in C major to a Trio in E major, and in the unfinished symphony in E minor/major of August 1821 a sustained octave E on the oboes does precisely the same thing as in the 1828 movement, leading from a Scherzo in C major to a Trio in A major. The 1828 Trio has had some slightly disparaging criticism in recent years, a time in which nineteenth-century criticisms of the symphony as a whole have usually been stilled. The melody has been called 'over-lush', 'too sumptuously upholstered', 'hovering too much round the mediant' and so on. There is, of course, truth in these criticisms, but one feels sometimes that the criticism should really be directed towards conductors who insist on slowing down the tempo at this point in the movement. There is no warrant whatever for this *meno mosso* in Schubert's own score; he obviously wished to retain the original *allegro vivace* of the Scherzo. It has been remarked, and with truth, that Schubert sometimes implied a *ritardando* when he wrote *diminuendo*: this is proved by the fact that he will add *a tempo* after the *diminuendo*. But there is no such indication at this point; on the contrary, the orchestral Trio is heralded by a *crescendo* indication, and the full orchestra announces the theme and its accompaniment. The shape of the melody is found in a *Winterreise* song 'Die Nebensonnen' composed only a few months previously. Both key and time are identical; the slower tempo of the song is compensated for by the longer notes in the Trio theme:

Example 34 *(a)*

This resemblance is not of itself greatly significant, but the course of the song reflects in miniature the course of the Trio. A short episode in A minor takes the melody into C major for the fourth couplet of the poem, in the same way as, in the Trio, Schubert passes through A minor to C major for the climax of the movement. In both song and instrumental work the music subsides to A minor and then to A major for the recapitulation of the melody.

But if this song gave Schubert a hint, an even more fruitful field of study of the origins of the symphonic Trio is found in a consideration of the Trio movement in the String Quartet in D minor — the 'Death and the Maiden' Quartet. Isolated quotations are no help, the whole conception of the quartet section was expanded and amplified in the symphony. Obvious points can be seen in the string quartet, in the transition from D major to D minor, and in the use of the rhythmic pattern in the inner parts:

Example 35

No other of the great symphonies of the classical and romantic periods has so divided opinion as this last symphony of Schubert's. Side by side with the glowing tributes of men like Schumann and Mendelssohn arose a body of outspoken denigration. The hostility it encountered from orchestral players in Vienna, London, and Paris — a hostility so great that performance was shelved — is a familiar if unwelcome episode in nineteenth-century music annals. In England, particularly, the almost vitriolic comments on the symphony make surprising reading. The work was performed for the first time in London in April 1856, and it was given in two parts at two separate concerts: the Finale omitted at the first, the first movement omitted at the second. The audience is said to have received the symphony 'with entire apathy'. The reason usually given for this cold reception was the great length of the symphony. In view of the fact that Beethoven's Ninth Symphony, which should take even longer to perform than Schubert's C major Symphony, and which, in those days, was treated as a mystical revelation of the godhead, frequently appeared in programmes of the period, one can only conclude that the tempos chosen for Schubert's movements must have been unconscionably slow; the Andante con moto especially was probably taken too leisurely.

One's own memories of performances in the 1920's seem to confirm this assumption: the tempo chosen for the slow movement by conductors in those days was certainly slower than that chosen today. But it is the Finale of the symphony that is the crux of this divergence of views.

Schubert's genius, it has been said, was expressive rather than constructive, but in this particular movement, by far the greatest of any of his instrumental finales, the constructive aspect dominates. Built on a massive interpretation of sonata-form, every component part of the Finale demands the full response of the listener, and Schubert, in yielding to the constructive needs of his movement, has become perhaps indifferent to the human limitations of his audience, however sympathetic. There is not a bar where the tension relaxes; even the silent bars that introduce the second subject are, by reason of their precipitous approach, tense with the expectation of what is to come.[1] This may be the reason why the movement has met with the detraction and criticism of musicians who require a more selfconscious approach on the part of a composer to his compositions. Tension, stress, and excitement in music to make their full effect must alternate with relaxation and repose. No composer understood this better than Wagner, and no composer was more aware than he of the continuing impact of his music on an audience. The Finale of the C major Symphony would have silenced its critics if it had demanded less from them; a few passages of inspired padding, such as all the great symphonists from Haydn to Brahms knew so well how to use, would have redeemed the work — in their view. The Schubertian seeks these reasons to account for the hostile com-

---

[1] Donald Tovey has an odd comment on this section of the Finale (*Essays in Musical Analysis*, vol. i, p. 211). Schubert's autograph shows here a cancelled theme; the second subject was a new idea. Tovey comments: 'He had got as far as the four premonitory notes of the horns; and then he dashed off into a schoolmasterly little fugue . . . the dingy little fugue-subject was struck out before the answer had well begun. . . .' But there is no hint in Schubert's autograph of any fugal treatment, and it must reluctantly be pointed out that Tovey's 'quotation', his Example 14, is a pure invention on his part.

ments that the movement has sometimes received; he himself does
not ask for a note to be altered.

The exalted mental state in which, as it has been suggested,
Schubert approached this symphony has in its final movement
produced the most remarkable reminiscences of earlier works. We
find the mood of the movement as early as 1816 in the C major
Magnificat, composed for solo voices, chorus, orchestra, and
organ (D. 486). The close of the offertory, Allegro vivace, a
setting of the words 'Gloria Patri et Filio', is full of prophetic
hints of the 1828 Finale. The same foreshadowing is to be found
in the two symphony fragments of 1818 and 1821. We find there
even the use of descending, imitative figures on the strings, so
marked a feature in the development section of the C major
Finale. It is, however, with the Finale of the third symphony that
the most striking kinship appears. Short quotations, again, are of
no use to illustrate this kinship, for it is in the spirit of the whole
of both movements that the common purpose is so clear. Schubert
can never resist the use of a triplet movement whenever he writes
a finale in 2/4 time, and the surging triplet-figures of the C major
Finale can be paralleled at once with the 6/8 time of the earlier
Finale. The high-spirited, almost unmastered, onrush of each
movement is achieved in a way that is easy to label; it is the use of
a series of prolonged and interrupted cadences. But the wayward-
ness of Schubert's harmonies by which he postpones the expected
cadence, and the totally unexpected plunge by which he avoids it,
these are impossible to label: we are faced with the illogical logic
of genius. The end of the exposition section of the D major Finale
comes very close in outward semblance to the Finale of the great
C major Symphony:

Example 36   (bars 107–129)

But in essential musical feeling, the close of the development section in the D major Finale comes closest to the Finale of the great C major Symphony, in spite of the very different dynamics.

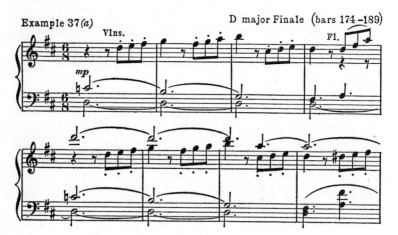

Example 37 (a)   D major Finale (bars 174–189)

(b) *Allegro vivace*   C major Finale (bars 76–90)

The two movements, the D major Finale of 1815 and the C major Finale of 1828, are noticeably akin in inward and outward matters. Quite as remarkable, but in external resemblances only, is the affinity between the Finale of the sixth symphony in C major of 1818 with the Finale of the 1828 symphony. Two of the most obvious analogies are cadential. In the last years of his life Schubert was fond of using a particular couplet of chords here quoted from the introduction of the C major Symphony:

Example 38

He did not use this cadential phrase in a general way, but always in the key shown above. Its only use before 1824 or so is to be found in the Finale of the 1818 symphony, where it occurs half a dozen times. The second cadential passage in the 1818 Finale is quite astonishingly like its fellow in the one of ten years later; it occurs at the end of the development section. A chord of G major is reiterated in various forms on woodwind, horns, and *pizzicato* strings. An F natural appears in the harmony and steers the course of the music into C major. One feels that Schubert was within an ace of reaching his later inspiration, in which the F natural falls not to the expected E natural, but to E flat, and so gives that wonderful burst of E flat major for the recapitulation of the 1828 Finale.

Quite the most interesting of these foreshadowings is to be found in the last few pages of the 1818 symphony. A rhythmic figure in the second subject evolves this phrase:

Example 39

and eventually the strings, in unison, utter the figure:

Example 40

The Finale concludes with cadences built on the C major form of this rhythmic fragment, so extraordinarily like the opening figure of the 1828 Finale. One feels that when Schubert laid down his pen on completing the 1818 Finale he was subconsciously half-prepared for the splendour of his 1828 symphonic Finale.

A small, but fascinating, correspondence between two ideas, one in the Finale of the C major Symphony and the other in the Finale of the Sonata in A minor, op. 42, of 1825, has been frequently mentioned in commentaries on the composer's work. The first appearance of the idea in the sonata movement occurs in bar 181; it is approached by a passage in E major:

Example 41

Allegro vivace

The symphonic potentialities of this phrase were realized by Schubert three years later when he wrote the second subject section of this Finale to the symphony:

Example 42

The codetta phrase marked 'A' in the quotations generated the superb pages that open the development section of the symphonic Finale.

It is both congenial and appropriate to find in the C major Symphony that Schubert resorted at several points in the course of the work to one of his most fundamental processes in musical thinking. Both the origin and development of this process are deeply imbedded in his creative gifts and their maturing. Since music for Schubert starts with melody, that might as well be our starting-point too. The personal style of all composers is brought to focus in their melodic styles; with Schubert it is undeniable that the mediant of his key, e.g., E natural in the key of C major or E flat in the key of C minor, is the hub of his melodies. If we also take into account his richly endowed capacity for harmonic colour, and the subsidiary tendency of that capacity towards shifting tonalities, we can see that for Schubert the key of C major inevitably suggested that of E major, the key of the mediant. In the same way the key of A flat is also obliquely suggested, since C natural is the mediant of the key of A flat. The whole aspect of Schubert's tonality is far more subtle and complicated than this simple analysis would suggest, but it is sufficient to illustrate the motives in the tonal eddyings of the Finale to the C major Symphony. One might conclude that the move from any one key to that a third below or a third above is for Schubert a melodically motivated move. Sometimes it is almost mechanical, but the results are far from mechanical or perfunctory and in later works it is often of supremely poetic quality. Quite early in his work the transition to a key a third below his tonic key was achieved by a descending phrase in the bass; the physical movement in the music, step by step downwards, also became associated in his mind with a diminution in the volume of sound. The result is that very characteristic 'hushing' of the music with its emotive suggestion of consolation or even, if one could be pardoned for a slight exaggeration, of a spiritual preparation for a revealed mystery. An early example, producing the *decrescendo* that Schubert desired for the recapitulation of his main theme, is found in the first movement of the sixth symphony:

Example 43

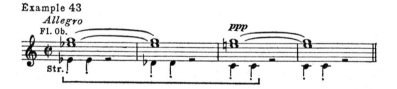

The emotional depths that this device can plumb are soon apparent in the songs and instrumental pieces of the years 1820–5. The song 'Totengräbers Heimweh' draws on the device at its most poignant moment; the text tells of the gravedigger looking with yearning eyes into the 'deep grave — the home of those at peace'.

In the very same month that Schubert composed this song, April

E

Example 44

hin - ab _ in's tie - fe, in's tie - fe Grab!

1825, he was at work on the Sonata in C major (the 'Reliquie'), which he left unfinished. The first movement contains two examples of the progression, both occurring at critical points in the constructional build of the movement. The first appearance is at the end of the recapitulation, where it is elaborated by a figure derived from the preceding codetta:

Example 45 (a)

The second, more profound in its emotional effect, even though it is of the simplest possible nature, occurs at the end of the movement, and forms a prelude to the coda:

Example 45 *(b)*

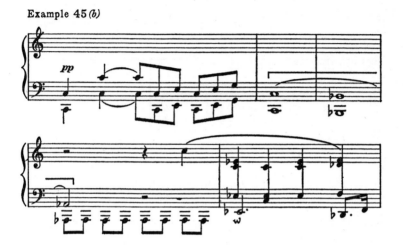

The correspondence between these two embodiments of the descending, step-wise motion, is obvious, but the achievement, technically, from the point of view of tonal experiment, and emotionally, is remarkably fine. That Schubert found, in this musical device, an appealing means of transition is shown by a further use of it in the Pianoforte Trio in B flat, op. 99, of 1826–7.[1] The particular form of the shift with which we are concerned here is used in the first movement of the pianoforte trio to set the stage for the entry of the second subject into the development section of the movement:

[1] The device is known to the Germans as *Mediantrückung* — the shifting between keys via their mediant-tonic links.

Example 46

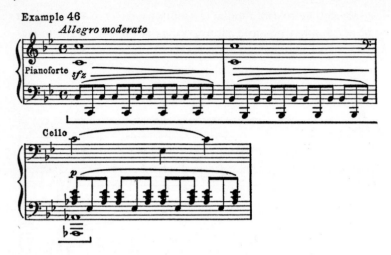

The culmination of this growth of an idea is found in its most perfect form in the C major Symphony. The lovely melody in the second section of the slow movement first appears in F major. The music glides into the key from A major thus:

Example 47

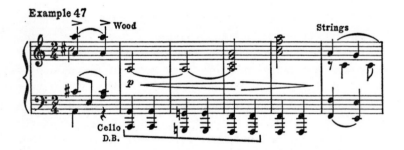

And, finally, there are its magical uses in the Finale. The exposition section ends in G major. The prolonged close has toned down the music from *fortissimo* fanfares in this key to a *pianissimo* octave G on the bass strings. The G moves down to F and then to E flat for the start of the development section. The progression is repeated for the coda of the finale, except that the music moves from C major not to A flat major, but to A major. But because the A major key is not designed to hold significant melody as was the

E flat key in its predecessor the emotional effect is heightened: we are left on tiptoe, so to speak, wondering what is to come. The whole passage is an excellent illustration of Schubert's achievement of sublime results with the simplest of strokes:

Example 48

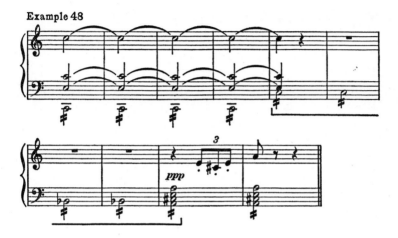

In an affectionate and favourite essay on this symphony Alexander Brent Smith writes the following paragraph on this passage:[1]

So far he has whirled us along in his wonderful symphonic machine over the beaten tracks of the world, but now a thrill greater than we ever imagined lies before us. Suddenly the earth recedes beneath us and we realise that we are rushing smoothly and swiftly over the edge of the world; that our machine is no longer a machine of man's device but a fiery, fiery chariot with fiery, fiery horses, and that we are in very deed going by a whirlwind into a heaven of new experience.

Consideration of this step-like descent from one key to another casts light on one of the famous moments in the symphony — one that has been mentioned already in passing. It is the extraordinary and unexpected plunge into E flat major for the recapitulation of the Finale when everything pointed to an orthodox move back into C major. The development section ends in G major. After a while the note F natural appears among the G major chords and

[1] 'The Musical Pilgrim' series, *Schubert: the Symphonies* (O.U.P., London, 1926), p. 28.

produces the dominant seventh of the tonic key. Then comes the surprising drop to an E flat, instead of E natural, and the opening figure bursts out, *fortissimo*, in the key of E flat major. Is not this whole passage a further example of the favourite move by steps from one key to another a major third below, and does it not therefore wonderfully parallel and complete the exactly similar way in which the development section was reached?

The C major Symphony was completed in March or April of 1828. In the six months or so left before he died Schubert produced four more instrumental masterpieces in extended sonata-form: the String Quintet in C major and the last three pianoforte sonatas. They unquestionably initiate a new phase in his development; only the Pianoforte Trio in E flat, op. 100, preceding the symphony, points to the future in the same way as do those four works: to the future that was denied him. The great C major Symphony was not only the climax of what one might call Schubert's first creative period; as this essay has tried to show, it was also, in a unique way, a magnificent summary and epilogue to that first phase of composition.

THE PART-SONGS FOR MALE VOICES

SCHUBERT composed his male-voice part-songs to meet a lively demand in his day. Music for male voices became increasingly popular towards the end of the eighteenth century and its cultivation was rapid and widespread. At the time when Schubert began to write such music, the male-voice chorus, both professional and amateur, was firmly established — one could almost say coagulated — in Germany, Switzerland, and Austria. When, later on in the nineteenth century, the movement collapsed, the thousands of part-songs that it had called into being fluttered into obscurity: autumnal leaves drifting away to mark the end of a long summer of popularity. Schubert's part-songs — there are between sixty and seventy of them — have not survived the wreck of the movement, for they receive today little esteem and rare performance.[1] The neglect is not altogether undeserved, for many of them are perfunctory, sliver'd in the moon's eclipse, so to speak, and only occasionally redeemed by an imaginative touch. They are also intensely of their period, and early nineteenth-century choral styles are now at the lowest ebb of esteem. Choirs of today, both male and mixed, absorbed in the choral styles of the sixteenth and seventeenth centuries, or in the ecclesiastical productions of the German masters of the eighteenth century, ignore them.

Among the many undistinguished pieces there are some half a dozen part-songs that do not deserve the fate of the rest. They may not reach the highest levels of his art, nor have they the over-mastering power of his finest songs, but they are valuable examples of his musical treatment of natural scenes, and of sentiments both homely and elevated. These few part-songs cannot be looked upon as isolated and chance inspirations, and it is hoped

---

[1] Performances are more frequent in Germany than anywhere else, but even there they are spasmodic rather than cultivated.

that a glance at the others may trace the sources of their greatness; the steps by which Schubert reached the heights are not without significance. It is sometimes said in connection with a masterpiece by any great creator: if he had written, or painted, or composed only this one work, it would have been sufficient to place him in the front rank. It is, perhaps, a naïve judgement, for the production of such an isolated masterpiece is incredible; a vast amount of creative work lies behind the devising and execution of any masterpiece, including the production of many other masterpieces by the same artist. For this reason Dr. Johnson's comment about bulk in the output of the poet strikes one as absolutely sound; no painter, poet, dramatist or composer who stands in the world's estimation as in the topmost flight has that reputation, unless it is based on the existence of a large number of works, each manifesting its author's genius. The words of the poet, Roy Thomas, are relevant here:

> The great poet is distinguished by abundance; his mental energy is extraordinary, and his output is large. 'Large', of course, is a relative term; the poet may have produced, as Homer produced, only two works, but those of such massive proportions that it makes the counting of titles absurd.[1]

As a possible exception to the rule, that uniquely isolated work the novel *Wuthering Heights* might be instanced; but it is unique only by reason of its form. The years preceding its creation were devoted by Emily Brontë to her poetry, and *Wuthering Heights*, as much a prose poem as anything else, is a masterpiece among her other masterpieces. So with Schubert's finest part-songs. We cannot say of 'Gesang der Geister über den Wassern' or of 'Grab und Mond' that if Schubert had composed only these two works he would stand in the forefront of composers for male-voice part-songs. They are the outcome of numerous experiments in the medium, a few of which fail, more of which completely succeed and in which his genius takes wing.

The part-songs that represent Schubert's genius at work, as opposed to those that he penned for performance, or as possible

[1] *How to read a poem* (University of London Press, London, 1961), p. 140.

money-spinners, are, in chronological order, 'Nur wer die Sehnsucht kennt' and 'Ruhe, schönstes Glück der Erde', D. 656–7, both of April 1819, 'Gesang der Geister über den Wassern', D. 714, of February 1821, and 'Nachthelle' and 'Grab und Mond', D. 892–3, both of September 1826. They are the peaks of his experiments in the part-song and display his efforts, sometimes deliberate, sometimes instinctive, to explore the use of the choral idiom to adorn different aspects of the poem in his hands: its pictorial qualities, its atmosphere, its philosophy. In one type of setting he blends, as in many of his best solo songs, the pictorial and philosophic aspects of the poem; the supreme example is the last, complete setting of Goethe's 'Gesang der Geister über den Wassern', but the poet has there already fused the concrete and abstract elements of his thought — the action of wind and rocks on water symbolizing the shaping of man's soul by the buffetings of fate. Schubert took the gift that Goethe offered.

Mention of Goethe recalls the fact that the texts of Schubert's part-songs are chosen from the poets whose names are familiar from his solo songs — Hölty, Matthisson, Schiller, Salis, and Goethe among others less celebrated. His friends Schober and Mayrhofer were responsible for the texts of a few part-songs, but the poets Müller and Heine, so prominent in the Lieder, were not used. Ernst Schulze, whose poetry inspired some fine songs in the years 1825–7, is the poet of only one part-song, and that of only mild interest, from February 1825, 'Ewige Liebe', D. 825.

Before considering the way in which the various types of part-songs culminated in the outstanding examples named above, a word or two might be devoted to the style of these works in general. In the early years, 1813–15, Schubert wrote only trios, T.T.B., usually unaccompanied. The trios gradually gave way to the quartet for T.T.B.B. during 1815 and 1816, and from March 1817 for the next ten years he composed only quartets or quintets. These too are usually unaccompanied, but instrumental accompaniments contribute an essential foundation to the 'Gesang der Geister' and 'Nachthelle'. The idiom, as was said earlier, is markedly of the period, that is, it is harmonic with an almost complete eschewal of counterpoint. Occasionally the voices enter in imitation, based on canon or fugato, but the device is soon abandoned. The necessary impetus is maintained by key-shifts — often very bold ones, and for unaccompanied voices extremely tricky to bring off — and by the use of emphatic metres in 2/4 or 6/8. The regular fall of the stresses in such metres, though invaluable in maintaining the chording of the voices, can often be monotonous or trivial. It becomes in some part-songs, e.g., in 'Das Dörfchen', D. 641, a mere strumming with voices.

The rejection of contrapuntal styles as an archaic process, not, of course, by Schubert only, but by all practitioners of the period, means that a heavy penalty is exacted. There is a sore lack of variety, of vocal colour and of interest (certainly to the listener and to an equal extent to the performers). The figuration in the voices and the regular pulse of the elementary metres — obviously a striving after a modern substitute for contrapuntal textures — are unsuccessful: they have elements of grossness instead of grace, and conjure up the full-throated roar of a German beer-cellar rather than the exquisite fantasies of Gothic chapel or Venetian salon. Quickly changing harmonies in vocal music defeat their own colourful aims; and when they are allied to rapid imitative entries in the voice-parts, as in Schubert's first setting of the 'Gesang der Geister', the confused noise affronts the ear. At other times the insipidity of the musical material, as in 'Nachtmusik' or in 'Geist der Liebe', produces work little more attractive than the average Victorian hymn-tune.

In one respect Schubert might have revolutionized the vocal quartet (for he is the first of the Viennese masters to treat it seriously) as Haydn and Mozart revolutionized the string quartet. Their aim was to make each instrument in the quartet of equal importance to the musical contribution. The idea that the string quartet was a violin solo accompanied by three subsidiary voices died hard; Schuppanzigh, Spohr, and even some of the mid-nineteenth-century violin virtuosi all spoke or wrote of *their* performance of string quartets — as if they were solo performers attended by three lesser partners. But the vanity of the solo violinist could not endure against the incontrovertible facts as set out in the quartets of Haydn, Mozart, and Beethoven; eventually the unity of the Viennese string quartet became an accepted fact. Schubert, right to the end, wrote his vocal quartets and quintets for a predominantly solo tenor voice with three or four accompanying voices. He never took the revolutionary step of writing a vocal quartet in which all four voices were of equal interest and significance to the pattern of the whole; had he done so he might have initiated a new, rich, and fruitful sphere in music, as he did in the Lied. Instead, in his hands, the male-voice part-song congealed as it were, and since no composer who followed him attempted the novel treatment, the part-song for male voices came to an ignominious end. If, towards the end of the nineteenth century, attempts were made by various composers to write such songs, in which the lower voices were vitalized and musical, they achieved only pastiche, for by then the form was dead, and the styles of previous centuries were the living stimuli. In most of Schubert's works for male voices the first tenor is the *melodieführende Stimme*, and even in the magnificent quintet 'Nur wer die Sehnsucht kennt' the voices are not equal participants. In 'Mondenschein' he entitled the score 'Quintetto', but also wrote against the first tenor part 'Tenore solo'; yet he intended the piece to be a quintet and referred to it as such in his letters to publishers.

This fact introduces a question, or a problem rather. Did Schubert distinguish between the part-song for a quartet or quintet of solo voices and the male-voice chorus? It is not always possible to judge from the title of his manuscript, or his published work, or from the actual music of any particular part-song what his wishes may have been in this matter. The doubt exists, of course, only in the case of the straightforward, homogeneous setting; certain part-songs, for example, 'Naturgenuss' of May 1816, contain interludes within the quartet setting to be sung by 'Tenor I' or 'Tenore I & II', and these interludes were, it is certain, intended for solo voices, as a pleasing contrast to the massed voices of the main sections of the part-song. In other cases, 'Nachthelle', for instance, there is no doubt at all: the song is for tenor solo with men's chorus; but in many others it seems likely that either medium would serve. As far as one can tell from the performances given in Schubert's lifetime, as they are set out in surviving programmes or concert-notices, his part-songs were given by an association of solo voices; this may have been due to economic factors, and the many performances of these part-songs in private, when doubtless a men's chorus performed, are unrecorded.

The consideration of the best of the part-songs that follows excludes any item from the church works, which, although for a similar medium, obviously require different terms of reference; nor have the numerous canons for three voices, composed in 1813 and 1814, found a place. The latter, although they clearly bear the stamp of Schubert's individuality, were written under Salieri's tuition and were never intended as anything but musical exercises. Another category of works that has been ignored consists of some half a dozen cantatas composed for the purpose of honouring various individuals and performed on a particular anniversary, birthday, name-day, or, in the case of Salieri, the jubilee celebrations of his arrival in Vienna. These, like the canons, are backwaters in the main stream of Schubert's music, and although, again like the canons, they have their moments of attraction, in bulk they are negligible.

One might fancifully entitle a large group of his part-songs 'Nature and Man'. All the poems depict the emotions aroused by the contemplation of nature, seen either as a benign mother offering solitude or invigoration or as a symbol and embodiment of the moods of the poet. The pathetic fallacy is freely evoked. Two early part-songs to words by Salis are 'Der Entfernten', D. 331, and 'Die Einsiedelei', D. 337; both are quartets for T.T.B.B. and both were composed in 1816. The poems are protracted and effusive, the first of five, the second of six, long stanzas. Schubert set each of them as solo songs at about the same period, and in these settings he indicated that all the verses were to be sung. Since the songs are Schubert at his plainest and simplest the result would be unbearably tiresome. In the quartet settings he selects verses. 'Der Entfernten' is a weak imitation by Salis of Goethe's 'Nähe des Geliebten'; as in this greater poem the sights and sounds of the natural scene arouse memories of the poet's beloved, but the lyric has none of Goethe's strength and grace. Schubert's setting is in C sharp major, the extravagance of the key being immaterial since it is for unaccompanied voices; nevertheless, the publisher, in 1867, transposed it to C major. It moves pleasantly in a slow, 6/8 measure, redeemed from insipidity by occasional astringent harmony; but it stands head and shoulders above its solo setting, and above most of the contemporary part-songs, by reason of an unusual and sustained cadence when the poet sees the dream-image of his beloved in the sunset:

Example 49

There is a touch here of the serenity of the Adagio in the String Quintet in C major. Before leaving this small part-song, one might note the introduction of that characteristic flourish in the melodic line, which Schubert is moved to introduce whenever his poetry deals with some specific natural reference, in this instance at the mention of the red rays of the sunset:

Example 50

The second poem, 'Die Einsiedelei', was first published by Salis under the title 'Lob der Einsamkeit'. The well in the oak-wood shall be his hermitage and chapel, and there he will dwell — the thought is somewhat confused — with his sweetheart. Schubert's two solo settings are negligible, but the short part-song is vigorous and likeable. Much of it is in unison, and the phrases, first in G minor, then in B flat minor, are almost angular; their lyricism redeems them from that, but a chorus would have to be on the watch against letting the chromaticism blur. The rising unison phrases of the opening are perfectly balanced by the fall of the phrase at the close, with its strong cadence in G major.[1]

The attraction of Salis for Schubert is easily understood; there is the same lilt in his verses, the same simplicity in his descriptions of scene and mood, as we find in Müller's work. His poem 'Lied im Freien', D. 572, was composed by Schubert in July 1817; it begins:

> Wie schön ist's im Freien,
> Bei grünenden Mai
> Im Walde wie schön!

Schubert sets off happily with a bouncing tune in F major, 2/4 time, in one of his easygoing and not too interesting styles. The end of the first section awakens attention by a well-tried, but effective device, a dive into D flat major, and in this key the jaunty rhythm slackens. The second verse, in which the poet stops in his tracks to rest in the shade of the lilacs and hazel-bushes, is more reflectively set, and the final verse entirely redeems the opening mediocrity. Half dreaming, half waking, the poet is lulled by leafy woods and the glint of the sunlight on the brook. Schubert's music takes on the mood wonderfully: the colours of D major, B flat minor, D flat major, and E major pass in the music, and a melodic figure in the first tenor part —

---

[1] The opening phrase of 'Die Einsiedelei' served later as the prelude for his solo song 'Atys': a mere coincidence, but an unusual one in Schubert.

Example 51

— is used as the basis of a page of fascinating music. The theme looks impossibly monotonous, but Schubert accepts it, and in his hands it serves as well as any more attractive melody. Technically, he achieves his purpose by grouping his voices into two duets; first tenor and first bass elaborate the theme, while the other two voices accompany; then the pairs change places:

Example 52

The close of the part-song reverts to the rhythmic bounce of the first page, but Schubert, his genius now awakened, introduces several touches that give point and variety to the music. One reaches the close of the piece with a renewed sense of admiration at the flexibility and resource of the composer who, although at times fettered by a chosen rhythmic scheme, in 'Lied im Freien' passes easily from and back to the scheme at the demands of the text, without any sense of violation or disunity.

The earlier part-songs in the 'Nature and Man' category close with 'Ruhe, schönstes Glück der Erde'. The poet is unknown, but he belongs to the Hölty–Matthisson–Salis fraternity, and his poem, a little deeper in sentiment than usual, seems to express a private grief, but its appeal is universal. He begs the beauty of the earth to give him peace so that dreams and tempests of the heart will pass away and his soul rise from its grave. Schubert composed the part-song in April 1819. It starts simply in C major with a slow 6/8 metre. But at once we are aware of a new beauty in the melody, and before very long the harmonic colouring and the shifting tonality arouse the highest interest. The words

> Dass es stille in uns werde
> Wie in Blumen ruht ein Grab.

are set to a short phrase in A major, and this is repeated at once a semitone lower. This is the earliest appearance of a feature that grows more prominent in the later part-songs. It is an extraordinary feature and demands a great deal from unaccompanied voices. The plea for peace is again sung in C major; the passage in which the spiritual agonies of the poet sink to rest is exquisitely treated and the melodic charm continues. As these dreams and longings rise, says the poet, so rises the pain of the soul. Schubert's response to these words is such as we find in his greater songs when they also touch on similar sentiments. A tortured chromaticism leads to a climax of pain:

Example 53

The passage is repeated in a higher key, but on the second occasion it becomes:

The words 'Ruhe, deinen Frieden gieb der Erde' bring back the music of the start, but given to the lower voices; above them the first tenor soars with a new, descant-like melody in Schubert's most lyrical vein. Again we have that typical feature, a phrase in E minor at once repeated in E flat minor, each time the cadence has a serenity that recalls the music of his last years, the 'Lindenbaum' or the String Quintet. The part-song closes with a *fortissimo*

F

cadence, which suggests that Schubert was changing the poet's hope that the soul will rise from its grave into an assertion that it shall do so. 'Ruhe, schönstes Glück' is a masterpiece. It is completely unknown, and I doubt if it has been sung in England this century. But given the performance it deserves, its effect would be most moving.

It is time to look at the Goethe part-songs, which all belong to this earlier period, 1817–21, and all of which can equally be included in the 'Nature and Man' series. At the same time as Schubert composed the 'Lied im Freien' he also composed his first setting of Goethe for male voices, that of the poem 'Gesang der Geister über den Wassern'. The poem had a powerful appeal for Schubert. A fragmentary setting for solo voice remains from 1816, and a year later he took it up again and produced an unaccompanied quartet setting.

Goethe's celebrated poem compares the souls of men to water: his use of symbolism, water cascading on rocks, smooth sheets reflecting the stars, the buffeting winds, was never more cogently used to convey his philosophy of life. The poem was written at Thun, during October 1779, at a time when Goethe was resolving to have done with the turbulence of his youth — the 'Sturm und Drang' phase — and to devote himself to cultivating the powers within him. The waters, after their stormy descent, should flow quietly, creeping through the meadows between smooth borders. Schubert's first setting, of March 1817, consists of a series of five independent episodes. A sense of approaching climax is contrived by quickening tempos and more elaborate figuration in the voice parts until the words describing the dash of water on rock are reached. The music is then excitedly chromatic and the turmoil is enhanced by syncopated rhythms, but there is a sense of contrivance, and the passage is not altogether convincing. Far more successful are the following episodes; the picture of the reflected skies is conveyed charmingly with short, melodic figures based on broken chords, technically far from easy for the voices:

Example 55   *Geschwind*

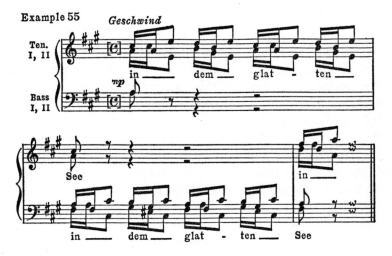

The music lessens in intensity to its close; Goethe repeats his opening lines at the end of the poem, justifying Schubert's return, in the last bars, to the music of the start.

Schubert must have felt that his setting had failed. For all that, it became known to his friends and was probably performed by them, for a copy of the score was made for Witteczek — the only source of the work that we have. Schubert may have destroyed his own manuscript, and he certainly made no effort to get the part-song published. Not until the appearance of the appropriate *Gesamtausgabe* volume, in 1891, was the work printed. A few years after this failure, in December 1820, he took the poem in hand again. The month is a remarkable one in the Schubert annals: it saw the production of the 'Quartettsatz' in C minor, the setting for female voices of Psalm XXIII and the song 'Waldes-nacht'. In this phase of heightened creative power he sketched out, in short score, the music for the first two-thirds of the 'Gesang der Geister'. The setting, in C sharp minor, is for a male-voice quartet with piano accompaniment. The slow, stately opening is fully composed, but from the verse beginning 'Von Himmel kommt es' only the voice parts are sketched in. The piano part of the first section consists of stormy, semiquaver octaves, typical of many of his 'water' poems — similar examples can be seen in the accompaniments to the unfinished songs 'Johanna Sebus', D. 728, and the second setting of 'Mahomets Gesang', D. 721, both of which were composed a few months after the part-song. The magnificent impetus of this renewed attempt on the poem slackens, and the final bars do nothing fresh with the text that had not been equally well done in the earlier setting. Schubert abandoned the sketch. We can be grateful to Mandyczewski that the fragment was printed in the *Supplement* (Serie xxi) to the *Gesamtausgabe* in 1897 instead of remaining in manuscript and to all intents and purposes unavailable to the majority of those interested. For as an insight into the raw outpourings of excited genius the musical material is of inestimable value to anyone who is moved by the phenomenon of musical creation.[1]

Almost immediately after throwing up his task, Schubert turned again to the poem, attempting a third and yet different version. His sketch for this setting begins in C major and is designed for eight male voices, accompanied by a quintet of bass strings — two violas, two cellos, and double-bass. The voices are strikingly grouped, not as a conventional double male-voice quartet, but as a tenor quartet in association with a bass quartet. The scope of the poem, becoming more apparent to Schubert as he studied it more deeply, seemed to call for these larger forces. The style of the music, noble enough in both the previous settings, now rises to majestic proportions. As with the previous sketch, voices and strings are fully composed for the first part of the poem, thereafter only the voice parts were written in. The music is more typical and much finer than that in the C sharp minor sketch. The stanza that starts 'Ragen Klippen, dem Sturz entgegen', telling of the cascading water, uses the turbulent chromatics of the previous settings, but its more open rhythm avoids the confusion of the 1817 setting, and Schubert, this time, is completely successful with its pictorial design. The calmer reaches of the river are described in a simple, flowing movement in E flat major until the lines on the 'reflected stars', where the

[1] The manuscript was lost sight of for many years. It is now in the library of Stanford University, California.

sketch breaks off.[1] But this was not the end. Schubert must have realized that here, at length, he had mastered the difficulties. Two months later he worked on the sketches for the first few stanzas and brought the part-song to a successful conclusion. The finished part-song is for the same medium, four tenors, four basses, with string quintet accompaniment. There are few changes between the sketch, as far as it goes, and the completed version, the most important being at the very start. The cadence in A flat major is altered to one in A major. This semitonal change, the result of what one would almost call 'semitonal indecision', in Schubert's composition is a fascinating quirk. Reference has been made to his tendency to repeat phrases a semitone lower, particularly noticeable in his part-songs. What was his reason for the alteration here?

Example 56

(a) Sketch: December 1820

Adagio molto

Ten. I, II III, IV

pp Des Men-schen Seel-e gleicht dem Was - ser.

Bass I, II III, IV

(b) Final version: February 1821

pp Des Men-schen Seel - e gleicht dem Was - ser.

The closing stanzas, missing from the sketch, are given a broad, extended treatment; the lingering cadences at the end of the lines,

[1] The manuscript sketch was sold in 1844 by Ferdinand Schubert to Ludwig Landsberg. After Landsberg's death it was bought by the Berlin Royal Library where it remains today (Deutsche Staatsbibliothek). It may be mentioned that in 1844 Ferdinand was in possession of both this sketch and the manuscript of the completed version: the latter was not published until 1858.

telling of the waters as they reflect the stars, are especially attractive; so is the way in which the cadential figure is elaborated by the cellos to usher in the section where the poet writes of the play of wind upon the water. As in the 1817 setting the last lines are sung to a modified form of the opening music, and the part-song ends with a long-held plagal cadence (nicknamed the 'Amen' cadence) in its minor form.

The work was performed, very shortly after Schubert composed it, at a concert in the Kärntnerthor Theater, Vienna, on 7 March 1821. Earlier in the concert there had occurred the famous performance by Vogl of 'Erlkönig' (on the eve of its publication). It was followed by the 'Gesang der Geister'. This was disastrously unsuccessful, and the failure, one feels, must have been due to inadequate interpretation.[1] The report of the concert in the Vienna *Allgemeine musikalische Zeitung* hits on a happy — if harrowing — comparison of the composer as a drayman who drives an eight-in-hand, swerving now right, now left, without ever getting along the road! The part-song was not published until March 1858, when it appeared from Spina as op. 167. It has long since taken its place in the forefront of Schubert's choral settings.

Schubert's second setting of a poem by Goethe is the quintet 'Nur wer die Sehnsucht kennt'. It belongs to April 1819, the month that also saw the birth of the quartet 'Ruhe, schönstes Glück'. The quintet is as celebrated as the quartet is obscure. The fame of Goethe's poem must contribute to this strange state of affairs. Many musicians feel that Schubert has shown a certain lack of sensibility in setting this intensely personal lyric, the cry of a desolate spirit, for male voices. Maybe! But the lines 'He who knows and loves me is far from here', which particularize the pathos, are lost in the general significance of the opening and closing lines, with their universal appeal: 'Only he who knows

---

[1] Accounts differ. Sonnleithner in his reminiscences (1857) says that the work was insufficiently rehearsed. Umlauff, on the other hand, says of it '... a deeply conceived and noble tone picture, which was excellently rehearsed and performed by the eight singers, all of them thoroughly trained and capable musicians' (1861).

longing knows what I suffer . . . lonely and torn from all joys, I
look on Nature's beauty in vain.'

The part-song, published in 1867 as 'Sehnsucht', is in externals
simplicity itself, a moving sequence of rich harmonies. Only at
the words 'My brain reels . . .' is the simple homophonic progress
broken by imitative entries. But the shifting harmonic colours
give an extreme poignancy to the appeal of the music. To name
the keys through which the music passes would mislead, for
Schubert's hold on his main key, E major, is firm enough, and the
chromatic cadences drive forward relentlessly through the heartbreak of the words to the resignation of the close. But clearly his
underlying scheme is the juxtaposition of E major and F major
and from the discordance to create in music Mignon's grief. Thus
when the opening phrases close, apparently in G major, the
progress of the music makes it clear that this G major is the
dominant of C major, and this in turn the dominant of F major.
We reach the first climax, to the words 'is far from here', in that
key, emphatically affirmed with *fortissimo* tone. The second half
of the part-song repeats the words, but the music derived from
the opening page is modified in many details. The tonality of F
major is this time merely hinted at, and the song seems to be
reaching its destined key for the close when, with an outcry of
pain, the wrench is made once more:

Example 57

From here the establishing of E major is by a lingering and pathetic cadence. In this masterly work Schubert has created an unforgettable embodiment not merely of Mignon, but of mankind, comfortless and alone.

The third and last poem by Goethe set to music by Schubert is 'Im Gegenwärtigen Vergangenes'.[1] Although Schubert's manuscript (undated) survives, the part-song is completely undocumented and the year of its composition is unknown. The verses come from the poet's 'West-östlichen Divan', and we know that Schubert composed, during 1821, several other poems from this source, including the two 'Suleika' songs, 'Geheimes', and 'Versunken'. Hence it is possible that 'Im Gegenwärtigen Vergangenes', D. 710, was also composed in 1821. The style of the music does not, at least, contradict the date, although the musical material is inferior; its inferiority is made more obvious rather than concealed by Schubert's evident attempt at a sweet, almost lush, presentation, inspired — or should one say instigated? — by Goethe's opening lines on roses and lilies. The form of the work, too, is unusual: it commences with a long tenor solo in D flat major, almost a self-contained song. The male-voice chorus that follows begins with a change of key, time-signature, and tempo, and is also complete in itself. Points of technique alone interest the student: the use of the little *fiorature*, which Schubert uses to illustrate his poet's reference to natural objects, in this song to the sight and scent of the flowers, and a casual device of canonic imitation between the two tenors at the start of the chorus:

Example 58

[1] The title might be translated as: 'The Past that lives in the Present'.

To this slight but not ineffective use of canon Schubert returned later.

During the next three years Schubert composed few part-songs and those few of small value. They were years mainly occupied with opera-composition, from *Alfonso und Estrella* to *Rosamunde*. Three sets of male-voice part-songs were composed and published during the period, opp. 11, 16, and 17. Apart, possibly from 'Liebe' and 'Die Nacht', op. 17, nos. 2 and 4, the pieces are of less merit than many of the juvenile pieces of 1816 and 1817.

Between the spring of 1824 and the autumn of 1826 he composed a dozen or so part-songs, of which half are typical of his best work. The two that close the series, conveniently labelled here as 'Nature and Man', are 'Mondenschein', composed in January 1826, and 'Nachthelle', composed in September 1826. Each poem celebrates the beauty of a moonlit night and the exaltation of soul felt by the poet as he contemplates the scene before him. The poem 'Mondenschein' is by Schober; it is over-consciously exquisite and his lines are plastered with typical German noun-doublets — 'Nebelschmelz', 'Zauberlicht', 'Liebesschmerz', and so on. Schubert's music, too, strikes us as just a little too studiedly sweet. The lower voices strum on a 6/8 rhythm, moving smoothly from A flat major and minor to E major and back again; above this guitar-like strumming the first tenor sings a rather florid serenata. Again we have the frequent appearances of those *fiorature* in the melody, evoked by the natural scene. 'Nachthelle' is a different matter. The poem, by J. G. Seidl, is shorter and pithier, and in a few stanzas it depicts the silvery landscape and the poet's sadness at the ephemeral quality of such beauty.

> Ich fass' in meinem Herzenhaus
> Nicht all' das reiche Licht,
> Es will hinaus, es muss hinaus,
> Die letzte Schranke bricht.

Although the poem of Seidl is quite unknown, it resembles a very celebrated German lyric, the 'Mondnacht' of Eichendorff —

> ... so sternklar war die Nacht.
> Und meine Seele spannte
> Weit ihre Flügel aus
> Flog durch die stillen Lande
> Als flöge sie nach Haus.   (EICHENDORFF.)

— familiar to music-lovers because of Schumann's and Brahms's settings. Schubert's response to Seidl's sincerity is immediate. The starry, moonlit night is depicted vividly in his pianoforte part; the tenor sings a melody of the true Schubertian gold, and the choral interludes are closely integrated with the solo to create the spacious air and the poet's emotions. The key-changes, very different from those in the mechanically sweet 'Mondenschein', are daringly novel, and at the close, where the poet cries out against the fact that such natural beauty will depart, the contrasting of B flat major chords with others in F sharp minor is hardly dimmed today, after a century and a half of such harmonic experiments. If this wonderful part-song is flawed at all, it is, first, in the extended nature of the music: words are rather excessively repeated to carry the massive proportions of Schubert's conception; and, second, in the almost impracticably high *tessitura* of the tenor solo part — 'with music by Schubert for a principal and damned high tenor voice', as one of his friends wrote to him.[1] But against these imperfections, the fresh, moving inspiration of the whole part-song stands undimmed.

The other four part-songs, composed between 1824 and 1826, are not based on poems dealing with man's reactions to Nature in her manifold aspects, nor do they fit into any such convenient category. But the music Schubert composed for them lends the group a unity in that he is concerned, within the limitations of his medium, to illustrate as vividly as he can the words of his texts, their images, and the sentiments aroused by the poets' chosen themes.

'Der Gondelfahrer', D. 809, is a poem by his friend Mayrhofer. The gondolier sings as his boat glides over the moonlit water and shrugs as the midnight bell sounds from St. Mark's — everyone is asleep, only he is working. The music, for quartet of voices with

---

[1] *Schubert: Documentary Biography*, ed. O. E. Deutsch, p. 597.

pianoforte accompaniment, is a charming barcarolle and the very lilting pianoforte chords of the accompaniment, though primarily intended to represent the dance of the gondola over the waters of the canal, obliquely suggest the pluck of Venetian lute-strings. The thought of the spectral glinting of the water in the moonlight brings Schubert's characteristic *fiorature* into the melody. Later in the part-song, the device of canonic imitation, used in 'Im Gegenwärtigen Vergangenes', reappears in a more captivating form:

Example 59

The melody of the second stanza develops the little flourishes of the first stanza to such a degree, under the influence of Mayr-hofer's rocking boat, that we get more than a hint of 'Auf dem Wasser zu singen', composed a few months previously:

Example 60

Midnight chimes in A flat major, and the main key, C major, is easily regained for the placid return to the opening music. The part-song was composed in March 1824, at the same time, probably, as the setting for solo voice. Both settings are similar in style (the main key in both is C major, and both modulate to A flat for the midnight tolling), but the solo song is one of Schubert's lesser songs and cannot bear comparison with the much finer part-song.

In October 1828 the music firm of Pennauer published three of Schubert's part-songs as op. 64 (D. 825). They are as diverse in style as can be imagined. The text of each is by a different poet, none of whose verses was used again by Schubert for a choral setting. They are 'Wehmut', poem by Heinrich Hüttenbrenner (the younger brother of Schubert's friends Anselm and Josef); 'Ewige Liebe', poem by Ernst Schulze; and 'Flucht', poem by Karl Lappe. (The last of these three poets was responsible for the texts of two favourite solo songs by Schubert — 'Im Abendrot' and 'Der Einsame'.) The second part-song is almost negligible, which is surprising in view of the fine series of solo settings that Schubert made of Schulze's verses. But the other two are in an attractive Schubertian vein. 'Wehmut' begins with the words 'Die Abendglocke tönt' ('The evening bell sounds'), and Schubert chooses to illustrate his text by giving the first bass a series of minims on F natural to sing in imitation of the tolling bell. Around this pedal note he builds his part-song. It is extraordinarily well done since nothing seems to be sacrificed to this very limiting condition. The melodies are delightfully easy and supple, the modulations seemingly quite spontaneous, although each of them, of course, centres round the pedal F: B flat major, D minor, D flat major, B flat minor. The bell stops, and the music moves into G flat major for the poet's meditation on his passing youth and his sensitive heart. The section ends in F major and the bell resumes its chime, that is, the first bass resumes the steady monotone on F. 'Oh, sound! soft bell, in the valley below; today is buried in tomorrow and grief is buried in the grave.' The short coda of the song telescopes the key-changes — D minor, B flat minor, and B flat major — in the space of half a dozen bars. It is a precious example of Schubert's absorption in his text and its elevation into a music greater than its own poetic worth.

The third number in the opus, Lappe's 'Flucht' is in complete contrast. 'I will live in the open air,' says the poet. 'Death is musty in the coffin.' Schubert's response takes the form of a bright, extrovert setting in C major, with striding melodies and a rhythm whose spring suggests the open air and bird-song; mock-sinister phrases, falling where the others rise, call up the picture of Death musty in the coffin or of Need squatting in the corner. But although the sight of these pages suggests at first a straightforward 'Wanderlied', a further look reveals a good deal of cunning craftsmanship. The part-song is actually more contrapuntal than most others, and although in general Schubert has a tendency to keep all his voices going full out in the chosen rhythmic pattern, this time it is held at bay. The short, two-part 'echo' motifs are not mechanically worked either; in the second episode Schubert recapitulates his music in C minor, and the whole vocal scheme is rearranged in an adroit manner, without any sacrifice of spontaneity. The third section of the work, reverting to the major key, uses a further, and for Schubert an almost unique, device, that of melodic inversions. Lappe, the poet of these verses, is forgotten in the annals of German literature, but Schubertians will always be grateful to his modest talent for the three vocal settings he inspired Schubert to compose.

The last of the part-songs showing Schubert's absorbed translation into music of a poem that deeply appealed to him, is the setting of Seidl's 'Grab und Mond', composed in September 1826, the same month that saw the birth of 'Nachthelle'. 'Grab und Mond' is the 'Doppelgänger' of the part-songs, a work that is unlike any other part-song and poses, like the 'Doppelgänger' also, a question. It promises possible developments; did Schubert's early death prohibit the fulfilment of the promise? . . . or is the unique quality of 'Grab und Mond' merely a 'sport' induced by the strange tone of Seidl's poem? The short, enigmatic verses ask one of man's eternal questions. The English version given here is a simple translation of the German and claims no merit other than that of attempting to convey the literal meaning of the words:

> Silver-blue moonlight
> Falls here.
> So many a ray sinks

Into the grave;
Dear Moon,
Friend of Sleep,
Be not silent.
Say whether in the grave
Darkness dwells
Or light?

Everything mute?

Now, silent Grave,
You speak.
You have drawn so many a ray
Into rest.
You have buried so many glances of the Moon,
Silver-blue,
Give back just one ray!

Come and see!

Schubert's music is in A minor, marked *Langsam*. Its extreme
simplicity covers many subtle touches of harmony and stress. The
first stanza concludes in C major, and the line 'Everything mute?'
starts the music in A flat major with this bare, hollow-sounding
questioning:

Example 61

The address to the grave is in A flat minor; with very little modification of rhythm, but that little most thoughtfully executed, it is a repetition of the opening music, and is the most remarkable instance of Schubert's practice of repeating music a semitone lower. But an even more remarkable instance occurs at the end. The phrase 'Give back just one ray' ends on a dominant seventh in A flat minor; the next line, 'Come and see!' begins in C flat major, leading the music back, via E major, to a close in A minor:

Example 62

An examination of Schubert's autograph manuscript shows that originally he wrote the last three bars in the above quotation, the *fortissimo* 'Komm und schau!', in C major. For the publication of the part-song (a year after its composition) he changed the C major phrase into C flat major! Is it fanciful to imagine that this is how he first conceived it, and that when the song came to be published he restored his original conception? The alteration was certainly not made to facilitate matters for the singers! C major may sound easier than C flat major to the instrumentalist; to the singer it is an immaterial difference. But in this song, the prevailing minor mode of the preceding passage and the pause before the entry on the word 'Komm' mean that either note is extremely tricky to pitch. These rapids past, however, the part-song ends quietly in a cadence in A major, conciliatory in a way that is Schubert's, but not, perhaps, Seidl's.

The male-voice part-songs of Schubert contain these isolated masterpieces: they do not, as a body of work, show any of the progressive development that other categories of his work so fascinatingly reveal, nor do they contribute anything obvious to those other categories. Only one small factor in his songs may derive from his part-songs: the necessity for sudden swerves into new keys, without preparation, in order to provide contrast and impetus to the unaccompanied voices, may have led to those similar shifts, so wonderfully effective, in his songs, for example, in 'Nacht und Träume' and 'Der Musensohn', and, in a different but related way, to the swerves to other keys at the end of each stanza in 'Die Sterne' (words by Leithner), D. 939, whose rhythm also reminds us of many of the part-songs. Otherwise their contribution is slight. But 'Grab und Mond', with its *gravitas*, its tragedy only hinted at by a half-irony, is new in Schubert, and contributed something towards the treatment of similar moods in Müller, when the composer encountered *Winterreise*. And when Schubert found Heine, in the 'Reisebilder', his realization in music of the new and ironic tone of the verses, half-tragedy and half-mockery, had its modest beginnings in the composition of 'Grab und Mond'.

THE FANTASIA IN F MINOR, OP. 103

In his schooldays Schubert composed three long fantasias for
pianoforte duet, but his worth-while work in this medium
began in 1818, some time after those juvenile efforts. From then
until his death he composed a substantial number of piano duets,
returning continually to the medium and using it for the expression of all kinds of music — music that ranges from small intimate
forms to full-scale sonatas. A remarkable fact emerges when we
glance over the list of his mature piano duets; it is that every single
one was published commercially. By that is meant that none of
them remained to be published by the editors of the *Gesamtausgabe* as a duty to be done in fulfilling the obligations of a complete
edition. There is an exception, the Overture in G minor, composed in October 1819, but since it did not come to light until
1896 it was never available to nineteenth-century publishers.
There are twenty major piano duets; fourteen were published in
Schubert's lifetime, and the remaining six appeared from various
publishing houses by 1840, only twelve years after his death. Each
of Schubert's duets, then, carries an opus number, however
irrelevant it may be. (Even the last duet of all, the short and
unimportant Fugue in E minor of June 1828, appeared in 1844
as op. 152.) This full publication is an indication of the immense
popularity of the piano duet in the last century, and it throws into
greater relief the almost complete disregard of the medium today.
In these times of broadcasting and gramophone records the piano
duet has lost its main purpose: it is now no longer the only
effective way of performing in the home works originally written
for orchestra or large chamber-music combinations. With the
disappearance from the musical scene of such arrangements,
much original work for piano duet, including Schubert's, has been
silenced too.

The music of the Schubert duets was cast in forms that are

G

varied but conventional. There are marches, polonaises, divertisse-
ments, fantasias, variations, rondos, and sonatas. The two years
1818 and 1824, the summers of which he passed as music master
to the two daughters of Count Johann Esterházy, each produced
a group of piano duets. The two groups have a noticeable simil-
arity of content — each contains a sonata, a series of marches, a
set of variations, a set of polonaises. The second group, from 1824,
includes such primary masterpieces as the Variations on an
Original Theme, in A flat, op. 35 (D. 813) and the Sonata in C
major (the 'Grand Duo'), op. 140 (D. 812). Nevertheless, it
yields first place to the final group, which he composed in 1828,
the Fantasia in F minor, op. 103 (D. 940), the Allegro in A minor
(known as 'Lebensstürme'), op. 144 (D. 947), and the Rondo in
A major, op. 107 (D. 951). In these three compositions the expression is, of course, more mature and the style more graceful than in
the earlier works, but the musical material itself is so much finer.
In the short, significant phrase or in the sustained melody
Schubert's devising is superb. One can only wonder at these
themes; analysis or explanation adds almost nothing. His use of
the material, however, is worthy of both analysis and investigation, for the discoveries add to our knowledge of his wide-ranging
powers and of his gifts for musical edifice. I have suggested elsewhere that the music he composed in 1828 shows new powers of
intellectual development and that the *Winterreise* songs first
tapped these depths of his musical being. The three piano duets
of 1828 are not surpassed, even by their companion masterpieces
of that year, in the revelation of those methods of development,
and the compositions of 1824, for all their endearing qualities,
contain nothing so magnificent in the treatment of theme and
pianoforte figuration as we find in the last three duets.

The Fantasia in F minor was first sketched in outline in January
1828 while Schubert was living in the home of his friend Schober.
The manuscript containing these sketches was discarded, but not
destroyed, by the composer as soon as his final version was
finished. For a reason that can be discussed later he kept the first
and bulkiest part of the sketches and took it with him when he left

Schober's home in August 1828 to live with his brother Ferdinand. The remainder, a few leaves containing notes for the last section, remained with Schober, and passed from him to his niece Isabella Raab. Either from Schubert's section, or from Schober's, a connecting leaf or two was lost, but the rest survived.[1]

The final version must have been completed from this preliminary draft in February 1828, for Schubert offered the work to the music publishers B. Schott's Sons of Mainz, on 21 February 1828, but the fair copy he made was not ready until April.[2]

A little later, on 9 May 1828, Schubert and his friend Lachner visited Bauernfeld and played the fantasia to him from manuscript. Bauernfeld, in his diary entry for that day, recorded: 'Today Schubert (with Lachner) played his new, wonderful four-handed *Fantasia* to me ...' and years later, in 1881, Lachner himself wrote some reminiscences of Schubert in which he recalled the performance of — in his own words — 'Schubert's glorious Fantasia in F minor, op. 103, for pianoforte duet. ...' These adjectives show the depth of the impression made on the two friends, and they are welcome comments for the fantasia tends to be undervalued amongst Schubert's piano duets. It is good to know that even in his own day friends were not lacking to appreciate its value.

B. Schott's Sons did not accept the work offered to them; it was published posthumously by Diabelli & Co. of Vienna, in March 1829, and called op. 103 (this was Schubert's own designation). The composer dedicated the work to his former pupil Countess Karoline Esterházy, the woman with whom he was said to be in love. Some biographers of Schubert, wishing to call the legend of the love affair into question, and indeed it has no serious foundation, have suggested that the dedication of op. 103 to Karoline derives from the publisher, not from Schubert himself. But the composer, in the letter to Schott's Sons already mentioned,

---

[1] The larger part, ten leaves, is now in the Louis Koch collection: Rudolf Floersheim, Muzzano-Lugano. It extends to the close of the Allegro vivace movement. The last part, two leaves, consisting of sixty-six bars, belongs to Dr. Max Josef Mannheim, London.

[2] The fair copy, dated April 1828, is in the Vienna City Library.

specifies the F minor Fantasia as 'dedicated to Countess Karoline Esterházy', which is conclusive.

The unassuming way in which the fantasia opens brings to one's mind a general thought about the big masterpieces of Schubert: how rarely they start with the bold flourish, or with the theme proclaimed emphatically by the full instrumental array! Rather do they steal on the ear, persuasive and appealing. One is reminded of the quiet, conversational scene with which Shakespeare will open one of his great tragedies. We recall, for instance, Schubert's two mature symphonies: the cellos and basses in the 'Unfinished', the *pianissimo* horns in the great C major; or the soft, accompanimental bass that ushers in the first movement of the A minor String Quartet. The powerful opening of the D minor String Quartet and that of the 'Wanderer' Fantasia in C are the exceptions rather than the rule. The scale upon which he will work during the course of the F minor Fantasia is not revealed by the surprisingly modest gesture at the start; it begins with two bars of simple, broken chords in F minor. Above their persistent, soft accompaniment the wonderful theme of the fantasia floats:

In the subsequent treatment of this theme, Schubert shows what I have called his powers of linear development. The theme is not used as the basis of a structural mass, there is no evolution of a pattern based on imitation, nor is there any scheme of key-contrasts exploiting the theme or part of it. Instead, by unexpected and detailed changes in its structure, he evolves a long, flexible, and varied melody. When this turns into the major key, the introduction of B natural (bar 2 of Example 64) leads to a sudden upsurge in the melody, delightful in itself, and which at once suggests further delights in the course of its linear development:

Example 64

However gently Schubert may open a movement, once he has ingratiated it with the listener, he usually proceeds to vigorous — even explosive — figures, which generate energetic and ornate episodes. Quite often these give the impression that the quiet theme at the start is merely a prelude, to be dropped as soon as it has served its purpose. This is rarely the case. It is one of the features of Schubert's constructions that, however modest-seeming his opening theme may be, it is, for all that, his *main* idea. The theme of the F minor Fantasia, after its appearance in the major form quoted in Example 64, leads to a lively, *staccato* figure in the bass, taken up directly after, and decorated, by the Primo part:

Example 65
Secondo (8ves)

Had Schubert been planning a 'first' movement in this section of his Fantasia, we could be reasonably sure that the development section would have concerned itself with the theme at the start of the work, and not with the more obvious, *staccato* figures of Example 65. As it is, one might now try to see what form he has actually planned for the fantasia, what is its underlying, basic structure, if so rigid an analysis can be applied to a form that, as its very title implies, may be formless if the composer chooses so. In fact, Schubert is attempting in this work in F minor to pursue the same kind of constructional efforts that he made in the Fantasia in C major for violin and piano, op. 159, of the previous month, December 1827. In both works he tries to loosen the conventional structure of the four-movement sonata: to loosen it: he will not entirely break with convention and avoid it altogether. The 'first' movement, i.e., the true 'sonata' movement, is dispensed with. In the C major Fantasia, for violin and piano, episodes from one section recur in subsequent sections in an attempt to fuse them together and give them a greater unity. In the F minor duet Fantasia the material of the opening section reappears at the end of the work and is there given an extended treatment, is developed, as it were, to form the Finale; a formal unity is obtained in a different way.

There is little development, in the accepted sense, of this material in the opening section itself. Apart from the melodic changes of the lyrical theme, the Allegro molto moderato consists of a series of alternations of his two contrasted ideas, the lyrical and the dramatic. The section ends with an F major version of the *staccato* theme in Example 65, so subdued and smooth that it is almost as if Schubert were trying to amalgamate the two ideas into one:

Example 66

The resemblance between the two phrases marked 'A' in Example 63 and Example 66 is apparent, and links one with the other. The next two 'movements' of the fantasia are a Largo and an Allegro vivace, corresponding to the slow movement and the scherzo of orthodox sonata construction. The first is short, little more than an interlude, but the second is a long, vividly written movement, containing some of Schubert's finest scherzo writing and forming the real, solid heart of the fantasia.

The Largo is in the remote key of F sharp minor. An earlier, parallel case can be found in another of his fantasias, the 'Wanderer'; the key of this work is C major, the slow movement is in C sharp minor. The choice of key in each case provides a further instance of Schubert's relish for the 'Neapolitan' shift to keys a semitone away from the prevalent key. The transition in the F minor Fantasia between F major at the close of the first section and F sharp minor for the start of the Largo is abrupt, almost gauche:

Example 67

It emphasizes, as nothing else does, that when Schubert dispensed with sonata-form, he dropped with it his careful and, in most cases, inspired transitional work from episode to episode. There are similar perfunctory moves between one section and the next to be found in the impromptus and moments musicaux: the sections are simply pasted together, as it were, by a few chords. Having reached F sharp minor, Schubert indulges in *fortissimo, ben marcato* chords and plentifully double-dotted — or triple-dotted — phrases where, as it has been said, he tends to mistake violence for power. But the outburst over, there comes suddenly one of those surprising interludes, soft and melodious, which he delights to add to his fiery expostulations. And the snatch of melody is one of his golden inspirations, all the more precious because it comes but once and is gone:

Example 68

This snatch of melody is full of the romantic sentiment to become so familiar during the middle years of the nineteenth century — one of the earliest manifestations of it. It is a striking example of the way in which genius, almost unwittingly, glimpses those intangible moves of the spirit of music, and first gives a tendency form and substance. Nearly contemporary with Schubert's melody, there is another, similar foreshadowing of coming events, and this, too, is a work of young genius; two years later, in Warsaw, Chopin penned his Étude in E major, op. 10, no. 3, and although his melody has nothing physically in common with that of Schubert's quoted above, both are unmistakably full of the spirit of the future — romantic themes akin to those we find in Liszt, Berlioz, and Verdi. More particularly, Schubert's melody has an affinity with the short, Wagnerian leitmotiv, those in the *Ring*, for instance. It could easily come from the Brünnhilde music of *Siegfried* or *Götterdämmerung*. Perhaps it is that fall of a seventh at 'B' in the quotation above, suggesting the melody associated in *Götterdämmerung* with 'Redemption':

Example 69

A short passage based on the *marcato* phrases concludes the Largo and leads to the third section of the work, a Scherzo in style, although not so called by the composer. The movement, an Allegro vivace in the same key of F sharp minor, is the longest section in the fantasia. It presents in rich array all the elements of the Schubert Scherzo and adds to them a polyphonic texture that is new and invigorating. The construction of the movement is conventional, with no deviation at all from the ground plan of the movement — that of a rondo. The first theme is quoted below, for several points of note arise in considering it. Only the outline is given:

Example 70 *Allegro vivace*

Primo

Secondo

The swinging gait of this theme, so typical of Schubert's on-striding rhythms, is maintained without relaxation throughout the section. The octave jump, the grace-notes, the small figurative elements in bars 9 and 10, and the broken chords a semitone apart in bars 13 and 14, all these are the ingredients of the Schubert Scherzo theme: they are rarely all present together as in this one, and all contribute to the general architectural mass of the movement. He seemed to be particularly fond, during the last three years of his life, of one of these features: the juxtaposition of chord arpeggios a semitone apart (bars 13 and 14). How the feature permeates the whole of the String Quartet in G of 1826! And the last four sonatas contain many passages based on the idea. It is, one feels, yet another embodiment of his addiction to the 'Neapolitan'-sixth chord and the possibilities of harmonic colour implicit in the progression. Before we leave consideration of the Scherzo theme there are deeper implications to notice. The first is the harmonic basis. Without being in any way extravagant, it has a quiet originality and the characteristic discovery of what I have called elsewhere the unimplied harmony of the note progressions. By that phrase I mean that the obvious harmonization of the melody is not so much deliberately avoided, as that an unusual, but perfectly convincing, scheme is found to support the notes of the melody, which is not necessarily implied by them. Once our ears have associated the melody with Schubert's harmony, how-ever, the substitution of the more conventional chords would sound extremely insipid. The result is that listeners tend to imagine that Schubert's harmonic schemes — here and in hosts of other places — are the obvious ones, and his quiet and unobtrusive originality in this way is overlooked. But is it obvious that the first four bars should be harmonized thus?

Example 71

The E natural instead of E sharp in the second bar, the plagal cadence in A major instead of in F sharp minor in bars 3 and 4, are surely both a little unexpected? But how much less vivid the passage would be if we restored the 'proper' harmonies! The second point of interest in this theme is the way in which Primo and Secondo exchange parts at the close of the passage — a small example of invertible counterpoint. This device awakens in Schubert an impulse towards canonic structure, and much of the splendid surge forwards of the Scherzo springs from this treat-ment. The next idea is a pure canon and is worked with tremen-dous verve in the short development of the movement. We are reminded of the Scherzo in the Pianoforte Trio in E flat, op. 100

(composed only a month or two before the present one), but that Scherzo is a purely melodic canon; in the fantasia, harmonies, contrapuntal figures, the very musical thought, all spring from the primary 'canonic' impulse. In one passage Schubert unifies his two ideas: for a moment the conflict is resolved, and, with a little adjustment, the two themes go together in a perfect contrapuntal fit. The adjustment gives a chance to hear how vital his initial harmonization was, since it is necessary for him to alter the E natural, for once, into E sharp to justify the counterpoint.

The central Trio episode, *con delicatezza*, in D major, continues the basic impulse. Light arpeggios, at a bar's distance, rise and fall between the players, and sparkle in various key-colours, F sharp major, C major, B flat major. This interlude finished, the music of the Scherzo is recapitulated. Another scissors-and-paste join occurs between the concluding bars of the Scherzo and the Finale, designed to pass as quickly as possible from F sharp minor to F minor for the introduction of the themes from the opening Allegro molto moderato.

There is always the possibility — one almost writes the word 'danger' — that the emotional overtones that are inherent in music may serve a composer in a merely mechanical way. A shift into soft, minor harmonies, whatever the quality of the music, conveys to the listener the sense of deepened, even saddened, emotion. The association of various sentiments with various musical devices has been so closely welded by all composers, great and small, over the centuries that our response, as listeners, is as closely welded to them. Nor need these emotions be so obvious as those associated with the quick march on the one hand, or the mournful elegy on the other; much subtler emotional responses are evoked by the chances and changes of music. It has been said of Schubert that his major to minor, or minor to major, changes are sometimes so mechanical as to be suspect.[1] This may be so in some of his lesser songs, for example. But the wonder of his craft in the greater songs and instrumental pieces is that these transitions of his, from one musical emotion to another, do always seem inspired by genuine feeling. They have the unmistakable

[1] Plunket Greene in *Music and Letters*, Oct. 1928, p. 317.

ring of sincerity. And so when the exhilarated mood of the Scherzo passes — by a somewhat mechanical bridge-passage, as has been admitted — to the sensitive, tender melody of the opening bars, the listener is subjected to a change of emotion that, one can be certain, was first experienced by the composer himself. The result is that when the short recapitulation of the initial melody is past Schubert can rise easily to a no less sincere, but nobly exalted, mood in which the music deals sublimely with the theme first announced in Example 65. It serves as a kind of *cantus firmus* to an elaborate web of counterpoint: the four hands of the players become four voices (using the term in its sense of parts in a polyphonic work). The various ideas, chromatic and highly individual, pass between the players and appear at all points of the keyboard. There is no doubt that Schubert was, in this impressive page, deliberately exercising his contrapuntal powers, making them the prime sources and not using them as a decorative, subsidiary background. The piano duets and the church music of 1828 all reveal this tendency towards conscious contrapuntal textures, and the composer's motives in displaying them were probably not unmixed. All the usual academic devices appear in the closing section of the fantasia, and the climax is prepared for by a 'pedal point' on the dominant, a long, rolling bass octave on C. The *fortissimo* chords at the climax suddenly break off; there are two bars of silence, and the soft, opening theme appears again; it concludes suddenly and the work ends with the most remarkable cadence in the whole of Schubert's work:

Example 72
(Outline only)

In conclusion, we might glance at the sketches for the fantasia, not only to trace Schubert's creative working on them, but also to see, possibly, why he kept those first ten leaves after he had finished the final version for the publisher. The whole of the opening section is sketched through and, in essentials of construction, is almost unchanged in the finished work; but the indications are almost entirely melodic, that is, the whole of the music springs, as it were, from a melodic conception. The appearance of these pages is of an unaccompanied melody, chiefly in the right hand of the Primo part; the other three staves are blank. The original form of Schubert's main theme was as follows:

Example 73

Although this was strengthened for the final version, the faltering effect at the close of the phrases is not unattractive. The melody appears thus throughout Schubert's sketch.

The slow movement is complete in the sketch. It was marked originally Andante molto, then Andante. The decision to have an even slower tempo, Largo, is, it will surely be agreed, a wise one. The Scherzo is also practically complete in the sketch. It is here that the most interesting point of the manuscript is to be found. Schubert's first idea was to write a march as a Trio to the Scherzo.

He has composed a continuous, though fragmentary, movement in common time, D major, marked Tempo di marcia. It is heralded by a sustained note on C sharp. The theme is an undistinguished motif based on heavily dotted chords, deficient in melodic interest, though rhythmically alive:

Example 74

As with other markedly rhythmic marches of Schubert's, this one also repeats its basic rhythm to the point of monotony. Unlike the present Trio, which replaced it, the march was to have made a second appearance after the recapitulation of the Scherzo. This would have lengthened the work to almost impossible proportions, and no one will quarrel with his decision to dispense with the protracted march in favour of the delicate and more homogeneous episode, in the same key of D major, which now serves as the Trio. That he decided to cut out the Tempo di marcia section, while still engaged on the sketches, is clear from the fact that ideas for the final D major 'Trio' make their appearance in the unfilled staves beneath the chords of the march theme.

But that he had got down on paper so substantial an amount of the march was doubtless the reason why he kept his sketches, intending to return to the half-finished draft and complete it later on, as a separate work, if the occasion arose. The only idea in the sketched march that he used was the sustained C sharp; this, becoming enharmonically a D flat, still serves as the link between the Scherzo, in F sharp minor, and the closing section in F minor.

The sketches for the transition between the two sections have been lost. The final two leaves of the sketch (four pages) resume at approximately the twelfth bar of the finale. Judging from these pages, Schubert did not find the devising of his contrapuntal finale an easy task: passages apparently complete were rejected, and another, of twelve bars, fully scored, is cancelled and recommenced at once. The final version, in every case, amplifies the first conception; unisons are made into octaves, chords more fully filled in. The remarkable coda, quoted in Example 10, belongs to his final work on the fantasia: in the sketch it is a plain, full close in F minor. As always, when one compares for the first time Schubert's unfamiliar sketches and the final version, with which one has always been familiar, one is struck by the enormous amount of work that went into the preliminary drafts for the fantasia. He does not jot down short ideas of melody, rhythm, transitional episode, and so forth and develop them individually on paper, nor does he record subsequent piano improvisation on them. The movement, still hazy in details, is there in his mind: the paper is the instrument on which he records, corrects, improvises, if so inspired, or amplifies. He is said to have composed while standing at a high desk; this implies work away from the piano, and the implication would seem to be borne out by his sketches. He composes right through, so to speak, and it is fascinating to see the strokes of poetic genius born on paper as he composed. It is fascinating, too, to examine the wealth of accompanimental detail used to support the melodic line that he has drawn so continuously and without deviation for page after page and to note his tendency to deepen the emotion whenever, momentarily, his melody darkens. This tendency to deepen emotion goes hand in hand with the tendency mentioned above to amplify and adorn the technical embodiment of that emotion. With some composers and poets the creative method is to select from profusion, to compress and refine; with Schubert the opposite is almost without exception the case. He amplifies his original ideas, he extends their emotional range and enriches their harmonies and accompaniments. But this is not the same thing as repetition of musical ideas; his sketches give no support to the criticism that he repeats himself, if by that is meant a mechanical repetition designed merely to lengthen a section or to hide an impoverished invention. Among the numerous sketches for his mature work, those for the F minor Fantasia stand almost alone in value, in interest, and in the light they shed on his methods of work. Only the sketch for the slow movement of the Pianoforte Trio in E flat, op. 100, surpasses them in importance.

'LAZARUS, OR THE FEAST
OF RESURRECTION'

THE author of the three-act drama *Lazarus, or the Feast of Resurrection* was August Hermann Niemeyer. He was born in Halle in 1754, worked in the city as pastor and university professor all his life, and died there in July 1828. Niemeyer became well known as a theologian and poet; he modelled himself on Klopstock, to whom he dedicated his collected poems when they were published in 1778. *Lazarus* is one among several sacred dramas from his pen, all obviously inspired by Klopstock's masterpiece in this line, *Messias*. His philosophy is made plain in the preface with which he introduced the 1778 edition of his poetry. He wrote:

There is no higher way for the fairest of all philosophies and the noblest of all arts than the way of religion . . . . I found in the story of 'The Resurrection of Lazarus' an admirable opportunity to show from every aspect three of the mightiest expectations which we men all have: Death, Burial and Resurrection.

He continued with these — to us significant — words in connection with his *Lazarus*:

I count a great deal on the musical setting of my drama by any composer, since on him rests the burden of bringing the narrative to life and giving it fluidity and movement.

Niemeyer's dramatic poem is mediocre, its sentiments either high-flown or emptily pious. The Biblical characters Lazarus, Mary, and Martha are supplemented by Jairus's daughter, here named Jemina (frequently misnamed, in English, Jemima) and two friends of Lazarus — the priest Nathanael and Simon, a Sadducee. The chorus is composed of friends and neighbours of Lazarus and his sisters. The characterization of the two sisters is

H

quite ably done, although it does not follow the familiar Biblical outlines; Mary symbolizes hope in the face of death, Martha despair. The two friends of Lazarus parallel this opposition; Nathanael's serene faith is contrasted with Simon's doubt and terror. The three acts embody Lazarus's sickness and death, his burial, and his being raised from the dead.

The obsessive concern in modern literature with imagery, symbol, and allegory has gone to absurd lengths, but the attempt of present-day critics to seek for the same tendency in the literature of the past is equally absurd; the delicate, partly unconscious use of allusion and symbolism in the poetry and plays of men who wrote in past centuries cannot plausibly be linked with the heavily selfconscious indulgence in such devices, which can be so tiring, in the work of writers today. In the seventeenth and eighteenth centuries, for instance, the Lazarus story was certainly looked upon as a symbol as well as an actual event; the fact that God, in Christ, raised the man Lazarus from the dead, was looked upon in those days as an indication that religion revivified the arts, gave new life to painting and music in contrast to the deadening influence of the secular in those spheres. The idea is set out in Niemeyer's words above. But it would be entirely false to the spirit of the period to read any attempt to exemplify the symbolism in the straightforward narrative of Niemeyer's drama and to see hidden subtleties and allusions in the phraseology he uses.

Still less can we seek for the symbolism, in any obsessive sense, in Schubert's music. It is a rich store of beauty, and an astonishingly mature and forward-looking piece of work, but completely straightforward in intention and device — a purposeful exemplification in music of the moods, actions, and interactions of the characters of the play.

Niemeyer's text had been set previously; in 1779 Johann Heinrich Rolle composed a cantata, and it was performed in Magdeburg in the presence of the poet. Rolle's music remained in manuscript and was unknown to Schubert when he encountered the text during the winter of 1819–20.[1] In biographies of Schubert

[1] Second edition of Niemeyer's poems, 1814. Kreissle was unaware of this second edition and attributed the poet's revisions to Schubert! There are,

it is customary to mention that the composition of *Lazarus* was something of a mystery — a secret activity of Schubert's, carefully concealed from his friends. This derives from Kreissle, who, in his account of the work, mentions that none of Schubert's friends knew anything about the inception of the cantata or the existence of the manuscript. He thus gives the impression that Schubert, for some reason, deliberately kept his friends in ignorance of this particular venture. Such unawareness on the part of his friends, however, applies to so many other compositions of Schubert that to single out *Lazarus* in this way is somewhat absurd. The first page of Schubert's manuscript is dated February 1820, and the supposition that he intended to compose the work in time for a performance at Easter of that year seems perfectly sound. But he never finished it, either in time for Easter 1820 or at any later period; it remains a fragment. He completed the first part and most of the second. The music concludes its course after the body of Lazarus is borne in by his weeping friends. Two short recitatives, sung by Nathanael and Martha, fill the last pages; it is clear that a few further sheets may be lost, but it is doubtful if the remainder of this second act was composed by Schubert. Ferdinand Schubert records only a completed first act in the catalogue of his brother's works, and treated it as an entity in his dealings with publishers.

Schubert called the work 'Osterkantate', and the three 'Abteilungen' (Parts) of Niemeyer, he entitled 'Handlungen' (Acts). Ferdinand separated the first act of the cantata from the rest of the papers and sold it to Diabelli, for eventual publication, in 1830. This autograph was absorbed into the piles of other unpublished works by Schubert in the publisher's offices and disappeared from view for nearly forty years. The score of the first act had, however, been copied for Josef Witteczek, and this copy was later acquired, through inheritance, by Spaun. The fragmentary second act remained with Ferdinand; after his death the opening completed sections of this fragment, together with other Schubert manuscripts, were taken over by the American scholar, Alexander Wheelock Thayer, who intended to negotiate their sale to collectors

nevertheless, a few places where Schubert has, either accidentally or deliberately, altered the poet's words.

on behalf of Ferdinand's widow. During the course of his work on the preliminary sketch for Schubert's biography, early in 1859, Kreissle examined the copy of the first act of *Lazarus*, in Spaun's possession, and was at once impressed by the quality of the music. By a strange coincidence he was invited in 1861 to visit Thayer, who showed him all the manuscripts he was trying to sell, among them, of course, the continuation of *Lazarus* in the autograph of Schubert. Kreissle visited Ferdinand's widow and discovered the remaining leaves of the manuscript: the total collection, that is, the copy of the first act and the autographs of the second act, were brought to the notice of Johann Herbeck, the conductor of the Musikverein orchestra and an ardent Schubertian.

Ferdinand Schubert had conducted a performance of the first act and part of the second act of *Lazarus* on Easter Sunday 1830 (11 April) at the Annakirche in Vienna. (The church is situated in the Annagasse, where also stood the Training College which Schubert had attended as a lad of sixteen.) This first performance of the cantata had also been the last. But Herbeck, like Kreissle, was deeply impressed by the music he saw for the first time early in 1862, and determined to perform the work as soon as possible. The first act and most of the second were given in the Redouten-saal (a small assembly hall in the Court Palace used for concerts and dances) on 27 March 1863. The audience was sparse, and the music aroused no great enthusiasm among the public; but in the case of several individual musicians the impression was very different.

The report that Herbeck's interest in the cantata *Lazarus* was to lead to a performance was not without its effect on the publisher Spina, who, as successor to Diabelli, still owned the autograph manuscript of the first act. At this period Brahms and Joachim, among others, were occupying themselves by studying these unpublished manuscripts of Schubert's, possibly with a view to advising Spina as to likely publication. We find Brahms writing on 26 March 1863 to Adolf Schuhring:

> The manuscript of 'Lazarus' really enchants me. It lies with many others on my desk and looks as if it had been written yesterday. I might add that this work is to be performed tomorrow for the first time (40 years after its completion).

A week or so after the performance Brahms wrote to Joachim as follows:

You will have read that a 'Lazarus' by Schubert has, after forty-three years, celebrated its resurrection here. I have copied out several scenes for myself; rest content: if you stay any length of time in Hanover, I might send them to you; I can promise you the greatest enjoyment.

(Vienna, 3 April 1863.)

In spite of the lukewarm reception of the work we find the critic of the *Donau Zeitung*, on 29 March 1863, inveighing against the publisher Spina for keeping *Lazarus* (and many other works) in dusty obscurity, and he concludes with the judgement that *Lazarus* is a work '... which has no equal in the whole literature of music'.

But Spina was not so indifferent as to the fate of Schubert's manuscripts as this passage suggests. The enthusiasm of Herbeck and Brahms was sufficient in itself, without these indignant reproofs, to bring about the happy sequel. In January 1866 Herbeck's vocal score of the cantata was published by Spina, and, if one takes a realistic view, this is a far more satisfactory appearance than publication of the full score would have been. This full score, in fact, was not published until it appeared in the *Gesamtausgabe*, Serie xvii, in 1892. Herbeck, naturally, used the original manuscript of the first act in Spina's possession, so that his arrangement is based entirely on Schubert's own score. The manuscript of the first act passed eventually into the possession of the National Library, Vienna; the fragmentary manuscript of the second act was bought from Ferdinand's nephew Eduard Schneider by Nicolaus Dumba, and from him it passed into the ownership of the City Library, Vienna.[1]

In England the cantata remains unknown. A misguided attempt to introduce it to English choral societies was made in 1909, when Novello's published a severely cut version of the cantata edited by Ivor Atkins (translation of the text by W. G. Rotherby).[2] In

---

[1] See pp. 185–7.

[2] This truncated score, one feels, must have been the version used by Professor Arthur Hutchings on which to form his judgement of the work, which is given in *Schubert* in the 'Master Musicians' series (Dent, London, 1956), pp. 138–9.

recent times two worthy attempts have been made to perform the cantata in full and bring to public notice the beauty of this strangely neglected work. On 11 March 1950 it was performed, with Richard Capell's new English translation, by the Birmingham Music Society under the direction of Anthony Lewis (the first act of this performance was broadcast). The Concert Choir of Itzenhoe, Germany, on 17 February 1958 performed the work under the direction of Otto Spreckelsen with great success. The difficulties of making the work known by public performance are not to be underestimated. To begin with, since the important third act, which recounts the miracle of the raising of Lazarus, is not part of the composition, it is a misnomer to call it an Easter cantata. It requires, moreover, six soloists, all of them able to meet demands on interpretative skill as well as vocal technique, and there is very little for a choir to get its teeth into. *Lazarus*, in other words, is a cantata for solo voices, and hence unlikely to be the choice of any established choral society. But such difficulties are not of the same order as those that keep Schubert's operas unperformed, and should not inhibit occasional performance. One does not, of course, subscribe to the judgement of the critic quoted above and deem *Lazarus* without its equal in the whole literature of music. None the less, one may feel that several sacred choral works of the nineteenth century — Brahms's *Requiem*, Berlioz's *Childhood of Christ*, Mendelssohn's *St. Paul* — which do receive fairly frequent performances, are no more admirable than *Lazarus*, which receives none at all.

The music was composed in February 1820. Very little in Schubert's previous work of a similar nature prepares us for the individuality that glows in nearly every bar of *Lazarus*. The only work that could, in any sense, be called a predecessor, is the setting of Klopstock's 'Stabat Mater', a German paraphrase of the famous Latin hymn, which Schubert composed in 1816; this has two sections, a chorus 'Wer wird Zähren sanften Mitleids?' ('Who will not weep tears of gentle compassion?') and a tenor solo, with oboe obbligato, 'Ach, was hätten wir empfunden?'

('Ah, what should we have perceived?'), both of which are outstandingly fine. The 'Stabat Mater', like *Lazarus*, was composed for solo voices, chorus, and orchestra. But its material is very definitely early Schubert and in general no more likeable than that in the earlier masses. It is remarkable, too, that Schubert had produced very little in other musical forms before February 1820 that could be looked upon as preparing the way for *Lazarus*. The 'Trout' Quintet had been finished a few months previously, and that is all. The major works, which are generally looked upon as heralding Schubert's maturity, such as the String Quartet movement in C minor (the 'Quartettsatz'), *Die Zauberharfe, Alfonso und Estrella*, the 'Unfinished' Symphony, all lay in the future. Only in some of the songs are there any true signposts to *Lazarus*, and they are unmistakable, especially in the songs that Schubert had composed during the previous year. They and *Lazarus* display two very characteristic features of those days, features that quite definitely appear in 1819 and disappear almost entirely in 1822. The first could be discussed adequately only by lavish quotation; it is a deliberate restriction of the harmony to diatonic chords of the key — almost a self-denying ordinance on Schubert's part. By reason of this restriction he achieves a purity and radiance that was never quite recaptured in the middle years of the 1820's, and appears only once more, in the great C major Symphony; yet warmth and colour are not sacrificed, for it was, after all, Schubert's genius using the diatonic devices, and anything less like, say, conventional hymn-tune harmony could not be imagined. Songs that display this harmonic practice are 'Der Wanderer' (not the famous song of that name, but the 1819 setting of Schlegel's poem 'Wie deutlich des Mondes Licht zu mir spricht'), 'Das Mädchen', 'Die Götter Griechenlands', and the two 'Mignonlieder' of April 1821. The pure harmonies of parts of *Lazarus* contribute essentially to the atmosphere, giving that 'shimmer of transfiguration', which, in Einstein's words, lies over the whole of the first act.

The second device is the immediate repetition, within the melody, of a short, lyrical figure. The most famous example is in the 'Unfinished' Symphony —

Example 75

— but it pervades the music of these years; it is particularly prevalent in the sketched symphony in E of August 1821. The arias and recitatives of *Laȝarus* are similarly ornamented with this unusual and attractive feature, often with a vivid and unexpected pointing of the words.

The 'Trout' Quintet was mentioned above; *Laȝarus* cannot compare in stature with this universally known and loved chamber work, Schubert's first masterpiece in instrumental music. The text of Niemeyer's Biblical play inspired Schubert to new and fascinating departures in music and at the same time set limitations on its general appeal. Those departures, nevertheless, are remarkable. If Schubert's *Laȝarus* had no noticeable predecessor in his own work, it certainly had none in other men's work; there is nothing like it in music anywhere else prior to 1820, and nothing resembling its novel styles is to be found after it until Wagner, unaware of what Schubert had achieved in *Laȝarus*, forged a similar procedure in *Das Rheingold* and *Die Walküre*. For the music of *Laȝarus* consists mainly of richly accompanied recitatives, in which the formal aria is not a break, but merely a heightening of the musico-dramatic progress. There are four arias in the first act, and not one of them is separated from the body of the music to such a degree, for example, as even Siegmund's song 'Winterstürme wichen dem Wonnemond' is individualized in the course of the music in the first act of Wagner's *Die Walküre*. Faced with the dialogue in Niemeyer's drama — the conversations of Mary and Martha with the dying Lazarus — Schubert resorted to the technique he had used over and over again with such fascinating resource and charm in his longer, dramatic songs, usually called ballads; and he poured into this accustomed technique a new and maturer poetry. The vocal recitatives are phrased lyrically and accompanied by short, modulating figures in the orchestra; by reason of their flexibility, these are capable of meeting any musical demands, they underline the meaning of the words; they serve as interludes to link differing sentiments, or they are used symphonically to excite the music to powerful climaxes. It was a style that obviously became more and more congenial to the composer, this bejewelling the text, so to speak, with short, musical figures, poetically developed. It is ultra-fanciful perhaps to draw attention to the appeal that such embellishment has to the eye; yet the feeling sometimes involuntarily arises, in reading these and similar pages of Schubert, that the composer delighted in these aspects of an adorned accompaniment. The audio-visual aspect is not wholly to be discounted: graceful-sounding phrases, after all, have a grace on paper as well, and it is perhaps not irrelevant to refer, once again, to Capell's words — 'the mere look of a composer's pages is characteristic'. The earliest examples of these embellished recitative-accompaniments occur in the Ossian ballads of 1815–17 and they not only gave rise to later, masterly songs like 'Der Zwerg', 'Der Einsame', and, eventually, 'Der Doppelgänger', but were to prove his mainstay in the non-lyrical sections of the operas — using the word conveniently to describe those parts of the text where, by dialogue or ensemble, the action of the plot is urged forward. So in *Lazarus*: the long recitatives that precede and follow each of the four arias give us the flower of Schubert's work in this style; only the greatest passages in *Alfonso und Estrella* and *Fierrabras* surpass them in power and beauty.

The scene opens in the garden of Lazarus's home. The dying man comforts his sisters, and the music flows with exquisite simplicity to his words. Martha replies with an outburst of despairing protest, and Schubert's treatment of her words gives a foretaste of the skill with which he will blend the varying moods of the characters in the drama into a unity of musical utterance; the substance of his music throughout can be described only by an *ad hoc* term and a clumsy one at that — it is a contrapuntal-harmonic

Example 76

style, and by that is meant that although each bar can be analysed into a harmonic progression, the harmonies are the result of orchestral part-writing. It can be seen simply in Example 76. But in the musical content both dramatic and lyrical powers are latent. Schubert heightens the one or the other to suit his text, but there is never any marked disparity between the various musical styles that are the result. The ensuing passage can be quoted since it illustrates the point.

Example 77

Example 77 (continued)

dass in ö - den Näch-ten in der ein sa-men

Hüt - te wir dich Kla - gen.

Several writers have called the fusion of lyrical and dramatic styles in *Lazarus* a blend of *arioso* and recitative; this is a true description if 'blend' is precisely defined and not considered the same as 'alternation'. The following pages, in which Mary reproves Martha's lack of faith, provide an example; her phrases are melodious and given a great variety of accompaniment; themes and ideas emerge, play their part, and give way to others, yet the family likeness between these figures provides an overall unity to the apparent diversity of recitative and cantabile passages. But the term *aria parlante* will not do for the style of *Lazarus*; the most frequently quoted example of this type of aria is 'Comfort ye' from Handel's *Messiah*; but this famous solo is formality itself compared with the free, spontaneously varying course of the music in *Lazarus*. Mary's aria, which succeeds her reproof, is an address to the Almighty, the Lord of Death, imploring Him to uphold Lazarus in his ordeal. The orchestral accompaniment is an antiphony of horn and string chords, with poignant interludes for solo clarinet. The pastoral smoothness of the F major melody is stiffened by this sturdy support, and any monotony avoided by the typical Schubertian shifts to darker keys.

The ensuing recitatives of Lazarus and of Nathanael, who

brings news of the advent of the Saviour, present an extraordinarily telling pattern of diatonic simplicity and restless,
chromatic passage-work as the sentiment varies between resignation and fear. Schubert is by now completely absorbed in the
poem, and there is a certain loss in this unselfconscious outpour-
ing; Nathanael's aria, 'Wenn ich Ihm nachgerungen habe' ('When
I have striven to follow in His footsteps'), is a broad, rhythmic
ballad in C major, its martial stride inspired by the opening lines.
A composer having an audience more in mind might have
wondered, possibly, whether such a robust effusion at this point
in the drama, full of a confident, almost jaunty, expression, would
not have an effect that was dangerously incongruous; only
thoughtful interpretation by singer and conductor here could
bring the tone of the aria into relevance with the rest of the work.
Yet in itself the aria is magnificent, with sustained and sweeping
phrases in the voice, echoed and urged forward by oboe and
violins in the orchestra.

Martha expresses her fears, brushing aside Nathanael's op-
timism and Lazarus's calm in the face of death. Mary, in a long
and varied recitative, encourages and comforts her brother. At
the close of this marvellously sustained music there occurs one of
Schubert's happiest touches, inspired — as so often in his songs
— by the poet's sudden interpolation of a question. The composer's treatment of question and answer should be universally
known as an example of genius using the simplest of means to
achieve its effect: 'When the hour of death comes,' asks the poet,
'what will hold a man so that he does not sink?' And the answer
is: 'God's Love.' Here is Schubert's way with the passage:

Example 78

The melodies and accompaniment figures spring from Mary's opening phrase, spreading and graceful; the allusions in the text to rock and tempest, vain against the stronghold of faith, bring a stormy motivation into the music, but it is skilfully blended with the prevailing mood of serenity and grace.

Jemina, the daughter of Jairus, enters. Her music is clearly differentiated from that of the two sisters, having a sweetness, and, in the orchestral accompaniment, a fragility of phrase that convey vividly the youthfulness and touching ardour of the girl. Ernest Newman was fond of drawing attention to Wagner's association of definite orchestral colours and sonorities with the various characters of the operas, designed to emphasize and delineate their personalities. Schubert unmistakably uses flutes and oboes, and the violins alone, to convey the youthful picture of this character in the drama. She enters to this passage:

Example 79

Lazarus thanks God for her coming as a sign of grace; Schubert sets his words to a typical phrase, and nowhere else has he so magically turned into the major key to convey the meaning of his poem.

Example 80

sterbe!

That this passage made its own impression on the composer will be obvious later.

The long and important aria now sung by Jemina describes her death-sleep, her vision of paradise, and her awakening by the Saviour. The verse opens with the words 'So schlummert auf Rosen' ('They slumber on roses, the souls of the pure in heart'), and Schubert, above a throbbing viola pedal, writes one of his endearing cradle-songs. The opening figure for the flutes, sung then by Jemina, remarkably illustrates a subconscious obsession of his; whenever he composes music to poetry that makes some reference to sleep, his melody is based upon a variant of rising or falling thirds. The feature is obvious in his most famous cradle-song, quoted here with its basic structure:

Example 81

Schla-fe, schla-fe, hold-er, süs-ser Kna-be

In Jemina's aria, the thirds rise, but the idea unmistakably inspired the melody:

Example 82

So schlum-mert auf Ro - sen, so —

schlum-mert die Un - schuld ein. —

The phrase proliferates among the instruments of the orchestra with exquisite musical skill; it is here that Schubert's self-forgetfulness shows tremendous gain, far outweighing the loss mentioned above in connection with Nathanael's aria. The essential purity and nobleness of his nature elevates this metaphysical fantasy to a moving and human poetry. Jemina's references to the Rose of Sharon leads the music into G minor, thence to G major, and so to the *da capo* in E flat major. A powerful, dramatic climax is whipped up in the music; Jemina describes how her spirit neared the throne of God. For a brief moment the radiance and bliss of the vision are depicted by a sequence of high, woodwind chords; Schubert actually suspends the sense of the text with the phrase 'yet too blinding, and . . .'.[1] Then his trombones, majestic and invocatory, announce the words of Jesus:

Example 83

[1] Even omitting a few words of the text to obtain his effect. Surely this is deliberate and not, as Mandyczewski thought, an oversight on the part of the composer?

The act closes with the death of Lazarus. The ejaculations of his sisters and Nathanael in brief, three-part harmony provide a welcome change of vocal colour, and then the music turns into C minor for Schubert's crowning inspiration. The accompaniment is scored for strings and trombones; the agitated *tremolando* bursts on the strings are punctuated by soft, crotchet octaves on the trombones, which give a powerful impression of the inexorable footfalls of approaching death — and this, when it comes, is presented with a miraculous simplicity:

The metaphysics and the theology are forgotten; Schubert, moved by the simple humanity of the scene, creates an unforgettably touching picture of the end to which all men must come. The music uses a variety of those chords whose technical names are so clumsy — French and German sixths and diminished sevenths — but which, as Paul Hamburger has so finely said, serve Schubert as granite for his bridges and gossamer for his dreams. At this point the dream is gossamer and shadowy, and the sleep is the sleep of death.

The chorus sings an invocation to the Almighty to receive the soul of Lazarus and to comfort the mourners. It is a short, funereal movement with a consolation in the B major cadences at the close.

The second act takes place in the burial-ground — a clearing surrounded by palms and cedars, with a path leading away to Lazarus's dwelling. It is night, and Schubert's orchestral introduction is a tone-poem designed to create not only the grisliness of the scene, but the terror felt by Simon the Sadducee who enters alone. Niemeyer's text invokes all the graveyard furniture of the Gothic horror-romance — mossy headstones, mouldering skeletons, general corruption, and so forth. Schubert does what he can with it; the music recalls in part the *largo* introductions to some of his early symphonies, in part the juvenile churchyard songs, such as 'Leichenphantasie' and 'Der Geistertanz'. Simon's terror is mixed with remorse and despair, since his youthful faith has gone. For this part of his soliloquy Schubert writes a long, scherzo-like section in F minor; the restless, urgent movement, and the use of the primary elements of the minor scale give a touch of early Verdian grace, but this is swept aside and the music mounts to an extended, *fortissimo* climax as Simon sees the open grave prepared for the body of Lazarus. The *da capo* is such in name only, being in fact a new treatment of the initial themes; Schubert throws the reins to his genius and pours out an excited, feverish scherzo, improvisatory in style, but finer far than anything he had composed hitherto in his symphonies; it has affinities with a later movement, the Scherzo of the String Quartet in G major:

Example 85

The solo ends with a repeated and anguished treatment of the
word 'Woe!' Nathanael enters. With his coming the music sinks
into the serene mood that prevailed in the first act; the priest
calms Simon and calls the blessing of God on the distracted man,
who pours out his grief and longing for the consolation of faith.
Schubert's pages show an unforced and melting lyricism, all the
more effective after his excitable and stormy exploitation of
Simon's hysterical grief in the opening scene. But for all the
apparent spontaneity of the phrases that spring up in voice and
orchestra, there is also a calculated use of reminiscence, which
offers an exciting promise; at the close of the Sadducee's words
about the consolation of faith in eternal life, there comes this
cadential phrase in the orchestra:

Example 86

The resemblance here to an earlier passage is surely deliberate, but if not, it must have been, on Schubert's part, a subconscious memory of great interest. Here is the cadential phrase he had used during the music sung by the dying Lazarus, expressing his confidence in the Good Shepherd:

Example 87

But a resemblance of even greater interest now occurs. As Simon continues, by saying how fortunate are they who have faith in the resurrection of the dead, his recitative closes with this melodic turn:

Example 88

This is unquestionably an allusion to the music in the first act sung by Lazarus to Jemina (see Example 80). It is possibly an exaggeration to call these two examples a use by Schubert of leitmotive, nevertheless we have here a novel departure from his usual practice and, had he lived to see the developments of Wagner in this line, it is one that in his hands would have become a very appealing feature of his work. The phrases that follow contain further echoes of the *Lazarus* theme, concluding with:

Example 89

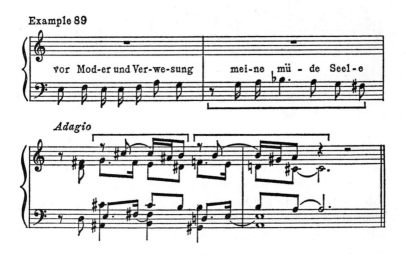

The priest informs Simon that the funeral procession is nearing the place where they stand; he expresses the hope that the steadfast faith of those who accompany the dead man and the words of the hymn sung by the mourners will comfort and sustain Simon. Again, in Nathanael's recitative, there is an allusion to earlier music, not so obvious on this occasion, but close enough to serve the composer's purpose. It reminds the listener of the very opening of the first act, when Mary and Martha attended their dying brother, linking that memory to the fact that the two sisters are now approaching the scene; but it also recalls the mood and the confident hope of Lazarus, which that music originally embodied:

Example 90

Herbeck's vocal score of the fragmentary second act ends with the choral hymn of the mourning friends. It is, as it happens, in A major, the key of the opening of the first act. And by another happy chance both the harmonic and rhythmic structure of the hymn are also similar to those of Lazarus's opening solo, so that in spite of the unfinished state of the cantata, the choice of key, the harking back to the original styles, and the substantial nature of this chorus (which Schubert fully completed) do provide a conclusion that is practicable for performance. The hymn is a plea to the Almighty to take Lazarus into His keeping: the heat of the day is over, the shadows of the evening have fallen. Schubert's music is devotional and untroubled, but he endeavours in several ways to give variety of vocal colour by assigning the melodies of the hymn now to male voices, now to female voices, using appropriate orchestral colours to accompany them. Later there are solos for the tenors, for the sopranos, then both together in duet passages, the orchestral part-writing growing more elaborate as, we are to imagine, the procession enters the scene and approaches the grave. Then, for the first time, the full chorus is used for the consignment of the body, and it brings the hymn to an end with a long-drawn and thoroughly idiomatic cadence in A major.

Although this chorus provides the cantata with a suitable conclusion, should it be performed, it was certainly not Schubert's intention to use it so. The remainder of Niemeyer's second act consists of Nathanael's benediction over the body, a protesting and grief-stricken outburst from Martha, a duet for Jemina and a youth, and a final chorus in which the friends sing of reunion with Lazarus beyond the grave. Schubert has set Nathanael's words melodiously, the long-held string chords and *pianissimo* clarinet phrases evoking to perfection the benedictory atmosphere of the scene. Martha is inconsolable. In a remarkably fine recitative she implores Death to give back her brother, recalling the flush of his youth as she gazes at his pale face. The textual symbols, Death and Youth, move Schubert deeply; the vocal phrases are free and wide-ranging, and, in the orchestra, musical images that we find in his songs associated with these symbols rise, flower, and give place to others; most remarkable is the use, once again, of the phrase associated with Lazarus, quoted above in Example 86.[1] Towards the end of Martha's recitative a *tremolando* figure played by the bass strings grows more prominent; it eventually sweeps up through all the strings and is used as the accompaniment figure in the aria, *allegro molto*, which Martha now sings. 'Raise me on the wings of the storm,' she cries, 'far from this grassy mound to the starry paths of heaven, where I can follow my brother.' It is a thousand pities that this aria breaks off when only half was composed — or, if Schubert completed it, that the latter half is lost. It is as fine as anything in the whole cantata. The impassioned phrases soar above the stormy, chromatic accompaniment, and although they have a seeming air of improvisation, the sequences and recapitulations are most skilfully devised. Schubert's excitement in the composition of these vivid, despairing words can be

---

[1] A small but interesting point here in Martha's recitative, and in earlier recitatives of Lazarus's and Nathanael's, is Schubert's unique use of occasional 5/4 bars within the regular metre of 4/4; he does not, of course, designate the bars with this time-signature, but the irregularities are not slips of the pen, for in one case he alters a correct 4/4 bar into one of 5/4.

deduced from his manuscript and from the fact that in his haste he occasionally scribbled 'Sonnenbahnen' ('paths of the sun') for the poet's 'Sternenbahnen' ('paths of the stars').

The features that make this cantata of Schubert's so fascinating a study, both for its intrinsic value, and for its possible significance as an example of the transition between the formal divisions of the classical dramatic work, whether secular or sacred, and the eventual emergence of the Wagnerian music-drama, have only been touched on in this essay, for far more extensive musical quotation would be necessary to exemplify such a thesis fully and convincingly. The pity of it is that such a thesis needs to be written and is not already part of musical history, as it would be if the music of *Lazarus* were as familiar to music-lovers as that of the *Flying Dutchman*, for instance. To what degree may Schubert have been consciously using leitmotiv procedure in *Lazarus*? To what extent was *Lazarus* a supreme culmination of his technique in the Ossian and Schiller ballads? What shaping of his future operatic styles resulted from his devoted work on this cantata? How can musicians give answers to these questions while the score of the work remains so obstinately closed?

Lazarus, it was said earlier, had no predecessor in the work of Schubert; nor was it to have any successor. The only other sacred cantata he wrote was *Mirjams Siegesgesang* ('Miriam's Song of Victory'), composed a few months before he died. This work, although fully mature in style and attractive throughout, evokes none of the absorbed interest that is aroused by page after page of *Lazarus*. *Miriam's Song* is competent in all its parts, whereas *Lazarus* sometimes falters; but Schubert was not in *Miriam's Song* endeavouring to achieve something novel and exciting; he was not exploring fresh paths and attempting adventurous, new ways in the treatment of dramatic verse as he was in *Lazarus*. This 'Resurrection' cantata remains a unique example, a masterpiece unlike any other in the work of the composer.

II

The Composer

SCHUBERT AND THE
KÄRNTNERTHOR THEATER

VIENNA'S Kärntnerthor Theater, so called because it was near the Kärntner — i.e., Carinthian — Gate of the inner, walled city, was the home of the Imperial Court Opera and as such the leading theatre in the city for the production of operas of all kinds. The modern State Opera House stands a little in front of the site of the original theatre. A first-hand description of the old theatre was written by the widely travelled English musician William Beatty-Kingston. He wrote of the building as Schubert knew it:

... it was an ugly, dirty, ill-ventilated den, stiflingly hot, and provided by an ingenious Court architect with the most distractingly intricate system of entrances and exits at that time in existence. To get into the house at your leisure was difficult; to issue from it in a hurry impossible.... The atmosphere inside the house was permanently sickly, conveying to at least one of the senses the impression that the quantum of interior air originally allotted to the Kärntnerthor Theater by the architect had been carefully poisoned early in the century and never changed since....[1]

Schubert's first recorded visit to the theatre was on 8 July 1811; the opera was Josef Weigl's *Die Schweizerfamilie*. During the next few years there were further visits, and he heard operas by Cherubini, Boïeldieu, and Mozart. His friend Josef von Spaun wrote that the young Schubert first heard the famous baritone Johann Michael Vogl, who was in after-years to achieve a yet wider fame as an interpreter of Schubert's songs, in Gluck's *Iphigénie en Tauride* in 1813. Vogl sang Orestes and aroused Schubert's intense admiration. Another friend, Moritz von Schwind, recorded that Schubert was so anxious to see *Fidelio* when it was performed at the Kärntnerthor Theater on 23 May 1814 that he sold his school-

[1] *Music and Manners* (London, 1886), vol. i, p. 3.

books in order to pay for his seat. At that performance he heard Vogl as Don Pizarro — according to witnesses the one failure in Vogl's career.

A few years later, in the spring of 1817, Schubert was introduced to Vogl, and so began the famous friendship between the young composer and the singer who was more than twice his age. The association brought Schubert into touch with the personnel of the Kärntnerthor Theater, for Vogl was full of praise for his young friend's music and spoke of him wherever he went. It was on Vogl's recommendation that Schubert was commissioned to compose a one-act operetta for performance at the theatre, a golden opportunity for so young and unknown a composer, and one that he seized eagerly. The play, entitled *Die Zwillingsbrüder* ('The Twin Brothers'), was by Georg von Hoffmann, one of the resident librettists of the Kärntnerthor Theater. The plot is remotely connected with the *Comedy of Errors*, although Hoffmann's play was based not on Shakespeare's, but on a contemporary French model. Schubert is said not to have cared for the play, but he did not allow this to damp his enthusiasm; the ten numbers were ready by the end of 1818, and the overture written by 19 January 1819. But the step from composing an operetta to the production of it in the theatre was no easier for Schubert in those days than for a young composer today, and various intrigues and postponements kept *Die Zwillingsbrüder* off the boards. One is reminded of Mozart's experiences with *Die Entführung*. On 19 May 1819 Schubert wrote a letter to his friend Anselm Hüttenbrenner, and in the course of it he said: 'In spite of Vogl it is difficult to manœuvre against *canaille* such as Weigl, Treitschke, etc. So instead of my operetta they give filthy things [Ludern] enough to make your hair stand on end.'[1] Josef Weigl, the composer of *Die Schweizerfamilie*, was the conductor of the theatre, Georg Treitschke the producer and chief librettist. Eventually, a year later, the operetta was put into production, and its first performance given in the Kärntnerthor Theater on 14 June 1820. Vogl doubled the parts of the twins, admirably distinguishing between the characters of the two men, one an army captain, the

[1] Kreissle, vol. i, p. 153.

other a farmer. Schubert, although present at the performance, refused to appear, and it was left to Vogl to thank the audience in his name. The operetta was only moderately successful. Public reports in the newspapers of Vienna and of the provincial centres of Germany were lukewarm, and private ones (in diaries and letters) even less than that. After six performances, the last on 21 July 1820, the operetta was withdrawn and never revived.

A few years ago a Viennese scholar, Dr. Ignaz Weinmann, discovered in the Vienna National Library some references to Schubert in the financial records of the Kärntnerthor Theater preserved in that library. We learn from these accounts that Schubert was paid 500 florins for *Die Zwillingsbrüder*. The money was paid in the old Viennese currency, and its equivalent in modern English money is not easy to assess. On the values given twenty years ago it would be about £20. The Kärntnerthor Theater accounts also record that Vogl was paid 150 florins in advance for Schubert.

No further direct commission of this kind was forthcoming for several years, but in the early part of 1821 Schubert applied to the directorate of the theatre for a position as official composer or conductor, furnishing testimonials from Ignaz von Mosel, a Court Secretary, from Count Moritz Dietrichstein, in charge of the music for the Court, and from Anton Salieri, his old master in composition. Dietrichstein, to whom Schubert had just dedicated his op. 1, the 'Erlkönig', was particularly interested in the young composer, but neither his influence nor that of the other men was enough to obtain such a post for Schubert. However, he was appointed a coach (*Korrepititor*) for young singers about to make their début at the Opera. This fact was first recorded by Leopold Sonnleithner in his biographical notes on Schubert written in March 1858; the notes were not published until 1919, and some doubts were cast by later biographers on such an appointment. But it is confirmed conclusively by the financial accounts of the Kärntnerthor Theater already mentioned. Karoline Unger, the young contralto, who had been trained by Aloysia Lange, Mozart's sister-in-law, was making her first appearance in Vienna as Isabella in *Mädchentreu*, i.e., *Così fan tutte*. The performance took place on 24 February 1821. On 13 April 1821 Schubert was paid 50 florins (£2, see above) for coaching her in the part. There are no other accounts of payments of this nature to Schubert, and this seems to bear out Sonnleithner's further remarks on the subject, for he says that Schubert was incapable of holding the post: 'He was unable to keep to rehearsal times punctually, and the mechanical nature of this work was vexatious to him.'

During the year between March 1821 and April 1822 several vocal compositions by Schubert were given at concerts in the Kärntnerthor Theater. At the first of these Vogl sang the 'Erlkönig', a celebrated performance, which was overpowering in its effect. Such popular acclaim could hardly be ignored by the theatre directors, and it may have been this success that led to a further small commission in the next week or so; it was to write two extra items for inclusion in the performance of Hérold's *La Clochette* at the Kärntnerthor Theater. The operetta was to be given under the title *Das Zauberglöckchen*. Schubert's two extra numbers, the words in all probability written by Georg Friedrich Treitschke, the man whom he had once designated *canaille*, consisted of a tenor solo and a 'comic' duet for tenor and bass. The performance took place on 20 June 1821. The solo, badly sung by Franz Rosner, was not liked at all by press or public. It was otherwise with the duet; this was loudly applauded. The singers were Franz Siebert and Josef Gottdank, the latter of whom had sung the part of the bailiff in *Die Zwillingsbrüder*. *Das Zauberglöckchen* was given eight times during the season, but the first of Schubert's two contributions, the tenor solo, was dropped after the first performance. In the Kärntnerthor Theater accounts we find that Schubert was paid 100 florins (£4, see above) for the two numbers.

It is worth noting that in the appendix to *Schubert: A Documentary Biography*, called 'Schubert's Income', O. E. Deutsch assesses 400 florins (Viennese currency) as the probable sum earned by Schubert for all his theatrical ventures (these include, of course, *Die Zauberharfe* and *Rosamunde*, composed for another Viennese theatre, the Theater an der Wien). In point of fact

Schubert earned 600 florins for the two Kärntnerthor Theater commissions alone.

In the autumn of 1821 Schubert began to compose his most ambitious opera, *Alfonso und Estrella*. It was not then commissioned by the directorate of the Kärntnerthor Theater, but was clearly intended by Schubert for production there. On 2 November 1821 he wrote to his friend Spaun at Linz that the opera had already progressed as far as the third act and added, optimistically as events turned out: 'I do wish you could be present at its production. We have great hopes of it.' Schubert concluded his letter by informing Spaun: 'The Kärntnerthor and Wieden theatres are actually leased to Barbaja, and he takes them on in December.' The leasing of the Kärntnerthor Theater to Domenico Barbaja, the Italian impresario, was considered ominous for the future of German opera, but facts seem to show that the fears were groundless. Weber and Weigl, as well as Schubert, were commissioned early in 1822 to compose operas for the theatre, and as many new German operas as Italian ones were eventually staged. Vogl was pensioned off, and at the same period other established German singers left the company. Future lamentations about the silencing of German opera during Barbaja's management of the Kärntnerthor Theater are to be explained by the intrinsic poverty of the operas that were staged, and which failed to keep the boards.

Schubert finished his *Alfonso und Estrella* at about the same time as he received the commission from Barbaja and at once submitted it. But it was declined. In December 1822 he wrote to Spaun: 'With my opera I did not do so well in Vienna. I asked to have it back, and back it came. Vogl has really left the theatre too.' Actually, although the services of Vogl as a singer were no longer required by the theatre, his advice on administrative matters was still sought, and he unquestionably refused to back Schubert's submission of *Alfonso und Estrella*. He disliked Schober's libretto and considered that Schubert was on quite the wrong lines. Although this temporary estrangement between Vogl and Schubert passed, there was by then no possibility of the opera being accepted by the authorities of the Kärntnerthor Theater.

Schubert reconciled himself to the idea that in Vienna, at any rate, any performance was out of the question.

Perhaps he was himself to blame, if blame is the right word, for the refusal of the Kärntnerthor Theater directorate to interest themselves in his work. There was every chance to become fully acquainted with the whole personnel of the theatre and with its day-to-day conduct of affairs had he cared to cultivate his association with the place. On the contrary, by the unpunctual and irregular fulfilment of what duties came his way he had spoiled his chances. The impression he had given was far from favourable. Sonnleithner, who knew the situation, said in this connection: 'Schubert was extremely fertile and industrious in composing. For everything else that goes by the name of *work*, he had no inclination.' These are rather hard words, for Schubert, in common with the rest of mankind, could not suddenly change his nature. To imagine him involved in the ceaseless attempt to dominate intractable managers and librettists, riding the storms of petty intrigue, cultivating the acquaintance of those who would further his interests, and triumphantly asserting his own claims on the Kärntnerthor Theater programmes is to attempt the impossible. He saw himself as a composer only, handing over opera scores, as soon as they were completed, for other men to bring to life. No opera composer can hope to begin — or maintain — his career from such an ivory tower, and no success-ful opera composer has ever done so.

With such an aim in view, but with no direct invitation from the Kärntnerthor Theater, he composed in April 1823 the one-act operetta *Die Verschworenen*, the title later altered to *Der häusliche Krieg*. A note in his own hand says *Der häusliche Krieg* was 'composed at father's, censored and passed for performance at the Court Opera'; but the words 'passed for performance' mean only that the censorship had been satisfied — there was no hope of securing an actual performance.

The next month he began another ambitious project, the composition of the three-act opera *Fierrabras*. The libretto was by Josef Kupelwieser, the younger brother of Schubert's friend Leopold. Josef was secretary to the directorate of the Kärntnerthor

Theater at the time he wrote the text, and it is even said that Barbaja commissioned the work. Schubert, struggling with ill-health, composed the work with incredible speed. The rigid censorship of the day objected to certain passages in the text, and on their deletion granted on 19 August 1823 the necessary permission for performance at the Court Opera. The following month Schubert completed the score of the opera and submitted it to the theatre directorate. Rumour spread through the city about the new Schubert opera and on 11 October the *Theaterʒeitung* published a paragraph in which the writer stated: '... the Kärntnerthor Theater is shortly to present the first grand opera by the much-promising Schubert, the ingenious composer of 'Erlkönig'; it is *Fierrabras*, after Calderón, by the Court Theatre Secretary, Herr Kupelwieser. It is also said that Herr Schubert is composing a short opera.'

Shortly afterwards Schubert's hopes received an unexpected setback, for Josef Kupelwieser suddenly left the theatre staff and any hope that his personal influence might be used to secure the production of *Fierrabras* vanished with him. A month later the same newspaper tersely informed its readers: '*Fierrabras* is not to be performed this season.'

It is hardly surprising, in view of the luckless fate of these two full-length operas and the one-act operetta, all composed within the space of two years, that Schubert's work on his last opera-text was desultory and inconclusive. Once again there were some grounds for his taking up the work, since we learn from two of his own letters, written during 1826, that the opera authorities had again approached him. The libretto was *Der Graf von Gleichen* by his friend Bauernfeld, and Schubert wrote to him during May 1826, saying: 'They have asked for my libretti here, to see what they can do with them. If your book were ready by now, I could submit that to them, and if its value were recognized, which I do not doubt, I might begin on it ....' The man who had asked Schubert for his libretti was Louis Antoine Duport, Barbaja's representative, but he evidently thought nothing of these plays and told Schubert of his poor opinion. Bauernfeld's *Der Graf von Gleichen* was not among them, and so, on 10 July

K

1826, Schubert once again wrote to Bauernfeld, begging for the libretto: '... come to Vienna as soon as possible. As Duport wants an opera from me, but the libretti I have so far set do not please at all, it would be splendid if your libretto were favourably received. Then, at least,' he cynically added, 'there would be money, if not reputation as well!' Bauernfeld handed him the completed text at the end of the month, and Schubert began to compose the music. But the censorship this time prohibited the libretto out of hand, for the plot turns on a bigamous marriage, and without that official permission the play could never have been staged at the Kärntnerthor Theater. Schubert wrote numerous sketches for the work, but brought nothing much to completion. For the next two years we hear occasionally of his working on the opera-text, and even on his death-bed he is supposed to have discussed it with Bauernfeld, but clearly the successive disappointments of the past three years had left him without heart for the work.

The commercial interests and by no means unmixed motives of the men who ran the affairs of the Court Opera and Schubert's completely unworldly and introverted disposition prohibited any kind of artistic co-operation between them. It was all bound to lead to a succession of disheartening and miserable failures. What seems a little surprising to a modern observer is that Vienna should still be so seemingly reluctant to stage these works of one of her greatest sons. It is true that *Die Verschworenen* was at length performed at the Kärntnerthor Theater in October 1861 and occasionally revived there in the next decade or so, and that *Die Zwillingsbrüder* and Liszt's cut-and-arranged version of *Alfonso und Estrella* were both given there in 1882, though not subsequently revived at all. But *Fierrabras* has never been performed in Vienna (or anywhere else for that matter, except in a truncated form, and in that shadowy substitute for the real thing — the broadcast version). After the war Vienna's State Opera House rose in splendour from its ruins; the opening of the theatre was an international occasion and the choice of which opera to perform must have been lengthily deliberated. From any point of view, national, historic, artistic, even the simple one of doing

belated justice, an obvious choice would seem to have been one of
Schubert's two big operas, staged, directed and sung with all the
magnificence of which the company was possible. Did such a
choice occur to no one in Vienna?

Any account of Schubert's relations with the Kärntnerthor
Theater would be incomplete if no mention was made of the story
of his supposed application, in 1826, for the post of assistant
conductor there. It was recorded by Anton Schindler, and
published in the Cologne music journal *Niederrheinische Musikzeitung für Kunstfreunde und Künstler* of 7 and 14 March 1857. The
details are familiar. Schubert was required to compose an operatic
scena for soprano and chorus; Schindler says that it was to consist
of an overture and five or six numbers, the text written by
Hoffmann. The extreme difficulty of one of Schubert's items, the
aria for soprano, combined with a lavishly orchestrated accompaniment, became obvious at rehearsals, and although Schubert
was made aware of this by the protests of the soprano, Nanette
Schechner, and by various friends of his, he refused to alter
anything. At the dress rehearsal the inevitable happened: the
soprano broke down, and an embarrassed silence fell over
performers and auditors alike. Renewed protests on the part of
Duport, Schindler himself, and musicians in the orchestra, led to
Schubert closing the score with 'a loud bang', shouting 'I will
alter nothing', and hurrying from the theatre, taking the score-
book with him.

No one has uncritically accepted this story. Kreissle, in his
biography of Schubert, written a few years after the publication of
Schindler's account (1864), reports the incident and proceeds at
once to call attention to its unlikelihood. Schindler's anecdote is
reproduced in full in O. E. Deutsch's book *Schubert: Memoirs by
his Friends* (1958). In the century from Kreissle to Deutsch all
comment has been unfavourable, and the tendency today is to
discredit Schindler, especially as his untrustworthiness in other
biographical fields has been established.

But before passing judgement on him, it is necessary to point out
first the facts that corroborate his story. To begin with, his dates

are largely unassailable. Duport was the administrator at the theatre in 1826, Hoffmann a librettist there, and 1826 was the year, the only one, during which Nanette Schechner was singing in Vienna. It is true that Schindler names Karl Krebs as the assistant conductor whom Schubert hoped to replace, but this could be a slip of the memory for Konradin Kreutzer, who actually was the retiring conductor. In 1826 Schubert was, as we have seen, considering the composition of Bauernfeld's libretto *Der Graf von Gleichen*; he hoped to get it performed at the Kärntnerthor Theater with Schechner as the soprano. It is very probable that that year, if any, he would attempt to obtain the post of conductor. Then Schindler names, correctly, three musicians in the orchestra of the theatre who, he says, were witnesses of the incident: Franz Zierer, flute, Georg Klein, clarinet, and Theobald Hurth, bassoon. Only the first of these men, as far as we know, was ever called upon for confirmation of the story. He told Kreissle that the aria was too much for Schechner, whose voice, he said, was 'failing' (she was twenty years old at the time!), but added that Schubert behaved in a quiet and controlled manner throughout the rehearsal.[1] According to him the aria was an 'independent' vocal *scena*, i.e., there were no five or six numbers and no chorus. He also denied that Schubert was ever a coach at the Kärntnerthor Theater. One way and another, it is obvious that Zierer, after the lapse of forty years, had so vague a remembrance of events that his testimony can be set aside. Another witness for the truth of Schindler's account is Ludwig Cramolina (1805–84), who for a short time was engaged to Nanette Schechner. He was a popular and attractive singer and in 1826 worked as a producer at the Kärntnerthor Theater. He said that the account was true.

It must be admitted that nobody who was in a position to do so ever denied in plain words the truth of Schindler's anecdote after its publication in 1857. But it is quite impossible to reconcile any of the accounts of those who did comment on the story. Josef Hüttenbrenner, for instance, in his reply to Kreissle's questions,

---

[1] In the *Quarterly Musical Magazine*, London, 1828, a correspondent, writing on music in Vienna, says that Nanette Schechner possessed 'a fine voice and great execution'.

implied that there was some foundation in fact, for he said that Nanette Schechner was delighted with Schubert's beautiful aria and that Schubert failed to obtain the post because of theatrical intrigue.

That the story may be a fabrication is the only reason for challenging it. We no longer share the nineteenth century's desire to demolish it because it shows Schubert in an unfavourable light. The obstinate refusal of Schubert to alter his music, alterations entreated by a young and charming *prima donna*, appeared to nineteenth-century biographers as ungentlemanly and did not square with their picture of the gentle and good-natured Schubert. To us it would commend itself, if it were true, as revealing the integrity of the artist, the inviolability of his art. To disprove the story, we must consider certain extraneous factors. And we might ask, for a start, what has become of the music that Schubert composed for Nanette Schechner and the chorus? If it consisted of an overture and five or six numbers, in parts and in score, it must have been fairly bulky: would it all have disappeared without a trace? Schubert, according to Schindler, walked out with the original score under his arm. It is true that a few works of Schubert have disappeared, but all of them belong to his early years, and apart from the 'Prometheus' Cantata (whose existence is proved beyond all doubt) none of them was at all bulky. No work from his maturity, if we exclude the hypothetical 'Gmunden-Gastein' Symphony from the argument, has been completely lost sight of.

Another question that arises is this: would Schubert have been so persistently obstinate in his determination to alter nothing? We read that when, on an occasion in that same year, 1826, a quartet of players was rehearsing his 'Death and the Maiden' String Quartet, and commented on the length of the first movement, he 'cheerfully made cuts' in the movement. If we are to believe this, then we can also believe that because of the much greater issues involved in the theatre experience, he would have been equally amenable to advice or persuasion. Finally, there is this question to be considered: was it customary, when the directorate of the Kärntnerthor Theater wished to appoint a probationer conductor, to require of him the *composition* of an operatic *scena*? Would it not have been sufficient, one wonders, and perhaps even more satisfactory, to test his abilities with an extract from a known opera of established success? Schubert's friend, Franz Lachner, was appointed in that year, 1826, as one of these probationer conductors: as far as we know, no operatic composition was required of him when he was considered for the post.

What are the origins of this story of Schindler? Is it, perhaps, to be taken as a kind of allegory, designed in good faith by Schindler to illustrate certain aspects of Schubert's character and abilities? (For notice that Schindler is not decrying Schubert's powers; the implication all along is that singer and orchestra were trying to cope with something too big for them.) Or did Schindler base it on an imperfectly remembered incident, which actually did occur — a few years previously? Was he thinking of that aria composed for Hérold's *La Clochette*, which was long, difficult, and with a lavishly orchestrated accompaniment, and which was so difficult that the singer, Franz Rosner, could not deal adequately with it? It was, in fact, abandoned after the first unsuccessful performance. These are unanswerable questions, which occur to anyone pondering over this strangely ordered anecdote and its ramifications.

SCHUBERT'S PORTRAITS

THE title of this essay — 'Schubert's Portraits' — is conveniently brief, but hardly comprehensive enough. It should be 'The portraits, pictures, and caricatures of Schubert executed during his lifetime by his friends and acquaintances', which is forbidding enough to discourage any reader. But the closing words would at least convey the fact that I am concerned here only with the contemporary portraiture of the composer. Posthumous drawings of Schubert, however attractive and well liked, could be based only on memory, description, or reference to the contemporary portraits, and they cannot claim the freshness and authenticity of those works drawn from the living model. Most of us would prefer Josef Kriehuber's lithograph of Schubert, drawn in 1846, or many of Schwind's numerous profiles of the composer made posthumously to almost all the portraits described in this essay.[1] They cannot, however, rank with contemporary work for one obvious reason; Schubert's fame was posthumous and Kriehuber and Schwind — yes, even Schwind — were pardonably guilty of idealizing their man.

A *catalogue raisonné* of the ten contemporary likenesses of Schubert is bound to owe a great deal to the work of Otto Erich Deutsch. His early years were spent in training as an art student (it is a well-known fact that his particular interest in the work of Schwind led him to Schubert), and that fact gives a unique value to his study of the Schubert portraits. The first results of his researches can be found in the supplementary remarks at the end of his pictorial volume on Schubert.[2] In 1922 Deutsch edited a

[1] Moritz von Schwind, a close friend of Schubert's, is fully discussed in the next essay.

[2] *Franz Schubert: sein Leben in Bildern*, Georg Müller, Munich and Leipzig, 1913. All portraits of Schubert mentioned in this essay, contemporary and otherwise, can be found in plates 1–30.

large folio volume containing excellent facsimile reproductions of the portraits; he expanded his earlier comments into a longer essay, which served as an introduction to this volume.[1] This volume presents nine portraits, omitting the oil-painting executed *c.* 1827 (see No. x below). The justification for the following essay is partly that both of these examples of Deutsch's work still remain untranslated into English and partly because of recent, newly discovered facts about the works themselves and the change in ownership since 1922.[2]

Mention made above of Schwind's attractive profiles of Schubert, drawn at various times, but many years after the composer's death, recalls the singular fact that he never attempted any serious portrait of Schubert during the years of their intimate friendship. Schwind's portraiture is admirable, and it is a strange fact that while Kupelwieser, Rieder, and Teltscher all occupied themselves with a Schubert portrait, and Schwind must have seen their efforts, he himself was never attracted to producing one. There is, it is true, a pencil sketch of Schubert in existence, which may have been drawn in 1825, and which is attributed, doubtfully, to Schwind: but it is quite negligible. Its questionable date, provenance, and authorship exclude it from the roll of authentic contemporary portraits. These are given here in the chronological order of their appearance, as far as it can be determined. In view of the rarity of Deutsch's pictorial volume, a reference is given at the end of each section to any reproduction of the portrait in his more accessible *Documentary Biography* (as *D.B.*) or *Memoirs* (as *M.*).

I. SCHUBERT: a profile silhouette in indian ink, 4·5 cm. high and 3 cm. wide. It is surrounded by ten concentric rings, the seventh from the inside being a broad band constituting a kind of frame to the profile. This silhouette, the earliest authentic portrait of Schubert to be preserved, was discovered in 1868 in the post-

[1] *Die historische Bildnisse Franz Schuberts in getreuen Nachbildungen*, Karl König, Vienna and Leipzig, 1922.

[2] A summary of the second of Deutsch's commentaries is to be found in appendix i of his *Documentary Biography* of Schubert, translated by Eric Blom, pp. 926–8.

humous possession of Anton Holzapfel. He was a fellow-pupil of Schubert's at the Stadtkonvikt. The silhouette is inscribed by him 'Franz Schubert 1817' and he may possibly have designed it. After his death, on 21 October 1868, it passed into the possession of his descendants and was exhibited for the first time in the great Schubert Exhibition, Vienna 1897, by his daughter-in-law Anna Holzapfel. In 1919 the silhouette was acquired by Otto Erich Deutsch; he resold it in 1925. Its present owner is unknown. (*D.B.*, 75.)

II. LANDPARTIE DER SCHUBERTIANER AUF EINEM 'WURST-WAGEN': an aquarelle[1] 23 cm. high and 32 cm. wide, by Leopold Kupelwieser. It is signed by the painter and dated 1820. It depicts an excursion by an open wagon to the neighbouring estate of Aumühl. (The German name for the wagon signifies a long, presumably sausage-shaped, vehicle with a knife-board.) A humorous incident is depicted in which a wheel of the wagon is crushing the top hat of one of the company (Spaun's, it is surmised). Schubert and Kupelwieser walk behind the wagon.

The aquarelle was painted for Schober. After his death, on 13 August 1882, there was a sale of his posthumous papers, etc., in Leipzig on 23 March 1885; the aquarelle was purchased there by Nicolaus Dumba, who bequeathed the picture (and its fellow, see next) to the City of Vienna. Dumba died on 23 March 1900, and the two aquarelles are now in the Schubert Museum. (*D.B.*, 336; in colour.)

III. GESELLSCHAFTSSPIEL DER SCHUBERTIANER IN ATZEN-BRUGG: an aquarelle, 34 cm. high and 44 cm. wide, by Leopold Kupelwieser. It is signed by the painter and dated 1821. This is the most fully documented picture of them all.[2] Not only have several

---

[1] Strictly speaking, the term aquarelle refers to a drawing in indian ink afterwards tinted with thin, transparent water-colour.

[2] It must also have been copied, for Kreissle's description of a drawing in the possession of Heinrich von Doblhoff fits this one too closely for there to have been another, original version of the scene; even the number of persons (excluding Schubert) is mentioned — seventeen. This was in 1865, before the original had left Schober's possession. (Kreissle, p. 222.)

people, including the painter's son, Max Kupelwieser, endeavoured to identify all the people depicted, but Schober himself has explained the occasion fully. He gave the key to a full understanding of it in a letter to Hyazinth Holland, written on 14 February 1876. Atzenbrugg Castle was owned by an uncle of Schober's, and there, for a few days in July, Schober invited a group of congenial friends. The annual visits took place in the years 1817–23. Schubert was certainly a visitor there in 1820, 1821, and 1822, and possibly in 1823.

The scene painted by Kupelwieser shows the performance of a charade in one of the rooms at Atzenbrugg Castle. Some of the company are miming a scene for the second syllable of the word 'Rheinfall', the rest are grouped round, watching and trying to guess it.[1] The actors had previously represented the first syllable, 'Rhein', by pretending to wash in the ponds and waterfalls painted on the walls of the room, after which — in Schober's words — 'they complacently assured one another, in pantomime, that they were clean (*rein*)'. They have now proceeded to the syllable 'fall', miming the Fall of Man. Eve (Therese Derffel) hands the apple to Adam (Franz Derffel) as they stand beneath the Tree of Knowledge (Leopold Kupelwieser). The serpent (Schober) peers from the branches, while Almighty God (Josef von Gahy, standing on the stove with broom as sceptre) broods over the scene, powerless to stop the course of events. The Angel with the Flaming Sword (Jeanette Cuny de Pierron) stands at the open doors ready to drive the miscreants from the Garden of Eden.

Among the spectators is Schubert, seated at the piano, having evidently provided introductory music; intently watching him is Phillip von Hartmann. Underneath the piano squats Kupelwieser's dog, Drago (yes, even the dog has been identified). The other people are minor figures in the Schubert chronicles, with the exception of the seated pair on the extreme right, who are Josef von Spaun and Schober's sister Sophie. Franz von Hartmann, consulting an old diary, recorded in after years that on 13 December 1826 he and his brother Fritz were invited to Schober's home to see his collection of pictures — among them, he wrote,

[1] Rheinfall was a charming district in the neighbourhood of the castle.

'a beautiful aquarelle by Kupelwieser, with Schubert at the piano, several friends including Kupelwieser himself, then, leaning over the piano, von Hartmann of Wels,[1] Professor of Zoology in Olmütz, who later became insane.'

The water-colour was, like the previous one, commissioned by Schober, who considered that the portrait of Schubert at the piano was the most faithful of all; its subsequent history is the same as that of its fellow. It was bought from the sale of Schober's artistic papers by Dumba, who bequeathed it to the City of Vienna; it is now housed in the Schubert museum there. (*D.B.*, 484; in colour.)

Dating from 1821, the charade-scene at Atzenbrugg is contemporary with the six lovely dances that Schubert composed there, known as the 'Atzenbrugger Deutsche', D. 728. His manuscript, dated July 1821, is in the archives of the Gesellschaft der Musikfreunde, Vienna. One other relic from that period is his first real portrait, now to be considered.

IV. SCHUBERT: a pencil drawing, 20·8 cm. high and 15·9 cm. wide, by Leopold Kupelwieser. Schubert is shown full-face. It is signed not by the artist, but by the composer — 'Franz Schubert mpia' — and dated by him 10 July 1821. The date suggests that it was drawn at Atzenbrugg; two days later Kupelwieser drew a similar portrait in pencil of Schober, which tends to confirm the idea. There is a possibility that Kupelwieser drew this Schubert portrait for the Sonnleithner family, and a copy of it came into their possession. The original, however, remained a private possession of the artist and was not discovered until his death on 17 November 1862. Several music journals announced in February 1863 the discovery among Kupelwieser's posthumous effects, and the drawing was photographed by the firm of Gustav Jagermayer, Vienna. Brahms secured one of these photographs and sent it to Joachim; in his letter, 13 April 1863, he wrote: 'I am sending you a lovely portrait of Schubert, which is not yet on sale.' The sketch was used as the basis of a woodcut, an inferior piece of work, which was reproduced as the frontispiece of Kreissle's biography

[1] A town on the river Traun, to the north of Steyr.

of 1865. The original portrait, pasted on cardboard, stayed with Kupelwieser's descendants until the early 1930's, when it was sold by Heck of Vienna. It is now owned by Antony van Hoboken, Ascona.[1]

Although not a favourite portrait, it is the work of an extremely competent draftsman, one who was a close friend of the composer; since it was presumably executed at one sitting, it has both spontaneity and veracity. The plain, matter-of-fact statement in Kupelwieser's portrait probably gets nearer the truth than do the more attractive, pictorial qualities of later, better-liked portraits. It was exhibited in both the great Schubert exhibitions in Vienna, in 1897 and 1928. (*D.B.*, 433.)

v. BALLSPIEL IN ATZENBRUGG: an etching made by Ludwig Mohn from a composite drawing by Schober and Schwind. It is not known exactly when the sketch was first devised; Schwind did not join the Atzenbrugg visitors until 1823 (see his letter to Schober of 24 December 1823), so that it probably dates from the July of that year.

Schober sketched the background, showing Atzenbrugg Castle; in the field before it Schwind drew the figures of the assembled company. He appears in the group seated in the foreground, with Vogl and Schubert, who is smoking a pipe. Schober, who has apparently thrown up the ball, stands behind and to the left of Schubert. The figure hurrying on to the left of the scene is probably Leopold Kupelwieser. The picture was then etched by Mohn, and below it he inscribed the caption 'Schober del... Schwind staf... Mohn fec...'.

Copies of the etching are very rare, but there are two in public possession. The first is in the Print Collection of the Albertina, Vienna; it is 14 cm. high and 20 cm. wide. The second copy is painted in water-colours by Mohn himself. It belonged to Schober and was found in his papers after his death. At the sale mentioned above it was purchased by Prince von und zu Liechtenstein (for 300 marks), who presented it to the Gesellschaft der Musik-

---

[1] See *Österreichische Musikzeitschrift*, Feb. 1959.

freunde, Vienna. This pleasantly coloured version, 9·8 cm. high and 16·7 cm. wide, is entitled 'Landpartie in Atzenbrugg'. It was exhibited at the 1897 Schubert Exhibition in Vienna (wrongly designated in the catalogue as a gouache) and again in 1928.

The value of the three pictures from Atzenbrugg, considered as studio portraits of Schubert, are almost negligible, but as revelations of the 'unbuttoned' Schubert and of the social circle of which he was an active member they are charming. (*D.B.*, 465.)

VI. 'MICHAEL VOGL UND FRANZ SCHUBERT ZIEHEN AUS ZU KAMPF UND SIEG' ('. . . go forth to fight and conquer'): a pencil caricature, 20 cm. wide and 18 cm. high, probably drawn by Schober *c.* 1825. The title is written in copperplate beneath the drawing; it refers, of course, to the popular and all-conquering partnership of Schubert and Vogl in the performance of Schubert's Lieder at the Schubertiade; the composer's coat-tail pocket bulges with a roll of manuscript songs as, no doubt, it did in real life. Vogl strides majestically ahead, and the caricaturist, no doubt with satirical intent, exaggerated Schubert's low stature, with the inevitable suggestion that it is the singer who, at least in his own opinion, is the more important of the two.

The caricature belonged to Schober's housekeeper, Babette Wolf, presumably a gift from her master (hence Schober's presumed authorship), but its existence was unknown until after his death. Babette seems to have given or sold it to an American collector some time in the 1890's, but it reappeared in a Berlin saleroom in January 1927. The drawing was then purchased by Dr. Curt Sluzewski of London, to whom it still belongs. The cartoon had been photographed by the Leipzig publisher Robert Kluckhart, and one of his reproductions, not the original, was exhibited by his son Julian at the Schubert Exhibition of 1897 (Cat. no. 132). There was a preliminary sketch for the cartoon, once in the possession of Otto Erich Deutsch. This, together with the Holzapfel silhouette, was sold in Berlin in 1925. The whereabouts of the preliminary sketch is unknown today. (*D.B.*, 657.)

VII. SCHUBERT: an aquarelle, 20 cm. high and 25 cm. wide, by Wilhelm August Rieder. The composer is seated, his right arm flung over the back of the chair, a book of poems in his right hand. On the left of the portrait is Rieder's signature with the date May 1825; on the right is Schubert's signature. In later years Rieder added remarks to these inscriptions: under his signature he wrote the words 'Nach der Natur [Drawn from life] von Wilh. Aug. Rieder 1825'; under Schubert's signature he added the date of the composer's death. It is the best known and most popular of the portraits, and deservedly so — a delicately executed piece of portraiture, combining refinement of detail with substance of form. It owes its existence to a sudden rainstorm in Vienna, from which Rieder sought shelter in Schubert's lodgings next to the Karlskirche (a house no longer, alas, in existence: it was demolished in 1961). While he was there Rieder started his drawing of the composer, and after a few more sittings completed it. The water-colour remained in Rieder's possession till his death on 8 September 1880. It was auctioned in Vienna on 22 February 1881 and bought by a lawyer, Georg Granitsch (for 1205 florins). It passed eventually to his son Robert and then to Robert's daughter, who sold it in December 1958 to the City of Vienna. It is officially a possession of the Historical Museum of Vienna, and is housed in a new building in the Karlsplatz — a stone's throw from Schubert's lodgings where it was first sketched. (*D.B.*, frontispiece; in colour.)

There are several old copies of this portrait made by other artists; all are inferior to Rieder's work, but often mistaken for it. The error must be due to the habit of editors and biographers, who are inclined to take the short cut of using reproductions from earlier books rather than go to original pictures for their illustrations. A copy of Rieder's picture was painted (probably by Michael Stohl) for Josef Witteczek's Schubert Library; Rieder himself signed the copy 'W. A. Rieder 1840'. Spaun inherited Witteczek's collection, and in his memoirs he wrote of this copy as if it were the original. On his death Spaun left all his Schubertiana to the Gesellschaft der Musikfreunde. Stohl's copy was used by Breitkopf & Härtel as a frontispiece for the *Gesamtausgabe* of

Schubert's works, without any indication that it was not Rieder's original painting. A second copy, signed 'S.T.' (?), was discovered in Diabelli's posthumous papers; this also was reproduced as the original portrait, first in *Die Musik*[1] and again in Walter Dahms's *Schubert*.[2] Two other copies are known, the earlier, dated 1857, painted by Schubert's nephew Heinrich.

Rieder's portrait of Schubert became widely known in the composer's lifetime, since shortly after its completion it was engraved on copper by Johann Nepomuk Passini and reproductions were on sale at the establishment of Cappi & Co. in Vienna. Their advertisement in the *Wiener Zeitung* of 9 December 1825 speaks of 'the Extremely Good Likeness of the composer FRANZ SCHUBERT'. A few years later Rieder made a lithograph of his portrait, which will be discussed later.

The likeness is not only a favourite one with music-lovers today, for Schubert's friends, with the exception of Schober, felt the same about it, and they all considered it to be the best one. It has formed the basis of nearly all the posthumous representations of the face of Schubert — distorted by the sentimentalist, the idealist, the romantic, and the frankly incompetent, yet always recognizable. Some of the subsequent versions are considered briefly later in this essay.

VIII. SCHUBERT: a lithograph, 45 cm. high and 30 cm. wide, executed by Josef Teltscher towards the end of 1825. In the diary of the popular young Viennese soprano, Sophie Müller, there are two references to the lithograph, on 11 and 24 January 1826, when Teltscher himself took the portrait to show her; these visits conveniently fix the date of the first appearance of copies drawn from the stone. The firm of Mansfeld & Co. later prepared and published copies, and these were on sale in the spring of 1829. The first edition carried a facsimile of Schubert's signature, together with the words 'Ehrenmitglied der Musik-Vereine zu Grätz und Linz' ('Honorary Member of the Music Societies of Graz and Linz') and the dates of his birth and death. Profits from the sale of

---

[1] Berlin, July 1906.
[2] Leipzig and Berlin, 1912, Plate 5.

this edition were given to the funds being raised to provide a monument over Schubert's grave. A second edition followed later, with merely his name and the death date. Copies of the original pressings and of the two later editions are extremely rare; two examples of Teltscher's own copies are preserved, one in the archives of the Gesellschaft der Musikfreunde and the other in the National Library, Vienna.

Teltscher was a very gifted portrait-painter. A younger man than Schubert (he was born in 1801), he became friendly with the composer during the various Schubertiade of the 1820's. His tragically early death by drowning, in 1837, cut short a life of great promise. His portrait of Schubert, a three-quarter face, is not greatly esteemed, although, like Kupelwieser's pencil sketch of 1821, it is probably a faithful likeness. The face is somewhat immature and static, with no suggestion of the latent fire that Rieder so admirably conveys. (*D.B.*, 688.)

Teltscher lived and worked for many years at Graz and was thus a friend of Anselm and Josef Hüttenbrenner and of Johann Baptist Jenger. When Schubert and Jenger visited the town in September 1827, however, Teltscher was away. It is tempting to consider the next portrait as a kind of souvenir of Schubert's stay in Graz, but it is not so. It was drawn earlier in 1827, possibly on the occasion of a visit by Anselm Hüttenbrenner to Vienna.

IX. JENGER, ANSELM HUTTENBRENNER, SCHUBERT: a coloured crayon drawing, 16·2 cm. high and 20·6 cm. wide, by Josef Teltscher. The head and shoulders only of each man are drawn: Hüttenbrenner's left hand rests on Schubert's shoulder. The artist had actually lithographed each man separately, and this composite portrait merely duplicates his previous work. So far as Schubert is concerned, the portrait contributes nothing new: it is prosaically like the single lithograph of the previous section. But the drawing commemorates the association of the three men and is a pleasant enough piece of work. (*M.*, 406; *D.B.*, 720; in colour.)

It belonged to Karl, Baron von Schönstein, and was sold after his death to the family von Schweitzer. In 1897, when it was exhibited in Vienna, it belonged to Baroness Ida von Schweitzer

4. Figure sketches for Schwind's 'Schubert Evening'

5. Sketch for the fully planned 'Schubert Evening'

and was preserved in the Gneixendorf Castle near Krems, well known to us because of Beethoven's sojourn there in the autumn before his death. It is still with the same family, belonging today to Baron Otto von Schweitzer of Sterbfritz-bei-Schlüchtern, Germany.

x. SCHUBERT: an oil, 56 cm. high and 44 cm. wide, painted c. 1827, by an unknown artist. The portrait was commissioned by Josef Sonnleithner to be included among his collection of musicians' portraits; it is owned today by the Gesellschaft der Musikfreunde. Josef's nephew Leopold von Sonnleithner considered it 'a very good oil-painting of him', a verdict with which we cannot, today, agree. The work itself is inferior, the face devoid of life; if Rieder's water-colour and Kupelwieser's pencil sketch are good portraits, this one is almost a travesty. For some reason the artist, whoever he was, painted Schubert without his spectacles, but it is not this omission that renders the likeness invalid. The devitalized impulse of the artist makes the painting uncongenial. (*D.B.*, 817.)

Schubert's portrait was associated in Sonnleithner's collection with that of Beethoven; since Beethoven's portrait was known to be by the painter Willibrord Josef Mähler, it was assumed that Mähler was also responsible for the one of Schubert. All reproductions of the portrait were therefore attributed to Mähler, sometimes definitely so, sometimes with the appendage '(?)'. In the journal *Musica*, February 1961, and again in the booklet *Mitteilungen der Österreichischen Galerie*, vol. 49, 1961, the scholar Fritz Novotny wrote of his doubts about the attribution to Mähler ('Zu einem Bildnis Franz Schuberts'). Novotny considers the portrait to be an early work of the painter Franz Eybl and gives quite convincing reasons, stylistic and documentary, for the new attribution. Eybl (1806–80) could have been in touch with Schubert, although the assertion that the painter of this portrait, whether he be Mähler or Eybl, must have known Schubert, loses force when we consider that a more successful result could have been achieved had the painter simply used Passini's engraving—then on sale in Vienna—as his model. Even Leopold

L

Sonnleithner went on to say that this engraving 'was the most speaking likeness'.

There are numerous likenesses of Schubert that claim to be contemporary, but only a few of them can substantiate the claim sufficiently to deserve mention here. The first is found in one of Schwind's oils, the scene known as 'Der Spaziergang vor dem Stadttor'; he painted it in Munich in 1827, that is, in the year before Schubert's death. It is 95 cm. high and 61·5 cm. wide, and is owned by a descendant of Schwind's. Five years later Schwind drew a pencil sketch of it for a lithograph version. Three figures in the left background pass the gate, the nearest, turning towards the observer, is Schubert. It hardly deserves the term 'portrait', being inferior even to the picture of the composer in the Atzenbrugg ball-game scene. But we do see a glimpse of Schubert through Schwind's eyes, as it were.

From Schwind's pen also there is a pseudo-caricature of Schubert in the title-vignette he engraved for a publication of Rossini's one-act *opera buffa, Il Matrimonio per Cambiale*. The scene shows the heroine on a sofa, with Schubert as her suitor standing before her; his rival peers through the half-open door. The drawing was made *c.* 1824 for an edition of the opera from the Viennese publishers Sauer & Leidesdorf.

A second caricature of Schubert also appears in a title-vignette. This was lithographed by an unknown artist for a collection of *Moderne Liebes-Waltzer*. The scene shows a father counting his money at a table, while the young man (Schubert) waltzes away with the daughter. The picture illustrates the couplet printed below it:

> Gar leicht sind Herz und Hand vermählt,
> Wenn Väterchen die Thaler zählt.

> (How easy heart and hand are wed,
> When by dear father's dollars sped.) (trans. Eric Blom.)

The collection of waltzes was published in 1827 by the same publishers; Schubert contributed the first one of the eight dances. Although scholars were fully aware of this publication, it was not until 1901 that a copy was discovered in the British Museum by William Barclay Squire. This discovery led to the republication of the waltz, and a reference to the Schubert caricature on the title-page.[1]

The most important of these likenesses, outside the canon of contemporary portraits, is the bust sculptured for Schubert's grave-memorial by Josef Alois Dialer. He knew Schubert, and it is not unlikely that his work was based on a death-mask of the composer. The bust was cast in iron and at a later date bronzed over. It must have been executed by Dialer at the time of Schubert's death, since small plaster models were on sale at Haslinger's a few weeks afterwards, advertised as on sale in the *Allgemeine musikalische Zeitung* of 17 January 1829. It is a noble work and, judging by Schwind's posthumous sketches, an excellent, if idealized, portrait. The bust was erected in July 1830, but removed in 1888; it is now housed in Schubert's birthplace — the Schubert Museum in Vienna. (*D.B.*, 848.)

A word must be devoted to a very attractive portrait, three-quarter face, of a youth with shirt-collar open at the neck, alleged to be Schubert at the age of sixteen. It is a chalk drawing and has been frequently reproduced in recent books. The artist is said to be Leopold Kupelwieser, and the date of the drawing is given as *c.* 1813. The existence of the sheet was unknown until 1891, when it appeared in the sale-room of C. J. Wawra in Vienna and was bought by Prince von und zu Liechtenstein; it is today in the Liechtenstein Gallery, formerly in Vienna, now in Vaduz. On the back is written by Andreas, Schubert's half-brother, 'Franz Schubert in his 16th year. Original chalk drawing by the friend of his youth, Leopold Kupelwieser, *c.* 1813'. This statement he then signed; the other half-brother, Anton Eduard, also added his signature. The authentication was probably written on the back of the portrait at about the time of its sale.

External evidence points to the fact that Kupelwieser was not the artist; his sons, Karl and Max, knew nothing of the drawing, and could find no mention in their father's work-catalogue of any

[1] *Zeitschrift der internationalem Musikgesellschaft* (Leipzig, 1902), pp. 317–20.

Schubert portrait drawn in 1813. Kupelwieser did not become acquainted with Schubert until 1820 (he was only seventeen years old in 1813). The evidence in its favour, given by Schubert's half-brothers, cannot be accepted without reserve. They were mere children, Andreas five and Anton two, when he died, and could not have had the least idea what he looked like in 1813! But the face of the youth gazing so steadfastly at us cannot be dismissed, in spite of assertions to the contrary, as quite unlike Schubert. He is unspectacled, although in 1813 Schubert was wearing spectacles, and this at once makes judgement more difficult. But the hair, the chin, and, in particular, the formation of the ear, can be compared with those in the other Schubert portraits, and one begins to feel, after doing so, that this *might* be the sixteen-year-old composer, idealized, as artists will idealize their sitters. Various other thoughts arise. The drawing evidently came to light in Germany, in the late nineteenth century: it might possibly have been part of the artistic possessions of Kupelwieser, kept by him as a memento of his old friend, although the work of a fellow artist. One might consider the fact that although Andreas and Anton Schubert could have had no personal memories of the appearance of their half-brother that have any weight in the argument, nevertheless the members of all families have a knowledge of facts and traditions about each other for which there is no particle of written evidence; it might have been common knowledge among the members of the second and third generation of the Schuberts that there was a chalk drawing of the composer, and that it was owned by Kupelwieser. But all these thoughts are pure surmise.

A few posthumous portraits, made within a few years of the composer's death, are sometimes accepted as contemporary portraits. The most important is Rieder's lithograph, based on his water-colour, which was probably made immediately after the composer's death. Copies were on sale at Artaria & Co., Vienna, in the early months of 1829. They are now extremely rare, but one is preserved in the City Library, Vienna. The well-known oil-painting by Rieder, in which Schubert is seated at a desk with quill-pen poised, was not painted, however, until 1875. This picture also portrays Schubert's pianoforte, which had passed into the possession of the Rieder family; it is now in the Schubert Museum, Vienna. Both the lithograph and the oil-painting were displayed in the 1897 Schubert Exhibition in Vienna.

A second early lithograph was made in Paris, in 1834, by Leon Noël. It is a delicate, transparent piece of work, but gives a definitely prettified version of Schubert's face — supposedly to satisfy the tastes of the mid-nineteenth-century Paris public.[1] There is a copy in the Gesellschaft der Musikfreunde.

With the possible exception of the oil-painting of *c.* 1827, the portraits agree remarkably well, in noticeable contrast to those of Mozart, for example, each of which seems to delineate the features of a different man. Schwind considered the Kupelwieser pencil sketch (No. IV) and the Teltscher lithograph (No. VIII) to be very good likenesses, but he implied that among the friends of the composer, Rieder's aquarelle (No. VII) was held to be the best portrait. This aquarelle is a charming piece of work: only examination of the original reveals its full beauty. Its delicate colouring and exquisite detail are largely lost in reproduction, but, compared with the productions of Kupelwieser and Teltscher, it clearly flatters the composer a little. Teltscher's representation of Schubert's features is probably very faithful, but the expression is distinctly flat. To see a faithful likeness, combined with an alertness of pose and expression, it seems that we cannot do better than look at Kupelwieser's painting of Schubert at the piano in the charade scene at Atzenbrugg (No. III). The pose is natural and relaxed, the face lifted and keenly interested. Schober, it may be remembered, considered this to be the best likeness of his friend; this opinion appears in a letter that he wrote to Maria Lipsuis ('La Mara') in 1878, when he sent her a photograph of this detail from the painting (in his possession at the time).

But if Schubert's portraits tally remarkably well, the descriptions

[1] The same glamorizing effect can also be seen in August Lemoine's lithograph, executed for the frontispiece to H. Barbadette's Schubert biography, Paris 1865. This was based on Kriehuber's famous lithograph of 1846; it omits the spectacles.

of his appearance, habits, and dress as we read them in the records and memoirs of his friends are comically irreconcilable. Most of these reminiscences are posthumous and clearly written with one eye on the public for whom they were intended. We may discount Bauernfeld's good-natured snub to a lady who asked him what Schubert looked like: 'Like a drunken cabby' was his retort. But Spaun's careful paragraphs, correcting the mis-apprehensions arising from Kreissle's biography, deserve careful attention. Spaun is particularly concerned to disprove the adjective 'negroid' applied to Schubert's features, and it is worth noting that he said, 'The portrait of Schubert, painted by Rieder, and engraved, is extraordinarily like him.' Coming from Schubert's closest and most trustworthy friend, the words seem conclusive.

SCHWIND'S 'SCHUBERT-ABEND BEI JOSEF VON SPAUN'

No man could have lived more obscurely than Schubert in view of the greatness of his creative powers and his post-humous eminence. Apart from the half-dozen or so expeditions to neighbouring Austrian towns, mostly in the nature of holidays, his days were spent in the Viennese by-ways. Two or three times the limelight played on his humble figure, when two of his operettas and one play, for which he had written incidental music, were staged in the capital; on one spring evening he was acclaimed and applauded by a public audience — largely made up of his friends and well-wishers. But anything like international, or even local, renown was denied him. And yet he numbered among his closest friends two painters and one author whose work, though not of the front rank, has adorned the obscurity of his life in a fashion not found with any other of the great composers. In this generous manner Fate certainly tipped the balance against the denial and seclusion of his daily existence. Bauernfeld in his writings and Schwind and Kupelwieser in their drawings have given us a continual source of delight, which enables us to contemplate first Schubert's power to charm and excite his friends with his music and second the Vienna so deeply loved by him and his circle of friends.

The most famous and frequently quoted of all the records of these friends is Schwind's picture 'Schubert-Abend bei Josef von Spaun' (frontispiece). It hangs today in the Schubert Museum of Vienna; this is housed in the preserved birthplace of the composer in the Nussdorferstrasse. Its conception, its composition, and its subsequent history are possibly interesting enough to discuss here.

Moritz von Schwind, born in Vienna on 21 January 1804, was a younger man than Schubert; this fact influences his admiration for the composer — it is touched with the veneration of a younger brother for an older one. He was a gifted musician as well as an extremely talented draughtsman, so there was no condescension in Schubert's attitude towards him. Schubert himself was by no means without a knowledgeable appreciation of painting, and he spoke and wrote enthusiastically of the work of his young friend. Each man admired whole-heartedly the art of the other. It was a valuable and fertilizing friendship. Although Schwind's professional life was not without its precarious aspects in the 1820's, he was beginning to undertake commissions and to establish a name for himself; his reputation was more surely grounded than Schubert's when the composer died in 1828.

Schwind heard of Schubert's death at Munich, where he was studying at the academy. He poured out his grief in a letter to their mutual friend Franz von Schober, concluding with the words:

It is to you that I bring all the love they have not buried with him, and always to live with you and to share everything with you is my dearest prospect. The recollection of him will be with us, and all the burdens of the world will not prevent us from wholly feeling for a moment now and then what has now utterly vanished.

Your Moritz.

Write to me soon about everything you still remember of him — but quite soon. For an hour with you all I would . . . .

The letter breaks off. These words have a tragically ironic ring when one considers that in later years the two men quarrelled, and in spite of an attempted reconciliation never resumed their former friendship. Schwind's old feelings of affection for Schober soured into dislike for the man. The fact is not without its bearing on the picture he painted.

The desire to pay tribute to Schubert in his paintings, not only to the friend and to his music, but also to the Vienna of his young days, which that music evoked, soon began to grow in him. As the years passed, an aura of romantic longing began to gather in Schwind's mind round the scenes of his youth: Vienna and Schubert aroused an emotion that, in his wanderings about Europe, grew stronger with the years. He wrote to Bauernfeld from Rome on 25 July 1835:

... I've designed a room in which Schubert's songs are to be sung. The 'Mayrhofer' wall is well advanced and could be sent next year for exhibition with that devoted to Goethe. Couldn't Witteczek order something of the kind? All could be done for a few thousand gulden. *Urania* and *Einsamkeit* as arabesques are ready in colour. But I'll have a look round in Pompeii. *Antigone und Oedip*, the *Zürnende Diana* and *Memnon* are composed ....

The drawings mentioned here were all executed by Schwind in Rome; his sketch-book containing them is still preserved. Nothing came of this project, but Schwind never forgot it, and he returned to the subject again in 1851 when he heard that the Viennese publisher C. A. Spina, a former partner and then the successor of Diabelli, intended to open a Schubert salon. It was to be situated in the Sailerstätte. The salon was opened with an inaugural ceremony on 28 February 1851; Bauernfeld wrote a 'Prologue' for the occasion. On 16 March 1851 Schwind wrote of his wishes to Bauernfeld: 'You say nothing about the Schubert salon. The more convinced I am that this will never come off, the more I dream of it, and "perhapses" run through my brain, and their frustration pains me.' A further Schubert 'celebration' was held in the salon on 25 November 1853, and the room itself survived until 1860, but nothing further came of Schwind's hopes to paint his illustrations to the Schubert Lieder on its walls.

At this period of his life Schwind was a professor of art at Munich, where he had once been a student. It was there, in 1852, that he painted for his own pleasure a picture in oils, which embodies some of his aspirations and ideals. The work had been planned for some time, as we learn from his letter to a colleague, Bernhard Schädel, written in November 1849. The picture is the first of a quartet that between them relate a love-story: a typical procedure of Schwind's, who was a master in the devising of a narrative picture series.[1] The oil-painting is called 'Die Symphonie' although actually it depicts a performance of Beethoven's

---

[1] The four pictures are designed to correspond with the four movements of a symphony. The other three — *Andante, Scherzo,* and *Allegro* — show a meeting between the lovers, a ball, and the bride's first glimpse of her future home. The picture discussed above is in the Neue Pinakothek, Munich.

Choral Phantasie, op. 80, for voices, pianoforte, and orchestra. Among the chorus on the left-hand side is a group consisting of Schubert, Schober, and Vogl; Franz Lachner conducts, and Schwind himself turns the pages of the pianist's album. The soft but vivid colouring is charming to a degree. Schubert's likeness begins to haunt Schwind's pictures: sometimes it is an actual portrait, as in the series of forty-six humorous water-colour drawings on the life of Franz Lachner, called the *Lachnerrolle*, which was produced in Munich in 1862; sometimes Schubert serves as a model for one of a group of people, as in one picture of the cycle of aquarelles called 'Gesichte eines Liebespaares'.

The prospect of painting his Schubert salon again became a possibility in 1862. On 30 May Schwind wrote to Bauernfeld and in the course of his letter said:

> . . . I received yesterday from the sculptor Schönthaler a letter asking if I would paint in the dining-room of a house belonging to a Herr Todesco a series of remembrances of the 'Baumanns-Höhle' — but I haven't any! Wouldn't it be a grand solution of the problem to suggest to this man that he should dedicate his walls to the memory of Schubert? I am full of it. The space would just do.

The Baumanns-Höhle was a kind of harmless secret society in the Vienna of the 1820's — closed, nevertheless, by the police in 1826. Word probably reached Eduard Todesco, a wealthy banker and art-lover, who had just acquired a new house in the Kärntner-thorstrasse, of Schwind's desires in the matter, and there may have been some talk about it in Vienna. We find Eduard Hanslick writing in the journal *Die Presse* on 31 January 1863 (an anniversary of Schubert's birthday) these words:

> According to report one of the most respected and one of the greatest art-lovers among the Viennese bankers is going to have a salon in his new house decorated with illustrations to Schubert's works, and has in mind for this undertaking Schubert's most gifted and affectionate friend M. von Schwind. There is something very attractive in the idea. A better man for this particular task it would be impossible to find anywhere.

But once more the project fell through, and Schwind's hopes were dashed.

The plans and frustrated hopes began to assume a new shape in his mind: if not a room devoted to illustrations from Schubert's songs, then a picture devoted to the memory of the performance of those songs. The new idea was suddenly precipitated by an unexpected approach from an acquaintance of his youth, Baron Karl von Schönstein. This man, a friend of Count Johann Esterházy, had an appealing tenor voice, and had been much admired for his sensitive interpretation of the Schubert Lieder. He owned a miniature portrait, painted by Josef Teltscher, of Karoline Esterházy, the daughter of Count Esterházy, to whom Schubert had acted as music master during the years 1818 and 1824. Schubert was believed by his friends to have been in love with her, but there is little evidence for the belief. Early in 1863 Schönstein lent Schwind the miniature — 'of a lady in a blue dress' — and Schwind made a copy of it. Schönstein had intended to bequeath the portrait-miniature to Schwind, but since, as he wrote with wry humour in a letter to the painter on 28 April 1863, '... it seems to be decided in heaven that I must go on bearing a life that has long become a burden to me ...', he changed his mind. Schwind was told to keep the miniature as a 'Donatio inter vivos'. Karoline Esterházy had never attended any of those social evenings in Vienna when the music was devoted entirely to the songs and pianoforte pieces of Schubert, evenings that were known among his friends as Schubertiade; although Schwind was fully aware of her place in Schubert's life, he had never set eyes on her. The miniature gave him a unique chance to incorporate her presence in the company without violating probability too much: her portrait, based upon Teltscher's, should hang on the wall of the drawing-room. And so the idea of the picture assumed a definite shape in his mind. Early in 1865 he began to put on paper sketches to embody his ideas. There are seven preliminary drawings extant, and although the order in which they were executed cannot be gauged exactly, their nature suggests a possible one. To begin with there were five small studies concerned with details in the complete picture. Three of them concentrate on the central pair of figures, Schubert and Vogl. It is of interest to see that Schwind's original idea of the profile of Schubert, bent over the keys of the piano, never varied, but the exact posture of Vogl gave him trouble. In each of the three studies it is slightly different; in two of them the singer holds a sheet of music, in the third he turns away from the viewer and is dramatically interpreting a song. The only factor common to all three is the representation of Vogl's affected gesture with his lorgnettes, behaviour that so exasperated Schwind during the actual Schubertiade. Two of the sketches, in pencil, belonged to Schönstein and passed from him to the Schweitzer family at Gneixendorf Castle. They are today in the possession of Baron Otto von Schweitzer, Sterbfritz-bei-Schlüchten, Germany. The third, a pen-and-ink study, is now in the possession of a descendant of Josef von Spaun, Christoph Cornaro, Vienna. Further sketches are found on a larger leaf (21·1 × 34·1 cm.). It was auctioned in Frankfurt-am-Main on 29 May 1925 and purchased by the City of Vienna. The leaf is now preserved in the Print Collection of the Albertina, part of the National Library in Vienna. Both sides are covered with pen-and-ink sketches of various women in the picture, notably of Marie Pinterics: she sits on the end of the couch to the left of the picture (Plate 4). The possibilities of her graceful pose evidently fascinated Schwind. The sixth drawing, a large pencil sketch (50 × 100 cm.), probably followed these small sketches. The painter outlines the horizontal line of heads on a level with Schubert's, deciding then on the identities and relative positions of the chief characters in his picture. The details are excellent and almost exactly as they appear in the final picture. The attitude of Vogl is decided on to the painter's satisfaction — the singer is turning a page of the song-volume. The faces of Spaun and Schober are fully and decisively drawn. This very fine piece of work was purchased by the City of Vienna c. 1904 and shown publicly for the first time at an exhibition that year of Schwind's work. It is now in the possession of the Schubert Museum, Vienna (Plate 6). Finally, Schwind sketched the whole scene, roughly, in pen and ink: it is a fresh and vigorous conception, although naturally without the finesse and detail of the foregoing pencil sketch. This final sketch is fairly small (15·5 × 25·3 cm.); it was offered for sale at Frankfurt-am-main at the same time as the sixth sketch, and it too was bought by the City of Vienna. It is preserved in the Albertina (Plate 5). Schwind was probably still dissatisfied with some of his figure-studies, particularly with the poses of Marie Pinterics and her companion and with the attitude of Vogl's wife (she sits to the right of the piano). But the work was sufficiently advanced for him to write on 25 May 1865 to the poet Eduard Mörike as follows:

... incidentally I have begun to work at something which I feel is due to the intellectual part of Germany — my admirable friend Schubert at the piano, surrounded by his circle of listeners. I know all the people by heart and a happy chance has put me in possession of a portrait of a Countess Esterházy, whom I've never seen, but to whom he used to say he had dedicated all his works. She had every reason to be satisfied . . . .

Later in the year Schwind was given the commission that, to him, was the proudest and most satisfying ever made. He was invited to paint a series of semicircular frescoes — lunettes — for the loggia and foyer of the newly built Opera House in Vienna. These tempera paintings are his best and most famous work. For the loggia he painted scenes from Mozart's *Die Zauberflöte*; for the foyer a cycle of scenes from famous operas. Among the foyer paintings we find one devoted to Schubert. This lunette is divided into three panels, separated by two standing figures, 'Der Wanderer' and 'Die zürnende Diana'. The centre panel shows the closing scene of *Die Verschworenen*, the left panel 'Der Erlkönig' and the right 'Der Fischer'. The work on the frescoes for the Opera House took him the best part of five years, during which he achieved, he says, the loveliest and richest work that he himself could wish: the Schubert lunette was evidently planned in his mind by the end of the year. On 31 December 1865 he wrote about it to Henriette von Spaun, a niece of Schubert's old friend Josef von Spaun; she was then living in Linz. Schwind ended his letter:

... what pleases me is that even in my old age it has come my way to paint a memorial where it will remain and where thousands can see it.[1] Our portly, gay Schubert, who considered himself less than the second best, indisputably and as a matter of course, takes his place of honour among the foremost and greatest. . . .

He was approaching the end of his work on the frescoes when at length he took in hand the painting of the 'Schubert Evening' as we know it today. In the autumn of 1868 the picture was almost ready. It was executed in sepia, that is, in the brown pigment applied with pen and colour-wash, and is of practically the same dimensions as the large pencil sketch — 56·5 cm. by 92 cm. On 29 October 1868 he wrote to Bauernfeld about it:

I have done something that in a way could be an illustration for your 'Letters of an old Viennese to a lady friend'.[2] But in these anxious times it is unmanageable, and I have placed it with its face to the wall *nonum prematur in annum*.[3] It would be 'Schubert am Klavier', old Vogl singing, and the whole society of those days, all the little ladies and gentlemen, round about.

By the end of the year the picture was completed and hung on a wall in his rooms at Starnbergersee, near Munich. 'A "Schubertiad" is also ready,' he wrote in December 1868 to Bauernfeld, 'but I've hung it on the wall; it may improve by keeping.'

Two further examples of his Schubert portraiture may be mentioned, both executed at this period. The first is a pen-and-ink drawing for a projected Schubert *Brunnen* — a public fountain — to be erected in Vienna. Schubert's bust, similar to that by Josef Dialer for the grave-monument, is on a column flanked by two female figures: one symbolizing the 'Gay' Lied, the other the 'Serious' Lied. Water gushes from the mouth of a trout. The second portrait was drawn in 1870. Schwind was in Vienna

---

[1] These words might easily have been tragically contradicted ; but the frescoes escaped any war damage and still appear on the walls of Vienna's Opera House.

[2] Reminiscences published by Bauernfeld, not under this title, but as 'Aus Alt- und Neu-Wien'. They appeared periodically from April 1869 onwards.

[3] A quotation from Horace: 'it should be kept nine years', i.e., said of wine, for the proper maturing.

working on the final stages of the Opera House lunettes; he learned that the much-talked-of Schubert monument was at last to become a reality and to adorn the city park. It was to be sculptured by Karl Kundmann, an artist whose reputation stood high in those days. Kundmann's memorial sculpture for Schubert and Grillparzer was much praised in after-years by Brahms, who, writing to his publisher Simrock in 1892, spoke of them as 'the best here in Vienna'. Schwind visited Kundmann in his studio, and in order to give the sculptor a definite idea of the cast and lineaments of Schubert's head he sketched the composer's profile in pencil on a slab of plaster. It is a spontaneous and satisfying piece of work in spite of its improvised medium.[1]

Whether his remarks in connection with the sepia drawing of the 'Schubert Evening', about its 'improving with keeping' and so on, meant that he still looked upon it as a stepping-stone to a yet more ambitious project is uncertain. But later in 1870 he began work on a version of the picture in oils.[2] He died before it was finished. The centre group, containing Schubert, Vogl, and the group of ladies, was completed and has great charm. There is a suggestion, perhaps, that the figures are more spruce than in the sepia drawing; they seem better groomed, better clad, and not quite perhaps so much of the period, and the impression is not altogether due to the different and more sophisticated medium. The alteration in the pose of Kunigunde, Vogl's wife, is a reversion to earlier ideas; her hand, instead of being lifted to her cheek, droops from the piano with touching grace.

Schwind died on 8 February 1871. The 'Schubert Evening' remained in the possession of his widow, Louise. We hear of it once during subsequent years; there was a Schubert Exhibition in Vienna, in 1892, organized by the Schubertbund, and Louise von Schwind lent the picture to be exhibited. It was photographed, too, at this time. But soon afterwards Louise died and the picture

[1] An even stranger medium had been used by Schwind — and with a similar purpose in mind. It well illustrates the humorous charm of the man. In 1866 he outlined Schubert's head for the Munich sculptor Max Widnmann on the windowsill of his studio with the burning end of a cigar!

[2] O. E. Deutsch, *Memoirs*, frontispiece.

was sold. Its history for a few years is obscure; it is supposed to have been taken to America. It was certainly not available for the Schubert Exhibition in 1897, arranged by the City of Vienna to celebrate the centenary of Schubert's birth. The authorities had to be content with the photograph. Eight years later the original reappeared in Europe, and in the autumn of 1905 was offered for sale in the Kunstsalon of Arnold of Dresden. It might have vanished again had it not been for the efforts of Otto Erich Deutsch. During the late autumn of 1905 and in January 1906 he made every effort to arouse private and public opinion in Vienna in order, in his own words, 'dieses lange verschwollen und damals plötzlich wieder aufgetauchten Bild für Wien zu retten' ('to save for Vienna this long-lost picture, suddenly emerging to the light again'). His efforts succeeded. It was bought by the City of Vienna, and from 1906 has been public property. Schubert's birth-house was also purchased by the city authorities in 1912, and both the sepia drawing and the unfinished sketch in oils were hung there.

The most striking aspect of Schwind's great achievement in this depiction of the Schubertiad is the fact that the observer feels at once drawn into the intimacy of the group of listeners. The circle, in fact, seems to be completed by the one who gazes at the scene; he even feels as if he is seated between the woman to his left and the man to his right at the points of the nearly completed circle. As his gaze passes round the company from head to head, Schwind's conception — individual portraiture combined into a unity by the shared emotion — is felt in all its grandeur; the observer is first drawn into the group and then shares in the absorbed listening. What song is Vogl singing? It is an idle question. Schwind left no inkling and probably had no definite song in his mind. But the song one would like to imagine being sung is surely 'An die Musik'. The rapt attention of these men and women in Spaun's drawing-room shows that the song has transported them, and which of all the Schubert Lieder has quite that power, that inwardness, as the miraculous setting of the lines beginning 'Du holde Kunst...' ('Thou gracious Art...')?

Schubert Museum, Vienna

6. Portrait sketches for the chief persons in the 'Schubert Evening'

Writers who have discussed the composition of the work point out that Schubert is at the centre of the scheme. True: but if one wishes to be finically accurate, then the actual, physical centre of the picture is not Schubert himself, it is the volume of his songs on the piano. It is the songs, the immortals, that are the hub of the circle. When Schwind painted his 'Schubert Evening', nearly all the men and women of those bygone days, whom we see listening to the song, were dead; the Schubert songs were becoming more celebrated every year. Was Schwind aware, one wonders, that the very year in which he was working on this picture saw the advent of an unprecedented outburst of renewed publication of the songs all over Europe? Even if he was, he could hardly have given us a more vivid representation of the scene he was striving to recall.

The identification of the men and women in the picture is now complete; one head, half hidden, is of doubtful attribution. The scene was inspired by an actual gathering in Spaun's house, but it is not intended to be a re-creation of any particular Schubertiad, nor were all the people depicted ever gathered together at one time. The identification of the individuals in the picture was first undertaken by Alois Trost in 1898, who used other individual portraits and generally accepted traditions, to establish the key, which is often reproduced side by side with the reproduction of the picture itself.[1] Schwind's grouping is of interest. If one considers what, as well as who, these people were, it is amusing to find that he has placed not necessarily kindred minds, but kindred arts or interests, together. This hardly applies to the five ladies on the right of the piano: the only factor in common there is that all were wives of various Schubertians, but their group enshrines the grace and charm of the occasion. But with the men it is otherwise. To Schubert's right is Vogl, the greatest of his interpreters, but standing behind Vogl is Karl von Schönstein, who was almost as good, and next to him is Benedikt Randhartinger, the first singer of the 'Erlkönig'. On the extreme left stand two men who were the first of the Schubertian collectors, Karl Pinterics and Josef Witteczek, and near by is Franz Lachner. Josef von Gahy, Schubert's friend, and his fellow in pianoforte-duet playing, stands

[1] O. E. Deutsch, *Documentary Biography*, p. 784.

M

immediately behind the composer-accompanist. On Schubert's left is a group of his friends, the nearest being Josef von Spaun. The painters of the Schubert circle stand together behind the seated ladies: Schwind himself (considerably older than he actually was in the days of the Schubertiade!) with August Wilhelm von Rieder and Leopold Kupelwieser. On the extreme right stand the literary figures, Grillparzer, Johann Senn, Mayr-hofer, Castelli, and Bauernfeld. Schwind's profile of Mayrhofer is, it is remarkable to note, the only portrait we possess of this close friend of Schubert's. Only one person in the whole assembly is not absorbed in the music; he turns to philander with the girl beside him. It is Schober. This touch of malice, a biting comment by Schwind on Schober's superficial response to the music of his friend, is sufficient indication of the bitterness of the breach between the two former friends. The girl is Justina von Bruch-mann, with whom Schober was having an affair during the years of the Schubertiade. The portrait of Karoline Esterházy hangs in the centre of the rear wall.

The two small pictures flanking the central portrait do not seem to have aroused any interest. They are hazy and merge into the background, giving the room merely a more comfortably furnished appearance; but Schwind was not painting a particular drawing-room, and none of the three pictures actually hung in Spaun's home. Since the painter's aim in placing a portrait of Karoline there is manifest, it might be worth trying to identify the other two pictures to see if he intended them to be more than mere furnishings, to contribute, perhaps, something towards that bygone atmosphere. I think they do. The one on the right is a landscape; it is identifiable as a picture of the mountains beyond Gmunden, on the shores of Lake Traun. Schwind and, later, Schubert and Vogl, all visited the district. But important as these associations are, the real point of the picture is that here is situated Traunkirchen, the little lakeside town to which Spaun retired in old age and where he died. On the left is the painting of a building; this is the Atzenbrugg Castle. It was for ever associated in Schwind's mind with that golden time of his youth when he, Schubert, Kupelwieser, and other congenial spirits had been

Schober's guests in the castle. There, in mid-July, they had passed the time in holiday mood, dancing, acting, and going for excursions into the nearby countryside. The period is enshrined in the paintings of Kupelwieser, in Schwind's own work, and in Schubert's dances, the 'Atzenbrugger Deutsche'. To the initiated those two paintings were anything but mere furnishings.

One or two figures in the gathering, kept discreetly in the left background by the window curtains, are anachronistic: they were contemporary friends of Schwind's, not even born at the time of the Schubertiade; but because of their love for the Schubert songs he paid them this compliment and included them in the assembled audience. On the other hand, one or two people who were fairly constant attenders at the Schubertiade are not to be found in Schwind's picture; names that occur to one are Fritz Derffel, Karl von Enderes, Fritz von Hartmann (the brother of Franz), the Fröhlich sisters, and a few others. One would certainly have expected to find in the throng Josef Huber, alluded to by the Schubertians as the 'tall Huber', for Schwind loved to draw and caricature him. There was certainly no personal grudge on the painter's part towards all these people that led to their exclusion.

By painting this picture Schwind eased the longing in his heart. Here he had evoked once again the beloved and never-to-be-forgotten friend, his music, the atmosphere of those long-past Schubert evenings in the Viennese homes of his youth. 'I am often homesick for Vienna; sometimes I hardly know how to bear it.' He wrote those words to Bauernfeld in 1845. After twenty years had passed, and on the eve of painting this sepia drawing of the scene at Spaun's house, he wrote to Spaun's niece Henriette: 'Our old friend [Josef von Spaun] was quite right when he said — "We were the happiest people in all Germany, yes, in all the world." And it was not only to the Schubert songs that we owed it, but also to the splendid, modest, warm-hearted people who were together then!' Vienna, her people; Schubert, the songs; the 'Schubert-Abend bei Josef von Spaun' is Schwind's re-creation of what they meant in his youth, and what they came to mean to him in maturity and old age. And having painted his picture he enables us to share, overpoweringly, in his emotions and in his vision.

FOUR SCHUBERTIANS

Kreissle von Hellborn, George Grove, Nicolaus Dumba, Eusebius Mandyczewski

F EW books on Schubert contain such a high proportion of unforgettably vivid comments on the character and work of the composer as Richard Capell's survey of the songs. His comments are often in the nature of asides uttered during his discourse on this or that well-known song; yet they impress themselves on the memory because suddenly, in these brief sentences, Schubert springs to life, suffering or exalting or striving as he must have done in reality. We are apt to lose sight of the humanity of the composer in contemplating his Olympic serenity as a creator, and to forget the Vienna of his everyday life in thinking of it as a phase in an artistic period. Capell himself never forgets these aspects, nor does he allow his readers to forget them.

For the Schubertian one of the most cherished of his comments concludes a discussion of 'An die Musik'. He says: 'Such a composition wins for its author a tenderness which is more than admiration from the coming and going generations.' The Schubertian can see, perhaps, a little deeper than others into the significance of the phrase 'the coming and going generations'.

At Schubert's death, not one of his friends, even the closest, not one of his most sincere admirers had any idea that they had witnessed the passing of a man who would eventually take his place among the dozen or so front-rank composers of the world. His greatest instrumental works and many of his supreme masterpieces of song were then still unpublished and completely unknown.

The fame won by his music had to be won almost alone by its spasmodic appearance during the long passage of the nineteenth century and by the accumulated impact of masterpiece after masterpiece upon a surprised and preoccupied world — preoccupied because the nineteenth century's interest in the music of the past was largely secondary to the absorbing business of Wagner and 'the music of the future'.

But the qualification 'almost alone' in the previous paragraph is, of course, necessary, since from the first Schubert was never without his ardent champions, and the 'tenderness which is more than admiration', in Capell's words, continued to produce dedicated men as the generations came and went.

In the course of this essay the labours and achievements of four of these devoted champions of Schubert will be briefly reviewed in the hope that they will thus become a little more vivid to the reader than mere names in bibliography or catalogue. Biographical backgrounds and character-sketches cannot, unfortunately, be given as fully as is desirable in two cases; the scholar, biographer, or patron is not honoured, as a rule, by official (or unofficial) biographies, and few details are available for Kreissle and Dumba. Comment is easy in the case of Mandyczewski, whose daughter, Virginia Cysarz, is still alive, and to whose kindness I owe a great deal of the necessary information. It is easier still in the case of Grove, who besides his musical activities was a noted public figure and a versatile worker in many fields; the excellent biography of Grove by Charles L. Graves is a mine of information although we are concerned here only with his work as a Schubertian.

The slow, but inevitable, realization of Schubert's greatness became evident very soon after his death. Even so, nearly forty years passed before the first full-length biography appeared. It was the work of Heinrich Kreissle von Hellborn, a Christian Jew, born in Vienna in 1812. Whether as a lad in his teens he ever saw Schubert is not recorded, but he came of a musical family, and it is impossible not to believe that his acquaintance with the music of Schubert, at least, came while the composer was still alive. Kreissle was a law student and took his degree as Doctor of Law at the University of Vienna. Among his fellow students was Adolf von Pratobevera, whose family was personally acquainted with Schubert. Adolf was the author of a one-act play *Der Falke* ('The Falcon'); the last scene contains a poem entitled 'Abschied von der

Erde' ('Departure from the Earth') for which Schubert composed a musical background. It is a unique form in Schubert, this so-called melodrama; the music was designed to give atmosphere while the poem was declaimed. Adolf's play was first given at a musical gathering to celebrate the birthday of his father, Karl von Pratobevera; the family home was at the Bürgerspital, very near the Kärntnerthor Theater. Whether Kreissle was present at this party we do not know, but his future wife was there. The youngest daughter of the family, Bertha von Pratobevera, became acquainted with Kreissle through her brother, and some time in the late 1830's she married him. As the years passed, Kreissle became an eminent figure in the social and civic worlds of Vienna. He was appointed Secretary to the Imperial Finance Office, and his musical interests and activities earned him a directorship of the Gesellschaft der Musikfreunde. His love of music and his growing admiration for the work of Schubert led his thoughts to the possibility of writing Schubert's biography; he began to collect material for the project, urged to do so, as he himself wrote later, by the desire to render the composer a long overdue honour. At that time he was unaware of the fact that several other men, attracted by the same desire, had also begun to assemble the necessary biographical material; each one, however, had lacked the stamina to finish the task, and had thrown it over. A glance might be given to these men and to what they had achieved.

There had been, of course, a crop of obituaries of a biographical nature following upon Schubert's death. His friends Mayrhofer, Bauernfeld, Sonnleithner, Spaun, and his brother Ferdinand had all contributed valuable work of this kind. Josef Witteczek and Franz Derffel had both collected useful material of a biblio-graphical kind, mainly copies of works, programmes, criticisms, and reviews; the famous autograph-collector, Alois Fuchs, had, in collaboration with Ferdinand Schubert, devised the first, though fragmentary, thematic catalogue. The earliest biographical essay, with a comparatively full catalogue of works, was written by Anton Schindler; it was published serially in the journal *Niederrheinische Musikzeitung* of Cologne in 1857. The cata-logue is valuable, but the biography is typically unreliable in a

Schindlerian way. By far the most extensive work had been done by Ferdinand Luib, for a brief period editor of the Vienna journal *Allgemeine Wiener Musikzeitung*; he had not only collected material available to any researcher of his day, but had written a number of letters to all the men and women whom he knew to be friends or relatives of Franz Schubert. The replies from these people were not always satisfactory and have not all been preserved, but many were of inestimable value, particularly those from Stadler, Schönstein, and Spaun. As late as 1862 it was still believed in musical circles in Vienna that Luib was completing, or had already completed, a comprehensive biography of Schubert, whereas in fact he had never so much as started it.

But Kreissle had firmer resolution, and his work of preparation was finally brought to a conclusion in 1860; at the end of the year a full and detailed sketch was published in Vienna called *Aus Schuberts Leben* (the book is dated 1861). Early in 1861 five extracts from it were published serially in the widely circulating Leipzig journal *Signale für die musikalische Welt* under the title 'Franz Schubert: eine biographische Skizze'.

The biography was very successful and produced, as a happy by-product of its success, an unlooked-for sequel. Kreissle became the fortunate recipient of much of the collected, but unpublished, material from other sources, including most of the Luib letters, together with many other memoirs of the composer, both verbal and written. In some cases these communications were made in order to correct errors of fact in his biography; in other cases they were unexpected additions to the store he was gathering.

For the next three years he worked over the enormous amount of material, and the outcome was his long and detailed biography, published as *Franz Schubert* by the Viennese firm Carl Gerold & Son at the end of 1864. In his preface, dated 7 November 1864, Kreissle briefly tells the story of his acquisition of the new material. Also, in paying generous tribute to the genius of his hero, he draws critical attention to one aspect of the then existent Schubert literature, and his comments are as relevant today as when he penned them exactly a hundred years ago. He deplores the fanciful, and often entirely mythical, embroideries round the

life and work of Schubert, which all tend, as he said, to give a
distorted picture of the composer.

Kreissle's biography may not be to the taste of the present-day
reader. It digresses from the main theme of Schubert's life to deal
fully with the personalities who crossed his path, with the places
he visited, with institutions and societies he encountered. It was
written while much of Schubert's work was unpublished or
otherwise unobtainable; many important letters and documents
were unknown, and their subsequent discovery has completely
changed the situation as seen by Kreissle. Nor, in spite of his love
and admiration for Schubert, was he aware, at that time, of the
composer's unassailable greatness, and his often defensive
attitude towards Schubert seems to us now rather ludicrous. But
the biography is by no means out-moded by subsequent and
better examples. It is a fruitful source of information for the seeker
after Schubert's background; it contains a very useful account of
the whereabouts of the then unpublished manuscripts; it gives a
profusion of details about performers and performances, both in
Schubert's lifetime and in the years that followed directly on his
death.[1]

Kreissle, in all innocence, offended one man by reason of a
statement in his first biographical sketch. This was Schober, who
became an implacable enemy. He had referred to the manuscript
of the opera *Alfonso und Estrella*, of which Schober had written
the text and Schubert had composed the music in the period
September 1821 to February 1822. Kreissle had been told by
Johann Herbeck, conductor of the Vienna Court Opera, that
Schober refused to return the manuscript to Ferdinand Schubert
in spite of repeated requests to do so; he reported this in his
preliminary sketch, and the passage was reprinted in the serializa-
tion by the *Signale*. Schober's indignation when he read the
passage is fully understandable — it is the reverse of the truth.
He was at the time spoken of (1848) secretary to Liszt and had
written to Ferdinand asking for the manuscript of his and
Schubert's opera, since the possibility of a performance under

[1] For information on the portrait of Schubert used as the frontispiece to
Kreissle's biography, see p. 143.

Liszt at Weimar had arisen. Ferdinand hedged; he had himself received the manuscript score back from Graz, where it had been kept by the Pachler family for fourteen years, and he was obviously reluctant to let it go from his keeping again. Since his right to Schubert's manuscript was a somewhat dubious one — he was never in any legal sense his brother's heir — and since, as librettist, Schober had a right to consider himself joint-owner of the manuscript, one can sympathize with Schober's subsequent action in writing a stinging letter to Ferdinand pointing out these facts. He demanded that the manuscript be sent to him and eventually received it. But the incident must have rankled, and when he read the garbled version in Kreissle's first book, his anger knew no bounds. Kreissle at once wrote a full apology, which was published in the *Signale* in January 1862; the offending passage was removed from the full-length biography of 1865 and a footnote inserted to rectify matters.

Another friend of Schubert's was likewise disturbed by many of the assertions in Kreissle's biography; this was Josef von Spaun. His feelings were not those of personal anger, rather of distress at what he considered misleading accounts of the composer's appearance, life, and methods of work and resentment over several definite errors of fact. On 29 December 1864 he finished writing an account of his reactions to the book in a long essay entitled 'Einige Bemerkungen über die Biographie Schuberts von Heinrich Ritter von Kreissle Hellborn' ('Some Observations on Schubert's Biography . . .'). These reminiscences were not published until 1934: Kreissle never saw them, and only a few people, prior to 1934, had access to the manuscript and so were able to make use of the valuable source-material contained in it.

Kreissle's book quickly inspired two others. The first biography of the composer to appear in France was by Hippolyte Barbadette and was published by the firm of Heugel & Co., Paris, in 1865; it leans heavily on Kreissle's and almost its sole interest for readers today lies in a very fine facsimile of 'An die Musik'. This was written by Schubert in the album of Albert Sowinski on 24 April 1827; Sowinski allowed Barbadette to reproduce this album-leaf, and the book was gratefully dedicated to him. The second biography was written by Edward Wilberforce and published by W. H. Allen, London, in 1866. It is actually a condensation of Kreissle's book, as the author states in his preface; he had been in touch with Kreissle, who had encouraged him to produce the work in England. Wilberforce's book appeared while another Englishman, Arthur Duke Coleridge, was engaged in a complete translation of Kreissle's work; but since Wilberforce had only summarized Kreissle, Coleridge fortunately continued with his task, and the English edition appeared in two volumes from the firm of Longmans, Green & Co., London, in 1869. The portrait used as a frontispiece, an engraving by H. Allard based on Kriehuber's famous lithograph of 1846, became the standard portrait of Schubert in England for the next fifty years. It is fortunate that Wilberforce's abortive book did not discourage Coleridge from continuing with his work, since his translated biography gained immense value by reason of a happy circumstance. This was the addition of an appendix by George Grove, embodying many of the firsthand discoveries he made during his visit to Vienna in October 1867 and including an annotated thematic catalogue of all the symphonies, the two unfinished ones in E minor/major and B minor as well as the seven completed ones. This was a magnificent contribution to Schubert scholarship, without parallel in Germany or Austria at that period. One might cynically add that Grove's *incipits* of seven of these nine symphonies were all that most musicians in England knew of them for the next sixty years.

It is doubtful, however, whether Kreissle ever saw the English edition of his biography with Grove's fine epilogue. He died in Vienna on 6 April 1869. The great service he rendered to Schubert and posterity by the unremitting work on the biography, with its full compilation of particulars about published music and unpublished manuscripts, is not easily assessed. No doubt, in course of time, someone else would have undertaken to write a full-length biography of Schubert, but the years were passing, and first-hand sources of information were gradually disappearing from the scene. When Kreissle started his work, all Schubert's brothers and many of his friends were dead, and his sister, though still living, seems to have provided little in the way of biographical material. Friends were difficult to trace, and were, in any case, ageing men whose memories were unreliable. Manuscripts, those that had survived, were uncatalogued and dispersed among many owners. These unpropitious factors would have become even less propitious had another ten or twenty years elapsed before a biographer settled to his task. Kreissle's biography was opportune, and the wonder is that it was so well done and so plentifully stocked with just those very facts that were vitally necessary.

Much still remained to be done, of course; happily a man was on the scene prepared and anxious to do it. The appendix to Coleridge's English edition of Kreissle's book was a significant pointer to the enthusiasm and ability of the one who took up Kreissle's pioneering work, and the magnificent contribution of George Grove to Schubert research is our next consideration.

George Grove was born in Clapham, London, on 13 August 1820 (just a few days, in fact, before the first public performance in Vienna of the overture to *Rosamunde!*). He was trained in youth as a civil engineer and became a remarkably successful one. His work, incidentally, took him abroad, and before he was thirty he had travelled widely in Europe and America. The impression one gets from reading his life, admirably written by Charles L. Graves, is that few men could have led a fuller life or been so well equipped by nature and training to do so. He was abundantly healthy, energetic, intelligent, witty, and blessed with that unmistakable air of capability, allied with friendly charm, which is irresistible. Everything to which he turned his hand was successful, no appointment that he strove to obtain was denied him. His interests were phenomenally wide. As well as his work in engineering, he was absorbed in theological matters, in the literary activities of his day, in geography, in politics, and in music. In all these spheres he produced work of solid value in committee activities, in propaganda, in organization, and in monographs and articles from his pen. It is hard to turn one's back on these interesting and fruitful studies of a life passed in such a fascinating period of English social history, but in fact the richness of one small sphere of his activities — Schubert — is almost overwhelming. Selection is necessary, though uncongenial.

His musical training was sketchy, consisting chiefly of domestic music-making such as piano-duet playing and part-singing. But his taste and judgement were impeccable. He became Secretary of the Crystal Palace Company in 1852, and two years later he took a hand in the organization of the musical functions there. From then onwards music dominated his interests, and his genius for organization led eventually to his appointment as the first Principal of the Royal College of Music. It was during the early years of his work in connection with the Crystal Palace concerts that his interest in Schubert was first actively aroused. The conductor of these concerts was August Manns; a few months after his appointment to the post he gave the first performance in England of Schubert's great C Major Symphony. The work was given in two parts: the first, second, and third movements on 5 April and the second, third, and fourth movements on 11 April 1856. No report of these concerts found its way into the musical press, and so little impact did they make that when, three years later, the first three movements were again given by the London Musical Society in St. James's Hall, the *Musical Times* reported the performance as the first in England. But the impact, in a subtler way, was far reaching. Years later August Manns related how he had persuaded the Secretary of the Crystal Palace concerts to attend the performance:

... and it was from that time that his enthusiasm for Franz Schubert's genius took root and gradually developed into that active participation in the researches concerning Schubert's composition which have borne such splendid fruit and benefited musical art in England and abroad to such a great extent ... (Letter to F. G. Edwards, 1 December 1896.)

Grove's knowledge of Schubert, prior to this time, had been confined to the songs, but henceforward his interest in the instrumental music grew deeper. The appearance of Kreissle's biography set the seal on his admiration. He was delighted with the catalogues and at once wrote to Schubert's publisher in Vienna, C. A. Spina, with whom as Secretary of the Crystal

Palace Company he had already had business dealings, inquiring about the *Rosamunde* music. Spina sent him the published copies of the two entr'actes, in B minor and B flat major, manuscript copies of the various sets of ballet music, and of the overtures to *Alfonso und Estrella*, *Fierrabras*, and the 'Italian' Overture in C major. 'They were all thrown into the shade', said Grove, 'by the unfinished Symphony in B minor ... which we received on 2 April and first performed at the concert of the following Saturday, 6 April 1867.' He continued: 'This most original and beautiful composition stimulated our desire to hear more of the same kind of music in the highest degree.' His inquiries from visiting musicians about the earlier symphonies were fruitless: no one had seen them or knew anything about them. Finally, Grove took the decision to go to Vienna and look for himself; accompanied by Arthur Sullivan — and there could have been no better companion — he arrived there on 5 October 1867.

There are two long and detailed accounts of his experiences in the short time he spent there, a week of crowded and very rewarding activities: they are in his appendix to Coleridge's book and in two long letters to Olga von Glehn, daughter of one of his oldest friends. He and Sullivan met Spina the publisher and, through him, Eduard Schneider, Schubert's nephew, the owner of a large store of Schubert manuscripts, including those in which Grove was most interested, the early symphonies, Nos. 1–4 and No. 6. (The autograph of No. 5, in B flat major, had been sent to Berlin.) Grove copied the *incipits* of each movement. Later in the week he added to his catalogue of the symphonies, by recourse to the archives of the Gesellschaft der Musikfreunde for Nos. 8 (the 'Unfinished') and No. 9 (the great C major symphony). There he met the archivist, C. F. Pohl, who became a lifelong friend, and in later years of great assistance when the *Dictionary* was in course of preparation. At the same time he also met Johann Herbeck and completed his catalogue of the symphonies from a manuscript copy of No. 5 in Herbeck's possession.

Before he left Schneider's rooms he had also seen many other of the bigger unpublished Schubert works there: operas, cantatas, masses, and so on. But, as he himself confessed, one of his objects had been to find the manuscripts of the *Rosamunde* music as well as the symphonies, and these had not been forthcoming. So far his account in the Coleridge appendix has been sober and restrained, but he now deals with a second visit to Schneider, and on this second occasion the lawyer allowed Grove to go into the large store-cupboard himself; Sullivan engaged Schneider in conversation, and Grove, free to explore, at length found in the farthest corner a two-foot-high pile of music, carefully corded and thick with dust. It was the missing *Rosamunde* music, tied up in the Theater an der Wien after the second and last performance on 21 December 1823 and evidently never disturbed since. The excitement of Grove's discovery breaks out in his hitherto sober writing and makes glorious reading.

Grove and Sullivan hurriedly returned with the music to their hotel, summoned Pohl, and, late as it was, all three men settled down and copied every note in the scores, finishing their work at two in the morning. Grove and Sullivan, in a burst of physical energy after their labours, high-spiritedly indulged in a bout of leap-frog round the hotel room.

The *Rosamunde* music that they had found did not, of course, contain any material that was completely unknown: the entr'actes and ballet music were already published; the 'Romanza' for alto voice and the part-songs were also published, but only with Schubert's arrangement for piano of his original orchestral accompaniments. By a happy chance Grove and Sullivan had found the copies of the missing instrumental parts for these accompaniments actually used in the theatre; Schubert's own manuscripts are lost. The old copies are now in the archives of the Gesellschaft der Musikfreunde. Grove's discovery, recounted by him in English, was not known in Germany or Austria for another twenty years or so; it is a lamentable fact that musicological discovery is so often confined, by reason of the language barrier, to its country of origin, unlike the music that it serves. Thus it is ironical to read that in 1877, nearly ten years after Grove's finding of these orchestral accompaniments of Schubert's own composing, the Leipzig firm of Rieter-Biedermann published orchestral arrangements by G. H. Witte of the pianoforte accompaniments to the *Rosamunde* music (*Allgemeine musikalische Zeitung*, 14 February 1877).

Grove's visits to the publisher Spina were also profitable. 'Spina the magnificent', he wrote to Olga von Glehn, 'has behaved like a prince.' Besides presenting Grove with some new publications of Schubert, he also put at his disposal a huge pile of unpublished manuscripts, which Grove and Sullivan thoroughly examined and assessed. Grove remained in Vienna two days after Sullivan left and took the opportunity to visit Brahms; he was shown more musical manuscripts, including some of Schubert's. He arrived back in England on 27 October, thoroughly satisfied with the results of his visit, his love for Schubert now combined with a love for Vienna that never left him.

In 1873 he was approached by Macmillan & Co. with a view to editing a dictionary of music; by the following year the work was under way. Grove was the ideal man for the task; his musical sympathies, his wide acquaintance with the world of musical practitioners and scholars, and, above all, the gifts of industry and enthusiasm that were part of his natural endowment eventually not only brought the *Dictionary of Music and Musicians* to a successful conclusion, but gave it a value and reliability that placed it — and has kept it — in the forefront of the world's musical dictionaries. He himself, and he makes this clear in his letters of the period, would have liked to have been personally responsible for many of the biographical entries; he abandoned the writing of the Schumann biography, for instance, only because of pressure of work. Eventually, he contributed three major biographies, those of Beethoven, Mendelssohn, and Schubert.[1] The last biography was started during 1880. He once again visited Vienna, arriving there on 23 September; he made copious notes, visiting all the houses, etc., associated with the composer, and, with the generous help of Pohl, examined afresh the manuscript-collections in the archives of the Gesellschaft der Musikfreunde. Among the surviving members of the Schubert family

---

[1] These three biographies, no longer part of the *Dictionary*, are published in one volume, *Beethoven, Schubert, Mendelssohn*, with an introduction by Eric Blom (Macmillan, London, 1951).

7. Sir George Grove (1890)

8. Eusebius Mandyczewski (1928)

he met Carola Geissler-Schubert, a grand-niece of Ferdinand's, from whom he obtained an important, unknown letter from Schubert to his brother.[1] Grove published it for the first time in his essay. Its interest lies in the fact that it establishes the *Deutsche Trauermesse*, D. 621, as a work of Schubert's; it had been composed for the use of Ferdinand, and he had performed and published it as his own.

Grove left Vienna on 30 October 1880, and for the next eighteen months he worked at his Schubert essay. From various people he begged for further help; Charles Stanford, who went to Vienna in September 1881, was given instructions to examine a variety of Schubert manuscripts; C. A. Barry, an old friend, who was on a visit that year to Munich, was asked to approach 'old Lachner' there for any reminiscences of Schubert. This latter source was unfortunate. Lachner's idea of musical biography was evidently that it should consist of a fund of good stories; he accordingly invented quite a number about Schubert, and some of them were good-naturedly provided for Barry. A well-known one deals with the niggardly payment of a publisher to Schubert: tenpence apiece for the *Winterreise* songs, said Lachner. Grove, in all innocence, included the story in his biographical essay, fulminating against such monstrous unfairness. Lachner, of course, knew nothing at all of what Schubert had received for these songs; the composer was probably paid about twenty florins for each song, and although it is impossible to convert this sum into present-day currency values, it would have been approximately equivalent to £2 in the England of Grove's day.

A letter of Grove's to W. Barclay Squire, written on 30 August 1881, contains a remark that will intrigue any who have written biographies! 'Schubert', he wrote, 'I have got down to 1825; this leaves '26, '27, '28 and all the wind-up still to do.' The biographical part of the essay was completed in March 1882, but the 'wind-up' gave him endless trouble. It consisted of a short review of the course of events in the years following Schubert's death, a discussion of the character of the composer, and a long appraisement of his music. This final section, comprising about a

[1] O. E. Deutsch, *Schubert: A Documentary Biography*, p. 94.

quarter of the whole, is an extremely well and warmly written tribute of a devoted admirer; Grove at his best. Whether by 'wind-up' he also meant his final pages — a full catalogue of Schubert's works — we cannot guess. But a word or two must be devoted to this catalogue. It was chronologically arranged, one section for each year of the composer's creative life. The works are numbered, and in each case particulars are given of the first edition, or, with unpublished works, the fact is indicated by 'MS'. It was for its day a superb compilation. A supplementary section contains those works for which no date of composition was known. Grove's enumeration reaches no. 1131 (works such as *Die schöne Müllerin*, containing twenty songs, are ranked as one item). It is practically certain that had Grove's list of works appeared in a German publication, or had a translation of his essay into German ever been published there, the excellent catalogue would have been used at once as a means of identification for Schubert's works, and the Grove numbers for Schubert would have been as familiar a part of our musical heritage today as are the Köchel numbers for the works of Mozart. As I have said elsewhere, it was intolerable that when further editions of the *Dictionary* were called for the editors deleted this wonderful piece of work in favour of a brief and largely uninformative summary of the *Gesamtausgabe* of Breitkopf & Härtel.

The *Dictionary* was published in parts, and the third volume, containing the essay on Schubert, appeared in the autumn of 1883. It was enthusiastically read and reviewed, and only the comments of one of the 'bloodhounds of Arthur's Seat' were adverse; they hurt Grove deeply. The criticism was not directed against his work, but sneered at the genius and culture of Schubert.

The essay on Schubert did as much towards the spread of Schubert's popularity in England as had Grove's personal achievements in the concerts of the Crystal Palace Company. It has the estimable quality of readability, and Schubert comes to life in it as in no other writings about him save one: the book on the songs by Richard Capell. If the Schubert who lives in their pages is a warmer, more golden figure than the Schubert of actual life, at least it is the Schubert we feel living in his music, in the

'Unfinished' Symphony, in the A minor String Quartet, in 'An die Musik' and 'Frühlingsglaube'.

The fifteen years that had passed between the appearance of Kreissle's biography of Schubert and Grove's preparations for his biographical essay had brought two decided advantages to Grove: the discovery of the 'Unfinished' Symphony and the publication of Nottebohm's *Thematic Catalogue*. The first of these facts contributed immeasurably to Grove's love for Schubert the composer; his words, written later in life to Mrs. Edmond Wodehouse, will be endorsed only by Schubertians, but by them fully endorsed:

... I listened to those two wonderful movements of Schubert's B minor Symphony. What *miles* they are above F.M.B. [Mendelssohn] ... in some particulars even above — ! [Beethoven] Please forgive me! you know my feelings for him — (B.), and yet, if one judges by the transport that is in it, one cannot doubt.   (Letter of April 1891.)

The second advantage, Nottebohm's *Catalogue*, was an essential aid to the bibliographical basis of his essay. If Nottebohm's book yields first place to Grove's catalogue, it is because the later compilation is arranged in chronological and numbered sequence.

Grove's last visit to Vienna was in August 1892; he went there to attend the famous musical exhibition arranged by the Schubert Society. He met an old friend, Eusebius Mandyczewski, then absorbed in the collection and editing of all the Schubert songs for Serie xx of the *Gesamtausgabe*. Grove's deep interest and enjoyment in poring over the manuscripts of these unknown songs can be imagined, and we have another example of his infallible judgement on the works of Schubert when he singled out for mention one of the songs he had never seen before. Mandyczewski had found it in an album, written there by Schubert for a friend: it is 'Herbst' ('Autumn'), a splendid song, composed in the last year of Schubert's life, and akin in spirit to the songs of *Winterreise*.

Grove was an indefatigable contributor to the 'Letters to the Editor' section of any magazine that dealt with one of his many interests; in the *Pall Mall Gazette* of 30 November 1883 he informed the musical public of the forthcoming complete edition of Schubert's works. His letter gives details not only of the publisher, Breitkopf & Härtel of Leipzig, but also of the part played by Nicolaus Dumba of Vienna in initiating the great publishing venture.

Nicolaus Dumba's name is an obscure one in the world of music; it should not remain so to any Schubert-lover, for without his ardent championship of the composer and his altogether rare generosity in providing financial backing for the publication of his compositions, there would have been no complete edition of Schubert's works at all. Even the word 'probably' refuses to write itself into that last statement. What incentive, for instance, would there have been to print the full scores of Schubert's operas, the hundreds of early songs, the obscure cantatas, the fragmentary pianoforte sonatas? These are never performed today, even though they are available in print; why should we assume that any publisher would have cared to print works for which there was no demand — merely curiosity on the part of a handful of scholars?

The man who made the *Gesamtausgabe* possible was, like Kreissle, of Jewish blood but Christian persuasion; Dumba's ancestors came from Greece and had settled in Vienna early in the nineteenth century. He was born there on 24 July 1830. A merchant by occupation, coming of a family of merchants, he was a wealthy man, and his interest in the arts, particularly in music, could be indulged as much as he pleased. He became well known as a collector, and since his chief love among composers was Schubert, he soon began to acquire a number of the composer's manuscripts, of both published and unpublished works. Transactions that have actually been recorded in various memoirs are these: from Herbeck he purchased the score of the 'Unfinished' Symphony and of *Lazarus*, and from Anna Fröhlich the manuscripts of the first version of Grillparzer's 'Ständchen', composed by Schubert for male chorus and solo voice, and of Psalm XXIII for female voices.

In 1872 the memorial statue to Schubert was installed in the city park; on 15 May Dumba was chosen to be the chief orator at the unveiling ceremony — sufficient evidence of his standing, in both the civic and musical life of the city. That same year saw the appearance in Vienna, from the newly established music-publisher J. P. Gotthard, of forty hitherto unpublished Schubert songs.[1] Three of the manuscripts had been provided by Dumba, 'Hoff-nung', D. 251, 'Die Perle', D. 466, and 'Der Knabe', D. 692, and to him the publisher dedicated these particular songs.

The continual publication during the 1870's by small publishers in Germany and Austria of haphazard items from the Schubert store prompted Dumba to raise the question of a complete edition; instead of this nibbling process, which barely reduced the mass of unpublished works, why not a concerted effort to categorize and issue, in a uniform edition, the whole of Schubert's works, those already published and those still unpublished? Eventually, Breitkopf & Härtel, secure in the knowledge that their work would be generously subsidized by Dumba, and assured that he would purchase the bulk of the unpublished works, agreed to consider the venture. Dumba approached Eduard Schneider, and as a first step he bought a great many of the Schubert manuscripts still in the lawyer's possession. He paid 1,500 florins for these manuscripts, but, as a businessman, would not pay for the publishing rights until he knew that the agreement with Breitkopf & Härtel would become legal. The manuscripts included all the operas and opera-fragments except *Alfonso und Estrella* and *Die Verschworenen*; the Mass in F major; the symphonies enumerated above, seen by Grove in 1867; many pieces of church and piano music, and something like seventy songs and other solo pieces for voice and pianoforte.

At this period, early 1883, the representative of Breitkopf & Härtel was Oskar von Hase. He hoped that Brahms would be chairman of the editorial board for the Schubert *Gesamtausgabe*, but Brahms was not only unwilling to accept the position, he even attempted to dissuade Hase from going ahead with the project. But his objections were overcome; Hase arrived in Vienna in the

[1] See p. 282.

spring of that year, and shortly after his arrival the individuals concerned with the organization of the complete edition gathered in Dumba's house for their first meeting. It had been hoped, at first, that Pohl would be secretary of the board, but eventually the position was offered to Eusebius Mandyczewski. As time passed the project took shape and was accepted by the Leipzig firm as an official undertaking. On 26 November 1883 Dumba purchased the publishing rights in his manuscripts from Schneider for 300 florins, and for a further sum of 4,500 florins he acquired almost all the Schubert manuscripts remaining in Schneider's possession.[1] All these were freely placed at the disposal of the *Gesamtausgabe* editors by Dumba. In a few months the final prospectus of the edition was published; it was further modified, but the work was afoot. By the end of the year (1884) the first volume, containing symphonies Nos. 1–4, was published; nearly seventy years had passed since their composition, and this was their first appearance in print.

During the closing years of the century Dumba was a familiar figure in the musical life of Vienna and an unfailing source of material for the various exhibitions and festivals that took place in the capital, particularly for the great exhibition in the anniversary year of Schubert's birth, 1897. Three years later, on 23 March 1900, Dumba died. Just before his death he had given his Schubert symphony scores to the library of the Gesellschaft der Musik-freunde, so that, with two exceptions, they now own the auto-graph scores of all the Schubert symphonies. The exceptions are No. 5, in B flat major, the score of which is in the National Library, at Berlin, and the sketch-symphony, No. 7, in E minor/major, bequeathed by Grove to the Royal College of Music and now housed in the British Museum. In his will Dumba wrote these words: 'The collection of manuscripts of Franz Schubert, that wonderful Viennese master, in my possession I

---

[1] Schneider still owned a number of interesting fragments, even after Dumba's double purchase; among them was an almost complete score of the overture to *Die Verschworenen*. This remained buried in the family archives and so was completely unknown. It was not discovered until a few years ago and the fact made known by Dr. Fritz Racek in 1963.

bequeath to my beloved Vienna.' They comprised approximately two hundred items, and Dumba, with one stroke, made the City Library of Vienna owners of the richest collection of Schubert autographs in the world — as is, of course, fitting.

Eusebius Mandyczewski, by reason of his position, was a frequent visitor to the Dumba residence; but the visits were not formalities: the two men were very close friends. To Mandyczewski, Dumba's house was a second home, and there he found not only the material for his work on the Schubert complete edition, but opportunities for relaxation of body and mind from his exhausting labours as teacher, conductor, and editor.

He was born in Czernowitz on 18 August 1857, the son of a priest in the Greek Orthodox Church. His father was a Ukrainian, to which fact Mandyczewski once referred in a letter to Brahms, calling himself, humorously, half a Slav. His mother was born in Romania. There were ten children of the marriage, Eusebius being the eldest son. He and his three brothers were educated in German primary and secondary schools and were all multilingual. Mandyczewski's extraordinary musical gifts were soon evident, and he began to compose at a very early age — chamber and choral music and settings of liturgical texts for use in the worship of the Orthodox Church.

He was conscripted and served in Bosnia during the Austrian military occupation of that country following the Berlin Treaty of 1878. After these duties were over, he went to Vienna as a student at the university, reading German Philology, History, Music (with Hanslick), and Composition (with Nottebohm). In his examinations for a musical scholarship he faced a professorial board including, among others, Brahms, seated next to Hanslick. But it is evident that Mandyczewski's outstanding gifts, allied to an extremely attractive sincerity — even nobility — of bearing and demeanour, made his path somewhat smoother than is usual in these affairs. Brahms was very taken with him and became a sincere and useful friend in after-years. Accounts vary as to how this friendship developed after student-days were over: in some we read that Nottebohm was the link between the two men, but it is more likely that Mandyczewski came into closer touch with Brahms in the home of a wealthy Viennese industrialist whose children were his piano pupils.

Mandyczewski abandoned the prospect of composition as the mainspring of his life; without the overriding impulse of genius, and yet with a conscientious attitude to the financial needs of his family and to the necessity of a stable position in life, he faced the decision without heartbreak. But his life settled into the exhausting routine of teaching, conducting, and administration. As teacher and conductor he became famous for his qualities of leadership and interpretation, but it is the work he took up in 1882 that has proved his most lasting monument and which has placed every musician for ever in his debt. His work in the preparation of the complete edition of Schubert's music, which will be considered later, was something new in the sphere of editorial supervision.

In 1887 he succeeded C. F. Pohl as archivist to the Gesellschaft, and at the same time undertook the duties of amanuensis to Brahms, continuing with this task until the composer's death in 1897. He became a conductor of the concerts of the Gesellschaft (frequently called the Musikverein, especially in its function as an organizer of public concerts and lectures), and in 1896 he was appointed a Professor of Music at the University of Vienna, where he taught History of Music and Composition. The last volume of the complete edition of Schubert's works had appeared in 1897; shortly afterwards, as an acknowledgement of Mandyczewski's supreme part in the production he received an honorary degree from Leipzig University. Somewhat late in life, in 1901, he married the great Lieder singer and teacher of singing Albine von Vest; there were three daughters of the marriage.

The years brought him fame, but did not lessen the ardours of his life. The continual drain on his energies entailed by his teaching and other musical activities left little time for writing. Yet his readiness to help and counsel his students — and, indeed, scholars already eminent in their particular musical spheres — was never failing.

We get glimpses, for instance, of his kindly and helpful

attitude in Graves's biography of Grove. When Grove visited Vienna in 1889, Mandyczewski clearly went out of his way to give all the assistance he could; as archivist at the Gesellschaft he provided Grove with all the information he required about rooms in the Musikverein building, the pupils, the arrangements for plays and concerts, and, naturally, about the store of manuscripts in the library there. Grove was writing his book on *Beethoven and his Nine Symphonies* and seeking material for it. Mandyczewski accompanied him to Schönbrun, to Hetzendorf, and to Vorder-brühl, places associated with Beethoven. They went to Mödling and later on to Krems and Gneixendorf. Grove's visit to Vienna in 1892, when Mandyczewski was deep in the preparation of the song-volumes for the Schubert complete edition, has been mentioned above.

It is, of course, Mandyczewski's care and concern for these song-volumes that is his chief memorial. When he started work on the collection and correlation of all Schubert's song-manu-scripts, he undertook a task of whose vastness no one, not even he himself, was aware. In 1887 or thereabouts, when he first began to collect the necessary information, some 480 songs of Schubert had been published; some of these were variants and a few were fragmentary.[1] There remained some two hundred still un-published. Mandyczewski was astonished to discover that the number of manuscripts for the songs was far in excess of the grand total obtained by listing all the poems set by Schubert. He found three, four, even five, differing manuscripts for the same song. In many cases these variants were obtained from copies made in Schubert's day by friends who admired the particular songs, and for which Schubert's own autographs are lost. The various collections of autographs and manuscript copies in the 1880's are too numerous for detailed description; the chief ones were the considerable number in the possession of Nicolaus Dumba, copies made by Albert Stadler, Josef Witteczek, and Josef von Spaun in the Gesellschaft library, unpublished auto-graphs still with the firm of Spina, and small collections in national libraries in Berlin, Paris, and Vienna.

[1] For details of the publication of the songs, see pp. 287–9.

As Mandyczewski began to realize the enormous extent of this section of the Schubert edition, he came to two conclusions: the whole field must be covered and all variants must be published; the complete series of songs must be arranged in chronological order from 'Hagars Klage', composed in March 1811, to 'Die Taubenpost', composed in October 1828.[1] His decision was by no means unanimously welcomed; Brahms, in particular, was not in favour of this scheme of publication. But when at length the song-volumes were complete, the tenth and last appearing in 1895, criticism was silenced. Indeed, the overwhelming impression made by the gradual evolution of the Schubert Lied, obvious as one turned the pages of volume after volume, earned for Mandyczewski praise from all musicians. Brahms was completely won over. He had undertaken the editing of the Schubert symphonies; when he looked over the ten volumes of Mandyczewski's edition of the songs and realized the care that had been lavished on them, he not only regretted the superficial manner in which he had discharged his own task, but even more deeply regretted his declaration that there was no sense in publishing the early examples of Schubert's Lieder — 'unprofitable rubbish' he had called them. In Mandyczewski's preface to the song-volumes and in his editorial report (the *Revisionsbericht*) on each individual song, there is revealed his scrupulous attention to the textual truth of the music itself, to the earlier publications, and to the poetry of the songs (in which field, incidentally, he was a specialist).

In addition to the songs he was also entirely responsible for the masses and smaller church works, the male-voice part-songs, the octets, string quintets, and string trios; he co-operated with other editors in the string quartets, the pianoforte duets, and the works for female and mixed chorus. In every department with which he was associated the editorial work is obviously carefully done; in those sections where he had no hand at all, the chamber works with pianoforte, the overtures, the pianoforte sonatas and —

[1] Grove always urged the chronological sequence for collections of the Schubert songs, and doubtless he had made his views known to Mandyczewski during their association together.

especially — the stage music, the work is definitely inferior and leaves much to be desired.

Apart from his work on the prefaces to the complete edition of Schubert, he wrote little else: a few introductory remarks to other men's writings on the composer, or to important Schubert concerts and exhibitions, or to commemorate the centenary of Schubert's birth.[1] But he wrote a valuable article for the *Chronik des Wiener Goethe-Verein* on Goethe's poetry in the songs of Schubert (10 March 1897) and two further articles of interest may be given in more detail. The first appeared in January 1907 in the Berlin journal *Die Musik*; a song had seen the light since the publication of the *Gesamtausgabe* and Mandyczewski published it there. It was the first version of the song 'Jägers Abendlied', D. 215, which Schubert had set on 20 June 1815. (At the same time Mandyczewski also published a work of secondary interest, the part-song 'Ruhe', D. 635, under the impression that it was unpublished; it had, in fact, been printed a few years previously.) The second article appeared in the annual report of the Schubert Society for 1923; it reproduced in facsimile and described a manuscript that has become known as the 'Three Masters Autograph'. This consists of Beethoven's song 'Ich liebe dich', on the back of which Schubert has sketched, in D minor, the slow movement of his Sonata in E flat major, op. 122; Brahms, once the owner of the autograph, has added his signature.

Mandyczewski continued to act as adviser and frequently as organizer of musical festivals and exhibitions in Vienna, his work being particularly valuable at the Schubert Exhibition of 1922. For the celebrations of 1928, the centenary of Schubert's death, he organized the great Schubert Congress held in Vienna from 25–29 November and attended by scholars from all over the world. He acted as chairman of the committee and, although by then an elderly man, did all in his power to make the congress a success and a worthy tribute to the greatest of Vienna's sons. In fact he worked beyond his strength and paid the penalty by a physical breakdown. A few months later, on 13 July 1929, he died. When

[1] For many years at the beginning of the century he was the Vienna correspondent of the *Musical Times*.

the report of the congress was published,[1] the editors had to face the sad fact that it must be dedicated not to Eusebius Mandyczewski himself, but to his memory.

In considering the tributes of friends to this great man and in trying to see him in the environment of his country and of his times one thing is immediately obvious. He was a representative of the best that the ancient Austrian empire with its picturesque background of nationalities could produce: a truly civilized human being. Vienna, the centre of a vast conglomeration of countries and nations, was for him a focus of attraction and unification. Nationalism was incomprehensible to him; he would not have considered himself a Ukrainian, Romanian, or German, nor could he understand the stressing of those dividing elements when there was so much common heritage. He was Austrian, without any ambiguity. Coming as he did from a remote eastern corner of the empire, he was free from national or cultural prejudice, and perhaps in an ideal position to feel the most essential quality of Schubert's music: its rich humanity.

It is giving an entirely false impression if, when Mandyczewski is called a supreme musicologist, a picture is conveyed of some remote, pedagogic brooder over manuscripts and editions shut up in an ivory tower of his own scholastic isolation. His scholarship and his application of it to printed music sprang from an absorption in the performance of music, in singing, playing, conducting, and composing, and in the teaching of all these branches of the art in actual sound. His whole outlook was practical and disinclined to speculation. The facts of music mattered to him, and everything pertaining to abstract theory, such as the speculations of Riemann or Schenker, went, for him, totally against the grain. Music was a living reality, and the knowledge of its history merely a way to the music itself. 'If you had asked him about Schubert, he would have smiled and said: "Schubert? Play his music, sing his songs, and you will know more about him than I can tell you!" ' That remark was recorded by Hans Gal, a pupil of Mandyczewski, who wrote to me the following words about his master:

[1] *Bericht über der internationalen Kongress für Schubertforschung*, Augsburg 1929.

He was for me more than my father: a teacher, a friend, and a model of the very best to be found among human beings; the only man I ever met who was totally free of the human frailties of ambition, selfishness, greed, or malevolence. I fancy that you should be able to see this in the noble, quiet beauty of his face, a face that perfectly harmonized with his character. His lack of ambition is the reason that he left no literary monument: his encyclopaedic knowledge went to the benefit of anyone who wanted information, suggestion, guidance. He never took the trouble of writing down what he knew. His very instinct led him to making music, rather than to thinking about it, but, being a thinker by nature, he knew more than anyone — and of the right kind — of the essence of music.

III

Manuscripts and Editions

TOWARDS AN EDITION OF THE
PIANOFORTE SONATAS

ONLY three of Schubert's twenty-three sonatas were published in his lifetime: Sonata in A minor, op. 42; Sonata in D major, op. 53; and Sonata in G major, op. 78. The next two to be published, the Sonata in A major, op. 120, and the Sonata in E flat major, op. 122, appeared shortly after his death. Neither Czerny nor Pennauer, their respective publishers, received them from Schubert himself. Vogl, it is almost certain, arranged with Czerny for the publication of the first (and also of the 'Trout' Pianoforte Quintet, op. 114); Ferdinand Schubert sold the second to Pennauer. The last three sonatas that Schubert composed, in C minor, A major, and B flat major, completing them two months before he died, were published by Diabelli in 1838 as a post-humous opus. At intervals during the next fourteen years other sonatas appeared and were allotted opus numbers: Sonata in A minor, op. 143; Sonata in B major, op. 147; and Sonata in A minor, op. 164. Two other sonatas, neither of which received from Schubert the finishing touches required for publication, were published in the middle years of the nineteenth century. The first is the Sonata in E major, which was published by C. A. Klemm, Leipzig, in 1843. Schubert composed it in August 1816 and made two attempts at the Scherzo. But his manuscript gave no indication as to which of the two he intended to retain. The publisher dropped the designation 'Sonata', included *both* Scherzo movements, and called the publication 'Fünf Klavier-stücke' ('Five Piano Pieces'). The second is the Sonata in C major of April 1825; it is unfinished, only the first two movements being completed. Yet the publisher, K. F. Whistling, Leipzig, engraved the work as it stood, the partially finished Menuetto and Finale appearing together with the first two movements. It appeared

o

under the title 'Reliquie' in 1861, and was the thirteenth and last sonata to be published as a commercial proposition by an individual publisher.

Ten sonatas, therefore, remained in manuscript when the *Gesamtausgabe* of Schubert's works was planned by Breitkopf & Härtel. The ten works, in varying degrees, are incomplete, either left unfinished by Schubert, or possibly broken up and the movements scattered during their passage through the nineteenth century. In one or two cases pages have been lost from a complete movement, and it seems likely that in others a whole movement has disappeared from its parent work. Serie x of the *Gesamtausgabe*, the one devoted to the sonatas, appeared in 1888. Besides, of course, republishing the already published sonatas, it gave for the first time four of the ten unpublished sonatas: Sonata in E major (1815); Sonata in C major (1815); Sonata in A flat major (1817); and Sonata in E minor (1817). But it omitted the 'Reliquie' Sonata, and since the editors were, in 1888, unaware that the 'Fünf Klavierstücke' was actually a sonata, that also was omitted.[1] It might be mentioned in this connection that the four works given above were probably the only ones from the ten unpublished sonatas that were known to the editors. In the same way they knew of only one movement, the first, from the Sonata in E minor of 1817: it was given, therefore, as a one-movement sonata in the tenth volume.

As the years passed the six remaining sonata-fragments saw the light (perhaps brought forward by their respective owners under the stimulus of the publication of Serie x of the *Gesamtausgabe*); in the *Supplement* to the edition, Serie xxi, published in 1897, five more sonatas appeared: Sonata in D flat major (1817); Sonata in F sharp minor (1817); Sonata in C major (1818); Sonata in F minor (1818); Sonata in C sharp minor (1819). The Sonata in D flat major was, of course, Schubert's first conception of the Sonata in E flat major, which had been published in 1829 as op. 122. The *Supplement* also included the 'Reliquie' Sonata in C major. The 'Fünf Klavierstücke' had been published in Serie xi

[1] The editors of the solo piano works were Julius Epstein and Eusebius Mandyczewski.

of the *Gesamtausgabe*, the volume devoted to the fantasias and other smaller pianoforte works.

It will be seen that in Serien x, xi, and xii of the *Gesamtausgabe* all of Schubert's sonatas, except one fragmentary work, seem to be available, fifteen in the first, one in the second, and six in the third. This is hardly the case. Quite apart from the fact that the twenty-two works are thus scattered through three large volumes of pianoforte music, it has become obvious during the past sixty years of investigation and discovery that many missing movements from the sonatas are masquerading as isolated pianoforte pieces. These orphaned movements should be rescued and restored to their parent sonatas. In addition to movements whose primary source is definitely known by now, there are other movements where a balance of probabilities suggests that they belong to a particular sonata, although documentary evidence of a definite kind is lacking. Scholars have suggested that this or that individual piece of Schubert's music for pianoforte solo was removed, either deliberately or accidentally, from a sonata. If the general consensus of opinion is in favour of relegating the movement to its original position in a sonata, it seems desirable that it should be so relegated.

My purpose, therefore, in this essay is to gather up all the available material and to present, item by item, these twenty-three works in a chronological sequence with the fruits of modern research given in connection with each one. In most cases no doubt whatever attaches to the particular sonata. It comes to us as it left Schubert's pen, and either the contemporary edition is there as evidence, or the extant manuscript, or both. In the other cases I have given the sonata as Schubert probably wrote it, quoting all the points of evidence in support of the scheme, and in no case, I trust, being dogmatic about the result. My reason for placing the two sonatas in E minor as nos. 8 and 9 in the sequence, is an attempt to give some significance to Schubert's own numbering of his sonatas in June 1817. He called the Sonata in D flat 'No. 2' (my no. 7) and the Sonata in F sharp minor 'No. 5' (my no. 10); since there must have been, in that case, two other sonatas between, I have assumed that they are the two in E minor of that same month.

The final sequence might form the basis of a future edition of his sonatas, giving the student, performer, or researcher the whole chronological process of Schubert's creative work in pianoforte sonata form. The justification for such a proposal, if it needs one, is simple: it lies in the excellence of the works themselves, an excellence that becomes every year more apparent, and to which more and more pianists, critics, and people who can only claim to be listeners pay enthusiastic tribute.

Such general and introductory remarks can now give place to a detailed consideration of each of Schubert's pianoforte sonatas in turn.

Sonata No. 1, in E major, D. 154, 157

    I. Allegro ma non troppo
    II. Andante (E minor)
    III. Menuetto: Allegro vivace (B major) and Trio (G major)
Composed Vienna, February 1815.

The first movement is dated 18 February 1815 at the start and 21 February at the conclusion. No Finale was composed. There is a sketch for the first movement entitled 'Sonata' and dated 11 February 1815; it is an Allegro in E major, published in the *Gesamtausgabe*.

Sources:
Manuscripts:
    City Library, Vienna.
First editions:
    (1) Sketch: *Gesamtausgabe*, xxi, no. 8 (1897).
    (2) Sonata in E major: *Gesamtausgabe*, x, no. 1 (1888).

Sonata No. 2, in C major, D. 279

    I. Allegro moderato
    II. Andante (F major)
    III. Menuetto: Allegro vivace (A minor) and Trio (A major)
Composed Vienna, September 1815.

There is another version of the Menuetto, with a different Trio in F major.

It is not known whether Schubert composed a finale for the

sonata. The manuscripts containing the three movements were very early bound with a white paper strip, which suggests that if a finale ever existed it was on a separate paper and never part of the sheaf containing the rest. Schubert has headed the work 'Sonata I'.

Walter Rehberg used the undated Allegretto in C major, D. 346, as a finale, when he completed and published this sonata (Steingräber-Verlag, Leipzig, 1928). The paper on which this Allegretto is written is similar to that containing the Andante of the sonata (same watermark, dimensions, etc.) and the hand-writing of each suggests the same pen and ink.

Sources:

Manuscripts:

   (1) City Library, Vienna.

   (2) Second version of the Menuetto and Trio: Marie Schubert, Vienna.

First editions:

   (1) *Gesamtausgabe*, x, no. 2 (1888).

   (2) Second Trio: *Die Moderne Welt*, ed. O. E. Deutsch (Vienna, December 1925).

Sonata No. 3, in E major, D. 459

    i. Allegro moderato
   ii. Scherzo: Allegro (E major) — there is no trio
  iii. Adagio (C major)
   iv. Scherzo: Allegro (A major) and
       Trio: *più tardo* (D major)
    v. Allegro patetico (E major)

Composed Vienna, August 1816.

The sonata was recorded in Aloys Fuchs's unpublished thematic catalogue of 1843, with the date of composition as given above. The manuscript, consisting of the first movement and part of the second, was said by Fuchs to be in the possession of Ferdinand Schubert. Kreissle also knew of this incomplete manuscript and mentioned it in his biography (p. 97: footnote). It cannot therefore have been the source of the first edition, which was published as 'Fünf Klavierstücke' ('Five Piano Pieces'). The fragmentary manuscript was lost soon after Ferdinand's death, and the fact that the five pieces actually comprised a sonata was not realized by the editors of the *Gesamtausgabe* in 1888. The re-establishment of the work as a sonata came in 1930 with the recovery of the manuscript with its definitive title.

Schubert, it is fairly obvious, would have excluded one or the other of the two scherzos had he himself prepared the manuscript for publication.

Sources:

Manuscripts:

    (1) First movement and part of the second: sold New York, 1947.

    (2) Fragment, the last eight bars of the Finale: City Library, Vienna. These bars are written on the back of the leaf containing Minuet No. 21, in F major, D. 41.

First editions:

    (1) 'Fünf Klavierstücke': C. A. Klemm (Leipzig, August 1843).

    (2) Finale fragment: *Revisionsbericht*, xxi, p. 4 (1897).

Sonata No. 4, in A minor, op. 164 (D. 537)
    i. Allegro ma non troppo
    ii. Allegretto quasi andantino (E major)
    iii. Allegro vivace (A minor)

Composed Vienna, March 1817.

As far as is known no scherzo or minuet was composed for this sonata.

Sources:

Manuscript:

    Conservatoire, Paris.

First edition:

    C. A. Spina (Vienna, 1852).

Sonata No. 5, in A flat major, D. 557
    i. Allegro moderato
    ii. Andante (E flat major)
    iii. Allegro (E flat major)

Composed Vienna, May 1817.

The unorthodox key of the Finale would suggest that it does

not belong to the work, but both manuscript sources confirm that it does.

Sources:

Manuscripts:

(1) Incomplete autograph fair copy, dated as above. It reaches to bar 25 of the Finale. Metropolitan Opera Guild, New York.

(2) A contemporary copy in another hand, somewhat faulty, of the whole work, undated but entitled 'Sonata'. This manuscript was originally part of the Witteczek collection. Gesellschaft der Musikfreunde, Vienna.

First edition:

Gesamtausgabe, x, no. 3 (1888).

Sonata No. 6, in D flat major, D. 567

I. Allegro moderato

II. Andante molto (C sharp minor)

III. Allegretto (D flat major)

Composed Vienna, June 1817.

This is the first conception of the following sonata, no. 7. As far as is known, no minuet or scherzo was composed in this version (but see the note to the next item). The third movement, as published, seems to lack the last seventeen bars: this is because the manuscript (3) has lost its last leaf, not because Schubert left the movement unfinished. This manuscript came to light after the printing of the sonatas in Serie x of the *Gesamtausgabe*. It was owned by Nicolaus Dumba at the time of its publication in Serie xxi. Schubert has headed both the manuscripts below 'Sonate II'.

Sources:

Manuscripts:

(1) First movement (incomplete): formerly with the Krasser family, now in the City Library, Vienna.

(2) First movement (the remainder): fifty-six bars written on the back of the song-manuscript 'An den Mond', D. 468: City Library, Vienna.

(3) All three movements, the last seventeen bars of the Finale lacking: City Library, Vienna.

First edition:
>   *Gesamtausgabe,* xxi, no. 9 (1897).

>   Sonata No. 7, in E flat major, op. 122 (D. 568)
>   I. Allegro moderato
>   II. Andante molto (G minor)
>   III. Menuetto: Allegretto (E flat major) and
>   Trio (A flat major)
>   IV. Allegro moderato (E flat major)

Composed Vienna, June–November 1817.

The sonata is not a simple transposition of the previous one, but follows it fairly closely.

The slow movement was first sketched in D minor, which indicates that D flat major was not Schubert's first choice of key for the sonata.

J. P. Gotthard, Vienna, published '2 Scherzi' by Schubert in August 1871. They are in B flat and D flat, D. 593. The publisher gave in the first edition the date of composition, November 1817. Both scherzos seem to be rejected movements from the sonata considered here, in both its keys — the D flat Scherzo from the first version, the B flat Scherzo from the second. This supposition is borne out by the fact that the Trio section of the D flat Scherzo (in A flat major) was retained by Schubert and used as the Trio for the third movement of the Sonata in E flat major.

Sources:

Manuscripts:

>   (1) Slow movement, D minor, Andante altered to Andantino, written on the back of Beethoven's manuscript of his song 'Ich liebe dich': Gesellschaft der Musikfreunde, Vienna (formerly in the possession of Brahms).

>   (2) Full sonata: lost.

First edition:
>   A. Pennauer, as 'Troisième grande Sonate', op. 122 (Vienna, 1829). (It was actually the fourth of Schubert's sonatas to be published.)

Sonata No. 8, in E minor (fragment), D. 994
1. Allegro

Composed Vienna, (?) June 1817.

The manuscript consists of thirty-eight bars of the first movement. It is entitled 'Sonata', but is undated. The material and style belong to the 1817 group of sonatas.

Sources:

Manuscript:

City Library, Vienna. The manuscript was reproduced in facsimile in the *Festschrift zum Hundertjährigen Bestehen der Wiener Stadtbibliothek*, p. 104, in the article by Fritz Racek, 'Von den Schubert-Handschriften der Stadtbibliothek' (1956).

First edition:

Schubert, Maurice J. E. Brown (Macmillan, London, 1958), pp. 58–59.

Sonata No. 9, in E minor, D. 566, 506
1. Moderato
11. Allegretto (E major)
111. Scherzo: Allegro vivace (A flat major) and
Trio: (D flat major)
1v. Rondo: Allegretto moto (E major)

Composed Vienna, June 1817.

A second autograph of the first movement, representing Schubert's attempt to begin a revision of the whole sonata, is extant; it was the only part of the sonata to be known to the editors of the *Gesamtausgabe*. The autograph of the first three movements had been purchased in June 1842 from Ferdinand Schubert by the Leipzig publisher K. F. Whistling, but never used. It was not discovered until 1903 and was then purchased by Erich Prieger of Bonn. The second and third movements were published at intervals (see below). The evidence for the Rondo as the Finale of the sonata is not quite conclusive, but very nearly so. There was a copy of the movement in another hand in the Witteczek collection, now in the Gesellschaft der Musikfreunde, headed 'Sonata: Rondo'. A sketch of Schubert's for bars 57–88 of the Rondo is written on the back of the song 'Lebenslied' (dated December 1816); but there is definite evidence that during 1817 Schubert was using up the blank pages of earlier manuscripts (see Sonatas nos. 3 and 10). Hence the date of the song is no guide to the date of the Rondo. The Rondo was separated from its fellow movements to form part of the pastiche 'Adagio and Rondo', op. 145. The possibility that the Rondo was the finale of the Sonata in E minor was first pointed out by Ludwig Scheibler in 1905.

Sources:

Manuscripts:

(1) First three movements: Hella Prieger, Bonn.

(2) First movement: National Library, Marburg, Germany.

(3) Rondo sketch: Roger Barrett, Chicago, U.S.A.

(4) Rondo (copy in another hand): Gesellschaft der Musik-freunde, Vienna.

First editions:

(1) Moderato: *Gesamtausgabe*, x, no. 4 (1888).

(2) Allegretto: Breitkopf & Härtel, ed. Erich Prieger (Leipzig, May 1907).

(3) Scherzo and Trio: *Die Musik*, ed. Adolf Bauer (Berlin, October 1928).

(4) Rondo: part of op. 145, Diabelli (Vienna, May 1848).

Sonata No. 10, in F sharp minor, D. 570, 571
 I. Allegro moderato
 II. Scherzo: Allegro vivace (D major) and
     Trio (B flat major)
 III. Allegro (F sharp minor)

Composed Vienna, July 1817.

The first movement is not completed, being composed as far as the start of the recapitulation. Schubert has headed the work 'Sonate V'. The final Allegro, similarly, is written out to the same formal point and left unfinished.

The evidence is not conclusive that the Scherzo and final Allegro do belong to the first movement, although all Schubert scholars agree that this is the case. The two movements are written on a folio of music-paper, which is separate from the first movement. But all three pieces were composed on blank sides of paper from the manuscripts of 1815: (*a*) the first movement on the back of the alto part of the 'Gloria' from the Mass in B flat (November 1815), (*b*) the other two movements on the blank pages left at the end of the unfinished song 'Lorma' (November 1815). The keys show a unity.

It is possible that the missing slow movement is the Andante in A major, D. 604. This is written on a blank page at the back of a sketch for the Overture in B flat, D. 470, of September 1816.

Sources:

Manuscripts:

    All three movements: City Library, Vienna.

First editions:

    (1) First movement: *Gesamtausgabe*, xxi, no. 10 (1897).

    (2) Scherzo and Allegro: *Gesamtausgabe*, xxi, no. 20 (1897).

Sonata No. 11, in B major, op. 147 (D. 575)

      I. Allegro ma non troppo

     II. Andante (E major)

   III. Scherzo: Allegretto (G major) and
         Trio (D major)

    IV. Allegro giusto (B major)

Composed Vienna, August 1817.

Schubert's fair copy is lost, but his preliminary sketches for all four movements are extant. The Scherzo precedes the Andante in these sketches. It is clear from the sketched slow movement that bar 29 was omitted from the first edition and it was restored by the editors of the *Gesamtausgabe* in Serie x.

The first edition was dedicated by the publisher to Sigmund Thalberg.

A copy of the sonata was made by Albert Stadler, inscribed 'Steyr, August 1818', for the young pianist Josefine von Koller.

Sources:

Manuscripts:

    (1) Sketches for all four movements: Gesellschaft der Musikfreunde, Vienna.

(2) Fair copy: lost.
(3) Stadler's copy: Otto Taussig, Malmö.
First edition:
    Diabelli, as op. 147 (Vienna, May 1846).

Sonata No. 12, in C major, D. 612, 613
I. Moderato
(?) II. Adagio (E major)
III. Finale (C major)

Composed Vienna, April 1818.

There is no conclusive evidence that the Adagio belongs to this work, except that all three movements were composed in the same month and it seems highly probable that they form a unit. Since the Adagio is the only one of the three to be completed by Schubert, that may be the reason for its separation from its fellows; it was published in 1870, while they were left in manuscript. The Finale carries no expression or tempo marks.

Sources:

Manuscripts:
    (1) First movement and Finale: City Library, Vienna.
    (2) Adagio: Conservatoire, Paris.
First editions:
    (1) First movement and Finale: *Gesamtausgabe*, xxi, no. 11
    (1897).
    (2) Adagio: Rieter-Biedermann (Winterthur, October 1870).

Sonata No. 13, in F minor, D. 505, 625
I. Allegro
II. Adagio (D flat major)
III. Scherzo: Allegretto (E major) and
Trio (A major)
IV. Allegro (F minor)

Composed Zseliz, September 1818.

The sonata, as published in the *Gesamtausgabe*, has no slow movement. The addition of the D flat Adagio as the slow movement is justified by the evidence of a very old manuscript catalogue prepared for Diabelli (possibly by Ferdinand Schubert).

It was once either in the possession of Kreissle, or consulted by him. At some time in the 1930's this catalogue, whose present whereabouts is unknown, was examined by O. E. Deutsch. It contains the *incipits* of works by Schubert for pianoforte solo, and for pianoforte and violin. For this particular sonata four *incipits* are given, including that of the D flat Adagio for the second movement.[1] Diabelli shortened the Adagio and transposed it into E major to serve as the introduction for the 'Rondo' in the same key (see the notes on Sonata no. 6 above).

Schubert's original manuscript of the Adagio is lost, but a contemporary copy in another hand was preserved in the Spaun–Witteczek collection. It is remarkable that in this copy one bar was accidentally omitted, but that the missing bar was preserved in Diabelli's corrupt and transposed version.

Both the first and final movements are not quite complete.

Sources:

Manuscripts:

(1) First movement, Scherzo and Trio, Finale.

(2) Adagio in D flat major.

All four manuscripts, in another hand, originally in the Spaun–Witteczek collection: Gesellschaft der Musikfreunde, Vienna.

First editions:

(1) First movement, Scherzo and Trio, Finale: *Gesamtausgabe*, xxi, no. 12 (1897).

(2) Adagio:

    (*a*) Shortened and transposed into E major: op. 145, Diabelli (Vienna, May 1848).

    (*b*) Clean: *Revisionsbericht*, xi, pp. 4–8 (1888).

Sonata No. 14, in C sharp minor, D. 655
1. Allegro

Composed Vienna, April 1819.

The movement is incomplete, extending only to the close of the exposition (seventy-three bars), with double bar-lines and repeat signs.

[1] See *Schubert: A Critical Biography*, p. 68.

Sources:
Manuscript:
>City Library, Vienna.

First edition:
>*Gesamtausgabe*, xxi, no. 13 (1897).

Sonata No. 15, in A major, op. 120 (D. 664)

i. Allegro moderato

ii. Andante (D major)

iii. Allegro (A major)

Composed Steyr, July 1819 (?).

No minuet or scherzo was composed for the work.

This sonata of Schubert's was not decisively documented during the early nineteenth century; Nottebohm's *Thematic Catalogue* of 1874 first provided a composition-date — 'probably 1825'. The date was accepted and attached itself to the work until Ludwig Scheibler in 1906 challenged the assumption. He suggested that the work was composed in 1819. His suggestion was based on a letter written to Ferdinand Luib in January 1858 by Albert Stadler; the relevant passage concerns Schubert's visit to Steyr, in 1819, where, wrote Stadler, he composed a sonata for a young pianist, Josefine von Koller. The only sonata that could possibly have been composed then is the one in A major. Scheibler, with reason, maintained that the style of the work is consonant with the idea that it was written for a pianist of brilliant attainments: though his further conclusion, that the pianist was a young lady, is perhaps too sentimental for us to follow him.

The reason for the wrong date, 1825, can be found in early catalogues of Schubert's works. In an obituary notice of June 1829 Bauernfeld gave, under 1825, three pianoforte sonatas, not specifying the keys. Schlinder, in 1857, published a catalogue of Schubert's works, which he based on material supplied by Ferdinand as well as on his own notes. He completed Bauernfeld's information with the keys A major, C major, and D major, adding that the last was composed at Gastein. A major might, of course, be either Ferdinand's or Schindler's slip for A minor, which would refer, correctly, to the Sonata in A minor, op. 42, composed in

1825. But that does not alter the fact that the sonata stood in Schindler's catalogue as in A major, and it became identified with op. 120. This accounts for Nottebohm's entry mentioned above. It is of interest to note that August Reissmann, in the chronological list of Schubert's works, which he devised for his biography of the composer in 1873, does not commit himself to this date.

The style of the sonata commends the possibility of the date 1819, but it must remain a likely, but not definite, date of composition.

A further point of Scheibler's is worth mention. Stadler, in the letter referred to above, went on to say that following a later visit to Steyr, Vogl took the sonata back to Vienna with him. 'Heaven knows', Stadler continued, 'where it is now.' Scheibler suggests, very plausibly, that both the sonata manuscript and that of the 'Trout' Quintet, op. 114, were in Vogl's possession at the time of Schubert's death, and that Vogl arranged with the publisher Czerny to publish the two works.

Sources:
Manuscript:
    Lost.
First edition:
    Josef Czerny, as op. 120 (Vienna, December 1829).

Sonata No. 16, in A minor, op. 143 (D. 784)
    I. Allegro giusto
    II. Andante (F major)
    III. Allegro vivace (A minor)

Composed Vienna, February 1823.

No scherzo or minuet was composed for the work.

Sources:
Manuscript:
    Otto Taussig, Malmö.
First edition:
    Diabelli, as op. 143 (Vienna, April 1839).

Sonata No. 17, in A minor, op. 42 (D. 845)
    I. Moderato
    II. Andante poco moto (C major)

III. Scherzo: Allegro vivace (A minor) and
Trio: *un poco più lento* (F major)

IV. Rondo: Allegro vivace (A minor)

Composed Vienna, early 1825.

Schubert took this sonata with him to Steyr when he left
Vienna on 20 May 1825.

The exact date of publication of the work is uncertain: it was
reviewed in Leipzig on 1 March 1826. For corrupt places in the
slow movement and in the Finale, see the bibliography, article by
Paul Badura-Skoda, p. 215.

Sources:

Manuscript:

Lost.

First edition:

A. Pennauer, as op. 42, called 'Première grande Sonate'
(Vienna, early 1826). It was dedicated by Schubert to
Cardinal Rudolf, Archduke of Austria.

Sonata No. 18, in C major, the 'Reliquie', D. 840

I. Moderato

II. Andante (C minor)

III. Menuetto: Allegretto (A flat major) and
Trio (G sharp minor) (unfinished)

IV. Rondo: Allegro (C major) (unfinished)

Composed Vienna, April 1825.

The manuscript was given by Ferdinand Schubert to Schumann
on the occasion of the latter's visit to Vienna in 1838–9. It passed
to Schumann's friend Adolf Böttger, who divided the manuscript among friends.

The work has been supplied with completions by Ernst Křenek,
1921 (Universal Edition, Vienna, 1923); Walter Rehberg, 1927
(Steingräber-Verlag, Leipzig, 1928).

Sources:

Manuscripts:

(1) First movement:

(*a*) bars 1–70: City Library, Vienna.

(*b*) bars 71–135: Fitzwilliam Museum, Cambridge.

      (*c*) bars 136–end: Ferdinand Rosen, Berlin.
(2) Slow movement: Ferdinand Rosen, Berlin.
(3) Menuetto:
      (*a*) bars 1–16: Ferdinand Rosen, Berlin.
      (*b*) bars 17–end: City Library, Vienna.
(4) Finale: lost.
First edition:
      'Reliquie: Letzte Sonate (unvollendet)', K. F. Whistling
      (Leipzig, Autumn 1862).

        Sonata No. 19, in D major, op. 53 (D. 850)
         I. Allegro vivace
        II. Con moto (A major)
       III. Scherzo: Allegro vivace (D major) and
          Trio (G major)
       IV. Rondo: Allegro moderato (D major)
Composed Gastein, August 1825.

The manuscript of this sonata is a corrected fair copy, not a rough draft; but it seems unlikely that it was the copy used by the publisher. There are minor differences and omissions apparent if the manuscript is compared with the first edition — e.g., the time-signature of the first movement is 2/2, not 4/4 as in the first edition.

Sources:
Manuscript:
      Albertina, Vienna.
First edition:
      Matthias Artaria, as op. 53, called 'Seconde grande Sonate'
      (Vienna, 8 April 1826).

        Sonata No. 20, in G major, op. 78 (D. 894)
         I. Molto moderato cantabile
        II. Andante (D major)
       III. Menuetto: Allegro moderato (B minor) and
          Trio (B major)
       IV. Allegretto
Composed Vienna, October 1826.

The title 'Fantasia', sometimes attached to this work, originated with its publisher, Tobias Haslinger. He published the sonata as 'Fantasia, Andante, Menuetto, and Allegretto', conveying the impression that there were four separate pieces for pianoforte in the opus. This impression was certainly made on the reviewer of the sonata for a Frankfurt journal of the day: he referred to 'the pieces contained in the book'.

The sonata was dedicated by Schubert to Josef von Spaun.

Sources:

Manuscript:

>British Museum, London. Schubert has headed his manuscript 'IV. Sonate'.

First edition:

>Tobias Haslinger, as op. 78: volume ix of *Museum für Claviermusik* (Vienna, 11 April 1827).

Sonata No. 21, in C minor, D. 958

    I. Allegro
    II. Adagio (A flat major)
   III. Menuetto: Allegro (E flat major) and
       Trio (A flat major)
   IV. Allegro (C minor)

Sonata No. 22, in A major, D. 959

    I. Allegro
    II. Andantino (F sharp minor)
   III. Scherzo: Allegro vivace (A major) and
       Trio: *un poco più lento* (D major)
   IV. Rondo: Allegretto (A major)

Sonata No. 23, in B flat major, D. 960

    I. Molto moderato
    II. Andante sostenuto (C sharp minor)
   III. Scherzo: Allegro vivace con delicatezza
       (B flat major) and Trio: (B flat minor)
   IV. Allegro ma non troppo (B flat major)

All three sonatas composed Vienna, September 1828. On the last page of the third sonata is the date 26 September 1828.

Sources:

Manuscripts:

(1) Sketches: City Library, Vienna.

(2) Final versions: Marie Floersheim, Wildegg in Aargau, Switzerland.

First editions:

(1) Sketches: Printed in part in the *Revisionsbericht* to the *Gesamtausgabe*, x, pp. 9–34.

(2) Diabelli, as 'Franz Schuberts Allerletzte Composition: Drei grosse Sonaten' (Vienna, May 1838). Schubert had intended to dedicate the sonatas to Hummel; by 1838 this composer was dead, and the publisher dedicated them to Schumann.

BIBLIOGRAPHY

BADURA-SKODA, PAUL: 'Fehlende Takte und korrumpierte Stellen in klassischen Meisterwerken', *Neue Zeitschrift für Musik*, Mainz, November 1958, pp. 637–41.

BROWN, MAURICE J. E.: 'Introduction to Schubert's sonatas of 1817', *Music Review*, Cambridge, February 1951.

CAPELL, RICHARD: 'Schubert's Sonatas', *Daily Telegraph*, London, 15 November 1938.

DEUTSCH, O. E.: *Schubert: Thematic Catalogue*, London, 1951.

HOLLAND, F. W.: *Music and Letters*, London, October 1955, p. 407.

KÖLTZSCH, HANS: *Schubert in seinen Klaviersonaten*, Breitkopf & Härtel, Leipzig, 1927.

RATZ, ERWIN: 'Schuberts Sonaten', *Schweizerische Musikzeitung*, Geneva, 1 January 1949.

Revisionsbericht, Gesamtausgabe, x, Breitkopf & Härtel, Leipzig, 1888.

TRUSCOTT, HAROLD: 'The two versions of Schubert's op. 122', *Music Review*, Cambridge, May 1953.

Only the Breitkopf & Härtel *Gesamtausgabe* can provide all the published material mentioned in the above list of sonatas. Two modern editions, both claiming to be based on original sources, make an attempt to give all the completed sonatas and the substantially completed fragments. But neither separately, nor even in conjunction, do they cover the entire ground. They are (1) *Klaviersonaten*, according to the autographs and first editions, edited by Erwin Ratz, Universal Edition (U.E. 257a and 257b), Vienna, 1953. Two volumes, containing fourteen sonatas. (2) *Klaviersonaten*, according to the manuscripts and first editions, edited by Paul Mies, G. Henle Verlag, Duisburg, 1961. Two volumes, containing eleven sonatas. A third volume of fragmentary sonatas is promised.

THE DANCE-MUSIC MANUSCRIPTS

THE background of Schubert's printed dance-music is more tangled and untidy than that of any other department of his music. Why trouble to sort it out, or, rather, *try* to sort it out? The usual reasons given for a tidying-up process of this kind are inadequate here. When the dance-music is chronologically arranged, the gains are small. There is very little artistic development to be found and profitably studied; there is no expansion in the technical treatment of the pianoforte, as we find revealed by the corrected chronology of the sonatas; not very much light is cast on other works of Schubert's composed at the same time as this or that collection of dances. When the autograph dance-music manuscripts have been sifted and correctly associated, they solve no problems, as the song-autographs do, for example, concerning texts or poets, because no such problems exist.

The answer seems to be that if the chronological ordering of the entire body of Schubert's manuscripts is to be undertaken at all, even if the necessary work on the dance-music yields little tangible profit, it must not be omitted. Unlike other departments of his music, it must be done simply as an end in itself. That is probably the reason why it has so far remained undone.

It must be admitted that O. E. Deutsch, in his *Thematic Catalogue* of Schubert's works, has broken the back of the task. Considering the scope of his book, it would be excusable had he devoted less time and trouble to the cataloguing of the dance-music, an inconsiderable part, artistically, of the composer's output. Instead of which he has paid considerable attention to the manuscripts and manuscript-collections of the many dances. But one must make two criticisms, however diffidently: the listing of dance-collections under their opus numbers has evaded the chronology of their composition, and the manuscript sources in the book inevitably bear a multitude of cross-references that entail a tremendous amount of page-turning.

The problem of ordering the dances in chronological sequence cannot be completely solved. In several cases the date of composition is almost guess-work; many manuscripts are lost and those preserved are not always dated. His friends frequently refer to his dances in their letters and memoirs, but, apart from the popular 'Trauerwalzer', they never specify any particular dance. Schubert, it is clear, looked upon his dances as a means of entertainment when performed and as a means of earning money when published. This is not to deny any primary creative impulse in them, for they were, so to say, his daily companions, and I have suggested elsewhere that they correspond in his case to the commonplace journals and notebooks of the literary artist. But the origin of many dances lay in improvisations at social evenings among his friends, from which he preserved afterwards, in manuscript, any of the results that pleased him. This is hardly the way he approached his songs or sonatas, for instance. The dances were popular, and copies of them were always being demanded by his friends. The dance-music manuscripts actually dedicated by Schubert to friends and acquaintances, and others obviously written out for friends, but not actually inscribed, are comparatively numerous. The dedicated copies are frequently dated, but their dates, inscribed months or even years after the composition of the dance, are of no assistance. As a consequence of this popularity we possess, in many cases, two or three copies of a particular dance; it may appear singly, or with a companion, or in a set of dances (sometimes as a member of different sets). One copy will be dated, another will not, and which is the earlier of the two manuscripts cannot be determined. The copies are frequently not exact, possibly because they were written out from memory by the composer; should they be looked upon as variants of the published dance and considered worthy of separate publication?

Another source of confusion is Schubert's apparent indifference to the formal categories of the dance. He called a piece a Ländler on one manuscript, a Deutscher on another, and it was published as a Walzer. Publishers were equally indifferent, and after his death they selected items from a collection of Deutsche and entitled them Ländler or Walzer. This categorization is a real difficulty; it has been met in the following pages by retaining the title used on publication. This is anything but satisfactory, but it has been done, first, because the dances are now known by these titles, and, second, because it is impossible in many cases to know what Schubert himself actually called them.

Finally, the publication of his dances has emphasized the problems outlined above and added others. The arrangements of sets of dances for publication, not only posthumously published, but also published while Schubert was alive, are haphazard and arbitrary. There is clear evidence that Schubert did take some trouble over his preliminary plans for the publication of op. 9, his first collection of dances, and we find at the end of a song-manuscript, 'La pastorella al prato', D. 528, of January 1817, the *incipits* of six dances, all in A major; this memorandum probably represents his initial attempt at an opus to consist of a set of dances. Another similar memorandum can be found on the back of the manuscript of the part-song 'Ruhe', D. 635, undated but of the same period. Here a further six dance-melodies are written down, four in A major and two in E major. But when the time came for the publication of Schubert's first set of dances, a varied assembly of thirty-six pieces, ranging in date from 1816 to 1821, was published in November 1821 as his op. 9.

Similar haphazard collections appeared as op. 18 in February 1823, and as op. 33 in January 1825. As for the posthumous publication, op. 127, the so-called 'Letzte Walzer', which appeared in 1830: the activities of the publisher Diabelli in compiling this set are remarkable. Various manuscripts of Schubert's were drawn on for the opus, his original order was altered, his keys transposed, here and there dances were omitted altogether, the trio section of one was deleted and another dance was substituted for it. Was anything gained by this interference with Schubert's originals? The question can be answered categorically: no, nothing. The original manuscripts are preserved in the Conservatoire, Paris, and in City Library, Vienna, available for anyone who wishes to compare them with Diabelli's final offering as op. 127. It will be found that neither from the point of view of actual dancing, nor from that of concert performance, has any advantage followed from Diabelli's adjustments. (MSS. 9 and 45 below.)

There follows, in the form of a *catalogue raisonné*, all the manuscripts of Schubert's dances; those irretrievably lost, but which are presumed to have once existed as entities, are listed in an appendix. The extant manuscripts are arranged, within the limits specified, in chronological order, and their contents described. The present whereabouts of the manuscript, if known, is given, and if unknown, the last owner's name is recorded. In a few cases the progress of the manuscript from Schubert's hands, through those of its owners in the nineteenth century, to its home today is included in the notes, if this descent, so to say, is of any interest. These particulars are all given in brackets at the end of each section. The term 'variant' indicates that the dance in the manuscript differs sufficiently from its form in the printed first edition to warrant such attention.

Every manuscript-collection is identified by its appropriate Deutsch number or numbers, and, *where necessary*, particulars of publication are supplied for any individual dance. All other details of publication and publication-dates can be obtained from Deutsch's *Thematic Catalogue* and are not, therefore, included here. Should any dance, however, have been published since the appearance of that catalogue (1951) the details are given in the appropriate place. Two important published collections of dance-music are abbreviated as follows:

1. *Deutsche Tänze*, edited by O. E. Deutsch and Alfred Orel (Edition Strache, Vienna, 1930): referred to as *Deutsche Tänze*.
2. *Schubert: Sämtliche Tänze*, vols. i and ii, edited by Paul Mies (G. Henle Verlag, Duisburg, 1956): referred to as *Sämtliche Tänze*.

MS. 1

Two Minuets, D. 995   *c.* 1811
   No. 1 in C major

No. 2 in F major

Each minuet has a trio in the same key. There are indications of orchestral instruments in the manuscript.

First edition: *Sämtliche Tänze.*

(Otto Taussig's Schubert Foundation, Malmö, Sweden)

MS. 2

Twelve 'Wiener' Deutsche, D. 128   *c.* 1812

The manuscript consists of four loose leaves with the dances given in the order below. The front side of the leaf is labelled (*a*), the back (*b*). No explanation was given for the changed order when the dances were first published in the *Gesamtausgabe*, Serie xxi, no. 23 (1897). But Schubert himself continually altered the numbering of each dance on the manuscript in order to obtain a satisfactory sequence. The number in brackets after each dance refers to its position in the *Gesamtausgabe.*

   I. (*a*) No. 1 in F major, with a short Introduzione (1)
         No. 2 in F major (12)
     (*b*) No. 3 in D major (11)
         No. 4 in B flat major (8)
  II. (*a*) No. 5 Duplicate of no. 4 in B flat major (8)
         No. 6 in A minor (5)
     (*b*) No. 7 in A flat major (3)
         No. 8 in D major (10)
 III. (*a*) No. 9 in D major (9)
         No. 10 in C minor (6)
     (*b*) No. 11 in F major (7)
         No. 12 in E major (4)
 IV. (*a*) No. 13 (?) in C major (2)
     (*b*) blank

The last dance may not be part of the sequence. It is a first sketch for the Trio of the String Quartet in C major (in its final form in F major), D. 32.

(City Library, Vienna)

MS. 3

Twenty Minuets, surviving from thirty, D. 41   1813

The manuscript is headed 'Menuetti' but the number is not specified. It consists of thirteen leaves, and these have been numbered consecutively by a later hand, although by the time this was done several leaves were missing. Some of the sides of these leaves were blank, and as was his practice in 1816–17, Schubert filled up the blank sides with sketches for later work. In the following description of the manuscript the thirteen leaves are given in order, the front side labelled (*a*), the back (*b*). An asterisk indicates a missing, or probably missing, leaf.

    I. (*a*) No. 1 in F major
       (*b*) No. 2 in C major
    II. (*a*) No. 3 in F major; Trio in C major
      (*b*) No. 4 in A minor; Trio in A major
    III. (*a*) No. 5 in B flat major
      (*b*) No. 6 in B flat major
    IV. (*a*) No. 7 in F major
      (*b*) No. 8 in C major
    * Leaf missing, with minuets nos. 9 and 10
    V. (*a*) No. 11 in F major; Trio in D minor
      (*b*) No. 12 in B flat major
    VI. (*a*) No. 13 in D major
      (*b*) No. 14 in D major
    VII. (*a*) No. 15 in D major
      (*b*) No. 16 in D major
    VIII. (*a*) No. 17 in D major
      (*b*) No. 18 in G major
    * Leaf missing, with Minuet no. 19
    IX. (*a*) No. 20 in C major
      (*b*) Fugue in E minor, pencilled sketches, Allegro moderato. A simple arrangement of 'Wiegenlied', D. 498, in C major, is written by Ferdinand Schubert, in ink, on some of the fugue sketches
    X. (*a*) No. 21 in F major

(b) Concluding eight bars of the last of the 'Fünf Klavierstücke', D. 459. Opening thirty-one bars of the Adagio in C major, D. 349

XI. (a) Continuation, fifty-three bars, of the Adagio, D. 349

(b) First sketch of 'Sehnsucht', D. 576

* Leaf missing (? with more of the Adagio, D. 349)

XII. (a) No. 22 in B flat major. The beginning, six bars, was cancelled and rewritten. Ferdinand Schubert has pencilled above the dance the word 'Gratias' (see note)

(b) Continuation, twenty-nine bars, of the Andantino in C major, D. 348

* Leaf missing (? with more of the Andantino, D. 348)

XIII. (a) Beginning, forty-two bars, of the Andantino, D. 348

(b) No. 23 in G major. The bass is in single notes with the indication 'Basso sempre con octavo'

Each dance has a trio in the same key, except in the three cases mentioned. According to Ferdinand Schubert these minuets were written by Schubert for his brother Ignaz 'in a very easy style'. He added in a footnote that they were lost. His note, 'Gratias', above Minuet no. 22 indicated that he intended to use it as the basis for that section of the text in his own 'Pastoral' Mass, published as his op. 13 in 1846. Large parts of this mass are based on the above minuets.

The twenty minuets, numbered 1–20, were published in the *Gesamtausgabe*, xii, no. 30 (1889).

(City Library, Vienna)

MS. 4

Minuet in D major for String Quartet, D. 86 (?) 1813

The manuscript is not dated. On the back page is Ferdinand Schubert's arrangement for piano of the minuet, dated 16 December 1844, and inscribed for Gustav Petter. The manuscript also contains the fragment 'Clamavi ad te', D. 85.[1]

(City Library, Vienna)

[1] 'Clamavi ad te' is not by Schubert. It is a copy, in his hand, of the soprano part from an offertory by Joseph Preindl, op. 16, published in Vienna. See 'Kleine Köcheliana', K. Pfannhauser, in *Mitteilungen der Internationalen Stiftung Mozarteum*, 1964.

MS. 5

Five Minuets for String Quartet, D. 89   19 November 1813

No. 1 in C major; Trio I in C major, Trio II in C minor
No. 2 in F major; no trio
No. 3 in D minor; Trio I in F major, Trio II in D minor
No. 4 in G major; no trio
No. 5 in C major; Trio I in C major, Trio II in C major

Only the parts are preserved, and the five dances are listed as belonging to volume ii. The first volume is lost.

(City Library, Vienna)

MS. 6

Five Deutsche Tänze, with coda, for String
Quartet, D. 90   19 November 1813

No. 1 in C major; Trio I in A minor, Trio II in C major
No. 2 in G major; Trio I in G major, Trio II in E minor
No. 3 in D major; Trio in D major
No. 4 in D minor; no trio
No. 5 in C major; Trio I and II both in C major
Coda in C major

As with MS. 5, only the parts are preserved, and the five dances are listed as belonging to volume ii. The first volume is lost.

(City Library, Vienna)

MS. 7

Two Minuets, D. 91   22 November 1813

No. 1 in D major; Trio I in A major, Trio II in D major
No. 2 in A major; Trio I and Trio II both in A major

The manuscript is headed 'IV Menuetti', but only these two are preserved.

(National Library, Berlin)

MS. 8

Ecossaise in F major, D. 158   21 February 1815

Schubert headed his dance 'Eccosais' [*sic*]. The date has been misread as 1805, which is just possible, but highly improbable.

(Pierre Cornuau, Paris, 1962)

MS. 9

Twelve Deutsche Tänze, D. 135, 139, 146   1815

No. 1 in E major, op. 127, no. 3;
    Trio in E major: *Deutsche Tänze*
No. 2 in A major : as the Trio to op. 127, no. 3 above;
    Trio in F sharp major, op. 18, Walzer no. 9
No. 3 in C sharp major; Trio in A major: *Deutsche Tänze*
No. 4 in B minor; Trio in G major: op. 127, no. 7
No. 5 in F major; Trio in A flat major (transposed into B flat major for publication): op. 127, no. 10
No. 6 in D major; Trio in D major: op. 127, no. 6
No. 7 in F major; Trio in F major (transposed into B flat major for publication): op. 127, no. 5
No. 8 in B flat major; Trio in B flat major: op. 127, no. 11
No. 9 in G flat major (transposed into G major for publication): op. 127, no. 8;
    Trio in G flat major (transposed into G major for publication): Trio to op. 127, no. 1
No. 10 in D major, op. 127, no. 1; Trio in D major, as the Trio for op. 127, no. 8
No. 11 in A major; Trio in A major: op. 127, no. 4
No. 12 in C major; Trio in C major: op. 127, no. 9

The manuscript consists of eleven leaves, twenty sides of which are filled. It is headed by Ferdinand Schubert '12 Deutsche sammt Coda für das Pianoforte von Franz Schubert, 1815', but there is, in fact, no coda. The manuscript reappeared in Bonn in 1900 from the collection of Alexander Poszonyi and was sold by the dealer F. Cohen to Charles Malherbe, archivist of the Paris Opera House. From Malherbe it passed to its present owners.

The Trio in B flat major, op. 127, no. 10 (no. 5 above) closely resembles the second Ländler in MS. 13.

(Conservatoire, Paris)

MS. 10

Eight Ecossaises, surviving from twelve, D. 299   3 October 1815

No. 1 in A flat major, op. 18, écossaise no. 1
No. 2 in E flat major
No. 3 in E major
No. 4 in A major
No. 5 in D flat major
No. 6 in A flat major
No. 7 in E major
No. 8 in C major

(Nos. 9 to 12 are missing from the manuscript.)

The last four dances are not lost, since Schubert copied the complete manuscript in 1816 for Marie von Spaun. His copy is lost, but it was itself twice copied by other people and their copies have survived. They indicate that the odd-numbered dances are to be repeated after the even-numbered dances are played.

Nos. 2 to 8 were first published in the *Gesamtausgabe*, xxi, no. 29 (1897). Nos. 9 to 12 were first published in *Die Musik*, 1 September 1912, edited by O. E. Deutsch.

(Gesellschaft der Musikfreunde, Vienna)

MS. 11

Four 'Komische' Ländler in D major, D. 354 ⎫
Eight Ländler in F sharp minor, D. 355   ⎬ January 1816
Nine Ländler in D major, D. 370   ⎭

The 'Komische' Ländler are written on two treble staves, probably as duets for two violins. For the other two sets of Ländler only the treble line appears on the manuscript. The seventh of the Ländler in D major is identical with the sixth of the eight Ländler in B flat major, MS. 13.

(City Library, Vienna)

MS. 12

Eleven Ländler in B flat major, D. 374   February 1816

Only the treble part is given in the manuscript, labelled

'Violino'. Certain of these eleven Ländler are identical with other dances, as follows:

Nos. 1–3: identical with the first three Ländler of MS. 13
No. 5: identical with the seventh Ländler in MS. 13
No. 7: identical with the fourth Ländler in MS. 13
No. 11: identical with the fifth Ländler in MS. 13, except that the two parts have been interchanged, i.e., 'A/B' has become 'B/A'
(City Library, Vienna)

MS. 13

Eight Ländler in B flat major, D. 378   13 February 1816

For identities between these dances and other Ländler, see MSS. 11 and 12. The second Ländler is similar to the Trio of the Deutsche, MS. 9, no. 5.

(City Library, Vienna)

MS. 14

Three Minuets, D. 380   22 February 1816

No. 1 in E major; Trios I and II in E major
No. 2 in A major; Trio I in A major, Trio II in D major
No. 3 in C major; Trio in C major (not complete)

The manuscript was published only in part in the *Gesamtausgabe*, xxi, no. 28 (1897). The complete set of dances is published in *Sämtliche Tänze*.

(City Library, Vienna)

MS. 15

Six Ecossaises, D. 421   May 1816

No. 1 in A flat major: identical with op. 18, écossaise no. 5 in B major
No. 2 in F minor/A flat major
No. 3 in E flat major
No. 4 in B flat major
No. 5 in E flat major
No. 6 in A flat major

The manuscript concludes with the remark 'Gott sey Lob und Dank'.

(Gesellschaft der Musikfreunde, Vienna)

MS. 16

Two Ländler in E flat major, D. 679   (?) 1816

The first Ländler is almost identical with the tenth dance in the set of Twelve Deutsche, D. 420; this accounts for the conjectured date.

(Weis-Ostborn family, Graz)

MS. 17

Minuet with two trios, in E major, D. 335   c. 1816
(City Library, Vienna)

MS. 18

Minuet and Trio in A major, D. 334   c. 1816
(City Library, Vienna)

MS. 19

Minuet and Trio in D major, D. 336   c. 1816

The manuscript is not in Schubert's hand, and the work may not be his.

(City Library, Vienna)

MS. 20

Nine *incipits* of dances, in A major, D. 528   *Post* January 1817

The *incipits* are written on blank staves at the end of the song 'La pastorella al prato'.

1. op. 9, no. 3.   2. op. 9, no. 1.   3. op. 9, no. 2.   4. op. 9, no. 4. 5, 6, 7, 8: lost dances.   9. D. 366, no. 16.
Cf. MS. 30.

(University Library, Tübingen:
Department of the National Library)

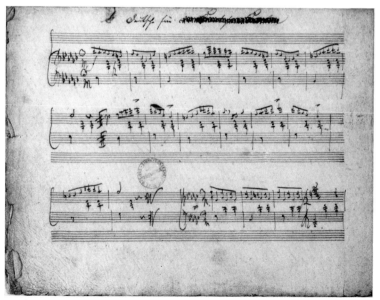

Conservatoire, Paris

9. Adagio in E major, D. 612; probably the slow movement of Sonata
No. 12 in C major, D. 613

Conservatoire, Paris

10. Deutscher Tanz in E flat major (MS. 41), showing the dedication to
Karoline Esterházy, cancelled by Schubert

MS. 21

Eight Ecossaises, D. 529   February 1817

No. 1 in D major	No. 5 in D major
No. 2 in D major	No. 6 in D major
No. 3 in G major	No. 7 in D major
No. 4 in D major	No. 8 in D major

The eighth écossaise is inscribed in the manuscript by Schubert 'Nach einem Volkslied' — but the folk-song has never been identified. Nos. 1, 2, 3, 6, and 7 were published in 1871 by J. P. Gotthard of Vienna. The rest were first published in the *Gesamtausgabe*, xxi, nos. 1–3 (1897).

(Erwin von Spaun, Vienna)

MS. 22

Minuet in C sharp minor, D. 600   Late 1817

The minuet is written on the back of some sketches for the Mass in F major of 1815. This practice of Schubert's, using blank spaces in the 1815–16 manuscripts, was customary in 1817. For a possible trio to this minuet see MS. 23.

(City Library, Vienna)

MS. 23

Trio in E major for a minuet, D. 610   February 1818

The manuscript is inscribed by Schubert: 'Trio, to be considered as the prodigal son of a minuet by Franz Schubert: written in February 1818 especially for his beloved brother [Ferdinand].' The minuet referred to here is almost certainly that of MS. 22.

(J. A. Stargardt, Berlin: February 1928)

MS. 24

Two Dances   Spring 1818

Deutscher Tanz in A flat major, op. 9, no. 3 (D. 365)
Ecossaise in E flat major, D. 511

The dances were written one on each side of an album-leaf for

Q

an unidentified friend of Schubert's. There is a humorous inscription at the foot of each page (see O. E. Deutsch, *Schubert: A Documentary Biography*, p. 77). In the sale-catalogue of Henrici the écossaise, then unpublished, was given in facsimile; it was published in *Sämtliche Tänze*.

(K. E. Henrici, Berlin: sale 23 August 1924)

MS. 25

Deutscher Tanz in A flat major, D. 365   14 March 1818

The manuscript is of the 'Trauerwalzer', op. 9, no. 2. It was written for Anselm Hüttenbrenner. The inscription on the manuscript can be read in Deutsch's *Documentary Biography*, p. 88. On the back of the manuscript is the first page of the text from St. John's Gospel, VI. 55–58. See illustration 11.

(Library of Congress, Washington. Former owner, Joseph Joachim, *c.* 1886)

MS. 26

Deutscher Tanz in A flat major, D. 365   March 1818

Another copy of the 'Trauerwalzer', written for Ignaz Assmayr. The inscription on the manuscript can be read in Deutsch's *Documentary Biography*, p. 89.

(Stefan Zweig collection, London)

MS. 27

Three Deutsche Tänze for Pianoforte Duet,
  D. 618   Zseliz, 1818
  No. 1 in G major; Trio 1 in G major, Trio II in C major, coda in
    G major
  No. 2 in E major   No. 3 in E major

The Trio of no. 1 is identical with the seventh dance in Seventeen Ländler, D. 366 (see MS. 28, no. 1). The third dance is intended to be a trio to the second. The manuscript belonged to Julius Stockhausen in 1872, and thence passed to its present owner.

(City Library, Vienna)

MS. 28

Five Ländler, D. 366, 974   (?) 1818

    No. 1 in G major, D. 366, no. 7
    No. 2 in D flat major, D. 974, no. 1
    No. 3 in D flat major, D. 974, no. 2
    No. 4 in D flat major, D. 366, no. 14
    No. 5 in D flat major, D. 366, no. 15

The manuscript has no title or date from Schubert. It was once in the possession of Nicolaus Dumba.

(Gesellschaft der Musikfreunde, Vienna)

MS. 29

Two Deutsche and two Ecossaises,
    D. 145, 365   Zseliz, November 1818

    Deutsche — No. 1 in A flat major (variant), op. 9, no. 3
             No. 2 in A major, op. 9, no. 16
    Ecossaises — No. 1 in A flat major, op. 18, écossaise no. 1
             No. 2 in G sharp minor (variant), op. 18, écossaise no. 8

See note to MS. 48.

(City Library, Vienna)

MS. 30

Six Ländler, note after D. 349   1818–19

    No. 1 in A flat major, op. 9, no. 3
    No. 2 in A flat major, op. 9, no. 2
    No. 3 in A flat major, op. 9, no. 1
    No. 4 in A flat major, op. 9, no. 4
    No. 5 in D flat major, op. 9, no. 15
    No. 6 in A flat major, D. 366, no. 16

The manuscript post-dates the *incipits* on MS. 20, as can be seen from the altered anacruses. It was originally in the possession of Brahms, who has written in blue pencil against no. 6 '? *ungedruckt*'. It was, in fact, unpublished, and Brahms included it as no. 16 of the *Zwanzig Ländler*, which he edited anonymously for J. P. Gotthard (Vienna, 1869). The manuscript has changed hands considerably, being offered for sale by Boerner in 1908, by Liepmannssohn in 1929, and recently by Schneider of Tützing. There is a facsimile of the first page, containing the first three dances, in Boerner's sale-catalogue of 1908.

(Unknown)

MS. 31

Six Ländler melodies, D. 640, 365   *c*. 1819

    No. 1 in A major, op. 9, no. 17

    No. 2 in A major, op. 9, no. 28*a*, op. 9, no. 18*b*

    No. 3 in A major, op. 9, no. 18*a*, op. 9, no. 28*b*

    No. 4 in E major, op. 9, no. 25, the two sections of the dance being interchanged

    No. 5 in A major and No. 6 in A major: the complete forms of these dances are unknown. They belong to the group that contained op. 9, nos. 17–21

The six melodies are written on the back of the vocal quartet 'Ruhe', D. 635. Nos. 5 and 6 are quoted complete in the article 'Von den Schubert-Handschriften der Stadtbibliothek', in *Festschrift zum hundertjahrigen Bestehen der Wiener Stadtbibliothek* (Vienna, 1956), by Fritz Racek, p. 112.

(City Library, Vienna)

MS. 32

Two Dances, D. 643   1819

    No. 1 Deutscher Tanz in C sharp minor

    No. 2 Ecossaise in D flat major

The Deutscher Tanz was written for Josef Hüttenbrenner, and Schubert has inscribed the manuscript 'Teutscher für He[rrn] Hüttenbrenner'.

(Gesellschaft der Musikfreunde, Vienna)

MS. 33

Nine Deutsche Tänze, D. 365 and note
    after D. 678   12 November 1819

The manuscript is headed 'Deutsche' and dated by Schubert. The dances were all published in op. 9, in which they appear in this order: 6, 7, 8, 9, 13, 10, 5, 11, and 12. All nine dances are in A flat major.

(Gesellschaft der Musikfreunde, Vienna)

MS. 34

Twenty Ländler, D. 145, 366, 970   1819–20

No. 1 in E flat major, op. 18, Ländler no. 1

No. 2 in E flat major, D. 970, no. 1

No. 3 in E flat major, D. 970, no. 2 (identical with op. 18, Walzer no. 7)

No. 4 in A flat major, D. 970, no. 3

No. 5 in E flat major, op. 18, Ländler no. 2

No. 6 in A flat major, op. 18, Ländler no. 3

No. 7 in A flat major, D. 970, no. 4

No. 8 in D flat major, D. 970, no. 5

No. 9 in D flat major, op. 18, Ländler no. 5

No. 10 in D flat major, op. 18, Ländler no. 10

No. 11 in D flat major, op. 18, Ländler no. 11

No. 12 in D flat major, D. 970, no. 6

No. 13 in B major, D. 366, no. 9

No. 14 in G major, op. 18, Ländler no. 15

No. 15 in D major, D. 366, no. 10

No. 16 in G flat major, op. 18, Ländler no. 16 (transposed into G major)

No. 17 in D major, op. 18, Ländler no. 17

No. 18 in D major, op. 18, Ländler no. 14

No. 19 in A major, op. 18, Ländler no. 13

No. 20 in A major, D. 366, no. 1

The manuscript was once in the possession of Brahms. It has no title or date.

(Gesellschaft der Musikfreunde, Vienna)

MS. 35

Six Ecossaises in A flat major, D. 697   May 1820

The first dance was published as op. 18, écossaise no. 6. The other five dances were not published until the *Gesamtausgabe*, xii, no. 28 (1889).

(Gesellschaft der Musikfreunde, Vienna)

MS. 36

Eight Ländler, surviving from twelve, D. 681   *c.* 1820

Nos. 1–4 missing from the manuscript.

No. 5 in E flat major	No. 9 in A flat major
No. 6 in B flat major	No. 10 in A flat major
No. 7 in E flat major	No. 11 in E flat major
No. 8 in A flat major	No. 12 in B flat major

The dances are numbered as above in the manuscript.

(Conservatoire, Paris)

MS. 37

Ten Ecossaises, D. 145, 977   *c.* 1820

No. 1 in D flat major	No. 6 in D major
No. 2 in D flat major	No. 7 in B flat major
No. 3 in A flat major	No. 8 in D minor
No. 4 in B major	No. 9 in A flat major
No. 5 in D major	No. 10 in B minor

Nos. 9 and 10 were published as op. 18, écossaises 2 and 3. The first eight were published in the *Gesamtausgabe*, xii, no. 26 (1889).

(Gesellschaft der Musikfreunde, Vienna)

MS. 38

Eight Ländler in D flat major, D. 145, 680   *c.* 1820

The first four of these dances were published as op. 18, Ländler nos. 4, 6, 7, and 8. The last two dances were published as op. 18, Ländler nos. 9 and 12. In this manuscript the last four Ländler have only the treble part, except for no. 6, which has the bass part in the first four bars only. The manuscript has neither title nor date.

(Gesellschaft der Musikfreunde, Vienna)

MS. 39

Seven Deutsche Tänze, D. 145, 365, 722   8 March–20 May 1821

Nos. 1–4: F sharp major: transposed to F major for op. 9, nos. 32–35

No. 5 in G flat major

No. 6 in F sharp major: transposed to F major for op. 9, no. 36

No. 7 in B major (the fourth 'Atzenbrugger' Tanz): op. 18, Walzer no. 2

The fifth dance was published in the *Gesamtausgabe*, xii, no. 19 (1889). Dances nos. 1–6 are dated 8 March 1821, no. 7 is dated 20 May 1821.

(National Library, Berlin)

MS. 40

Four Dances, D. 145, 365   (?) 1821

No. 1 in E flat minor: transposed to E minor for op. 18, Walzer no. 5

No. 2 in E flat minor/G flat minor, op. 18, Walzer no. 8

No. 3 in A flat major⎤
No. 4 in A flat major⎦ op. 9, nos. 6 and 7 — see note

The last two dances have interchanged their second halves in this manuscript.

No. 3 = op. 9, no. 6*a* + op. 9, no. 7*b*

No. 4 = op. 9, no. 7*a* + op. 9, no. 6*b*

The second part of the fourth dance is a marked variant of that in the first edition.

(Stargardt, Marburg, May 1963: formerly with Max Friedlaender, *c.* 1886, then John Bass, New York)

MS. 41

Two Deutsche Tänze, D. 145   May 1821

No. 1 in E flat minor: transposed into E minor for op. 18, Walzer no. 5

No. 2 in E flat minor, op. 18, Walzer no. 8

These dances are written on the back of the manuscript containing the copy of 'Rastlose Liebe' made by Schubert for Count Johann Esterházy. There was a dedication to Karoline Esterházy after the title, which has been carefully cancelled by Schubert. Although separated in the first edition, it is clear from this manuscript, and the previous one (MS. 40), that Schubert intended them to be a couplet of dances, possibly a Deutsche and trio. See illustration 10.

(Conservatoire, Paris)

MS. 42

Six Deutsche (the 'Atzenbrugger Tänze'), D. 728,
  second and third entries   July 1821

No. 1 in E major, op. 18, Walzer no. 1
No. 2 in A minor, op. 18, Walzer no. 3
No. 3 in D major, op. 9, no. 29
No. 4 in B major, op. 18, Walzer no. 2
No. 5 in A major, op. 9, no. 30
No. 6 in C major, op. 9, no. 31

Cf. MSS. 39 and 43.

(Gesellschaft der Musikfreunde, Vienna)

MS. 43

Four Deutsche Tänze, D. 145, 365, 728:
  fourth note   August 1821

No. 1 in G major: transposed into F major for op. 9, no. 32
No. 2 in G major: transposed into F major for op. 9, no. 33
No. 3 in B major (the fourth 'Atzenbrugger' Deutscher): op. 18, Walzer no. 2
No. 4 in E flat minor: transposed into E minor for op. 18, Walzer no. 5

(Gesellschaft der Musikfreunde, Vienna)

MS. 44

Twelve Ecossaises, D. 781, 783   January 1823

No. 1 in G flat major	No. 7 in B minor
No. 2 in D major	No. 8 in D major
No. 3 in E flat major	No. 9 in B major
No. 4 in E flat major	No. 10 in G sharp minor
No. 5 in A flat major	No. 11 in B minor
No. 6 in G flat major	No. 12 in B minor

The last écossaise was published as op. 33, écossaise no. 2. No. 3, transposed into E minor, and no. 6, transposed into G major, were published in *Nouvelles Galoppes Favorites et Ecossaises*, Sauer & Leidesdorf (Vienna, 21 February 1824) as nos. 7 and 9 respectively.

(Gesellschaft der Musikfreunde, Vienna)

MS. 45

Seventeen Deutsche Tänze, D. 146, 779, 783   February 1823

No. 1 in D major (variant), op. 50, no. 8
No. 2 in D major (variant), op. 50, no. 9
No. 3 in A major (variant), op. 127, no. 2
No. 4 in D major, op. 127, no. 20
No. 5 in G major, the Trio of op. 127, no. 20
No. 6 in D major (variant), op. 50, no. 12
No. 7 in G major, op. 127, no. 14
No. 8 in D major (variant), op. 50, no. 14
No. 9 in B flat major (variant), op. 33, no. 6
No. 10 in B flat major (variant), op. 33, no. 7
No. 11 in G minor, op. 127, no. 12
No. 12 in C major (variant), op. 127, no. 13
No. 13 in F major, op. 127, no. 19
No. 14 in G minor, op. 127, no. 15
No. 15 in F major, op. 127, no. 16
No. 16 in B flat major, op. 127, no. 17
No. 17 in B flat major, op. 127, no. 18

(City Library, Vienna)

MS. 46

Nine Ländler, D. 779, 973   Early 1823

No. 1 in B major (variant), op. 50, no. 1
No. 2 in B major (variant), op. 50, no. 2
No. 3 in G major, op. 50, no. 3
No. 4 in G major (variant), op. 50, no. 4
No. 5 in E major, D. 973, no. 1
No. 6 in E major, D. 973, no. 2
No. 7 in A flat major (variant), op. 50, no. 33
No. 8 in A flat major, op. 50, no. 34
No. 9 in A flat major, D. 973, no. 3

(City Library, Vienna)

MS. 47

Twelve Ländler, D. 790   May 1823

No. 1 in D major
No. 2 in A major (identical with op. 33, no. 1)
No. 3 in D major
No. 4 in D major
No. 5 in B minor/major
No. 6 in G sharp minor
No. 7 in A flat major
No. 8 in A flat minor (the second part identical with that of
    op. 33, no. 10 in A minor)
No. 9 in B major
No. 10 in B major
No. 11 in A flat major
No. 12 in E major

Schubert indicated 'Deutsches Tempo' on the manuscript, i.e.,
the tempo of the 'Deutscher Tanz'. Brahms secured the publication of these dances, the only collection from Schubert's maturity
published exactly as he left it. They constitute op. 171, published
by C. A. Spina (Vienna, December 1864).

(Gesellschaft der Musikfreunde, Vienna)

MS. 48

Ecossaise in G sharp minor, D. 145 and
    entry before D. 769   c. 1823

This dance was written on a leaf in the album belonging to Serafina Schellmann of Steyr. It had been composed before 1818, in the key of B minor, and in this form published as op. 18, écossaise no. 8. This 1818 manuscript is lost. For a version similar to that on the album-leaf, also in G sharp minor, and dated November 1818, see MS. 29. In the key of G sharp minor the note-values have been doubled. There is a facsimile of the Schellmann album-leaf in O. E. Deutsch's *Sein Leben in Bildern* (1913), p. 46, which constitutes its first edition.

(Helmut Tenner, Heidelberg, April 1960)

MS. 49

Two Deutsche Tänze, D. 769   January 1824

No. 1 in A major   No. 2 in D major

The first dance is identical with the second on MS. 50. It was published in the *Gesamtausgabe*, xii, no. 18 (1889). The second dance was published in an *Album Musicale*, Sauer & Leidesdorf (Vienna, 19 December 1823).

(Unknown, formerly with Alfred Rothberger,
Vienna. It is reproduced in facsimile in Walter
Dahms's *Schubert*, Plate 67)

MS. 50

Four Deutsche Tänze, D. 146, 769, 783   1824

No. 1 in A major, op. 127, no 2
No. 2 in A major, *Gesamtausgabe*, xii, no. 18 (1889)
No. 3 in A major, op. 33, no. 1
No. 4 in D major, op. 33, no. 2

The second dance is identical with the first on MS. 49. This manuscript was once in the possession of Schober, who left it to his niece Isabella Raab. Her daughter Maria sold it *c.* 1919.

(Unknown: formerly with Heinrich
Hinterberger, Vienna, 1937)

MS. 51

Fourteen Ländler for pianoforte Solo and Duet,
    D. 366, 618, 783, 814   Zseliz, July 1824

Pianoforte Solo:
  No. 1 in C major, D. 366, no. 4
  No. 2 in D major, op. 33, no. 2
  No. 3 in C major, op. 33, no. 12
  No. 4 in E flat minor, D. 366, no. 12

Pianoforte Duet:
  No. 5 in E flat major, D. 814, no. 1
  No. 6 in A flat major, D. 814, no. 2
  No. 7 in C minor, D. 814, no. 13
  No. 8 in C major, D. 814, no. 4
  No. 9 in C major
  No. 10 in E flat major

Pianoforte Solo:
  No. 11 in A major, D. 366, no. 2
  No. 12 in D major, D. 366, no. 8
  No. 13 in A minor, D. 366, no. 3
  No. 14 in A minor, D. 366, no. 5

Nos. 5, 9 and 10, for pianoforte duet, were also composed by Schubert in a version for pianoforte solo as follows:

No. 5, in E flat major, manuscript lost. It was published in Vienna on 22 December 1824 (see D. 366, note)

No. 9, in C major, MS. 56. This is called the 'Wiedersehen-Deutscher', published as op. 33, no. 9

No. 10, in E flat major, manuscript lost. It was published as op. 33, no. 8

The dances for pianoforte duet, nos. 5, 6, 7, and 8, were arranged for pianoforte solo by the publisher J. P. Gotthard: see D. 814, first edition. They were first published in their original form by Peters (Leipzig, 1870), in a *Supplement* to Schubert's pianoforte duets.

The dances for pianoforte duet, nos. 9 and 10, were first

published in *Ländler für vier Hände*, Schott (Mainz, 1934), edited by Georg Kinsky (wrongly dated there as 1818 instead of 1824).

(Unknown, formerly with Helene Hauptmann, Leipzig, whose father, Moritz Hauptmann, was a member of the Brahms circle)

MS. 52

Four Deutsche Tänze, D. 968 (note 2), 146, 366, 783   *c.* 1824

No. 1 in F major, op. 33, no. 16
No. 2 in A major, op. 127, no. 2
No. 3 in B flat minor, D. 366, no. 13
No. 4 in C major, D. 366, no. 6

On this manuscript the first dance begins an octave higher than in the first edition. The date is conjectured from other dated copies of these dances, see MSS. 45 and 50. The manuscript was once in the possession of Brahms.

(Gesellschaft der Musikfreunde, Vienna)

MS. 53

Three Ecossaises, D. 816   Zseliz, September 1824

No. 1 in B minor   No. 2 in D major   No. 3 in B flat major

Published in *Sämtliche Tänze*, vol. ii.

(Unknown: offered for sale by V. A. Heck, Vienna, 1937, but withdrawn by the owner)

MS. 54

Six Deutsche Tänze, D. 820   Zseliz, October 1824

Nos. 1–3: A flat major
Nos. 4–6: B flat major

The dances were written for Karoline and Marie Esterházy by Schubert while he was their music teacher. The manuscript remained with the Esterházy family until, in 1866, Wilhelmine and Melanie, daughters of Karoline's cousin, Countess Rosa von Almásy, gave it to their music teacher. It then disappeared from view until it was discovered in 1930 by Hans Wagner-Schönkirch. Although the dances were numbered 1 to 6 on publication, there are actually only two Deutsche, each with two trios.

(George Steinbach, New York)

MS. 55

Two Deutsche Tänze for Pianoforte Duet in
    E flat major, D. 820, note 1   November 1824

The first dance is entitled by Schubert 'Allemande'. Both dances were also composed in a version for pianoforte solo (see note to MS. 51: nos. 5 and 10).

(Louis Koch collection: Marie Floersheim,
Wildegg, Switzerland)

MS. 56

Six Deutsche Tänze, D. 146, 783, 975   1824 (? November)

No. 1 in D major, op. 33, no. 2
No. 2 in D major, D. 975
No. 3 in A minor, D. 366, no. 4
No. 4 in C major, op. 33, no. 9
No. 5 in B flat major, op. 33, no. 6
No. 6 in G minor, op. 127, no. 15

In this manuscript the sixth dance starts with an anacrusis on D, not given in the first edition. The fourth dance is the 'Wiedersehen-Deutscher'; Schubert's version of it for pianoforte duet is found on MS. 51. The manuscript once belonged to Brahms.

(Gesellschaft der Musikfreunde, Vienna)

MS. 57

Walzer in G major, D. 844   16 April 1825

This dance was written in the album of Anna Hönig, engaged for a time to Schubert's friend Moritz von Schwind.

(G. Henle Verlag, Duisburg)

MS. 58

Two Deutsche Tänze, D. 841   April 1825

    No. 1 in F major   No. 2 in G major
           (J. A. Stargardt, Berlin, 1926: there is a facsimile
           of the manuscript in the sale-catalogue)

LOST MANUSCRIPTS

A. Twelve Deutsche Tänze, D. 420   1816
B. Cotillon in E flat major, D. 976   *c.* 1817
C. Sixteen Ländler, two Ecossaises, D. 734   *c.* 1822
    Published as *Wiener Damen-Ländler*, op. 67
D. Galop and eight Ecossaises, D. 735   *c.* 1822
    Published as op. 49
E. Three Deutsche Tänze, D. 971   *c.* 1822
    These dances are not in the Vienna City
    Library, as stated in Deutsch's *Thematic
    Catalogue*
F. Ecossaise in D major, D. 782   January 1823
G. Three Deutsche Tänze, D. 972   *c.* 1823
H. Walzer in A flat major, D. 978   *c.* 1825
 I. Twelve 'Valses noble', D. 969   *c.* 1826
    Published as op. 77
J. Walzer in G major, D. 979   *c.* 1826
K. Two Walzer, G major and D major, D. 980   *c.* 1826
L. Twelve 'Grazer Walzer', D. 924   September 1827
M. 'Grazer Galop', D. 925   September 1827

SOME PROBLEMATICAL
PUBLICATIONS CONSIDERED

1. 'Die Advokaten', D. 37.   2. Introduction and Variations in B flat, D. 603.   3. *Rosamunde* Overture, D.
644.   4. Pianoforte Trio in B flat, op. 99, D. 898.
5. Variations for Flute and Piano, op. 160 (D. 802).
6. 'Mondenschein', D. 875.

QUESTIONS concerning six of Schubert's published works are
asked in this essay, but not one of them can be given an
entirely satisfactory answer. Need they, in that case, be raised?
Justification for doing so, and for reviewing fully the problems
that give rise to them, lies in the fact that the answers already
provided to many of the questions are either wrong or misleading.
Even if the right answer cannot be given to a particular question,
it is worth trying to check, or destroy, a wrong one. Four, and
possibly five, of these publications were the result of Schubert's
own negotiations with publishers, and it is astonishing, therefore,
that a problem of any kind should exist; the remaining work, 'Die
Advokaten', D. 37, was published in his lifetime, but apparently
without his knowledge. It is the earliest, and so the first, of the
works to be considered.

In December 1812, while he was still a schoolboy at the
Stadtkonvikt, Schubert refashioned a male-voice trio by another
composer, which had been published seven years previously by
the Viennese music-publisher Josef Eder. It was entitled 'Die
Advokaten: Komisches Terzetto', the words by Baron Engelhart
(of whom nothing is known), the music by Anton Fischer,
conductor in those days at the Theater an der Wien. It is for
T.T.B., with pianoforte accompaniment, and is an undistinguished
piece of musical buffoonery. Schubert added very little, chiefly
elaborating the accompaniment. Walter Dahms, in his biography

of the composer, suggests that this version was prepared by Schubert for himself and a few fellow-pupils to perform at a New Year concert in the college.

There are two autograph manuscripts. The first is headed 'Die Advokaten: Terzett: Frz. Schubert mpia: 1812'; the second is headed similarly and carries the date 25–27 December 1812. It cannot be said which of the two came first, but the detailed date suggests a later manuscript. On both manuscripts the author's name is altered to 'Rustenfeld'. Some other person has written on the first manuscript the words 'for 2 Tenors and Bass'; the manuscript also bears a censor's stamp dated 12 May 1827.

The censor's permit was given in connection with the publication of the work under Schubert's name; it appeared from the firm of Diabelli as op. 74 on 16 May 1827. It is an incomprehensible business. In 1827 Schubert had by him a large number of mature works, all of which he was trying to publish in Vienna and in towns in Germany; that he should have taken this boyhood arrangement of another man's hopelessly inferior work to Diabelli and palmed it off as his own is simply not to be believed. The conclusion is inescapable that one of his friends, without Schubert's knowledge, and under the impression that the work was an original one, passed it to Diabelli. Who was it? In order to attempt an answer, let us consider the manuscripts.

The one dated simply 1812, which was the source of Diabelli's publication, subsequently became dismembered into four parts. (a) One leaf, containing bars 1–30, with the heading and date, was not discovered until 1927; formerly owned by Otto Taussig of Malmö, it was sold in 1961 by Stargardt of Marburg. (b) Bars 31–57 are lost. (c) Bars 58–175 were once owned by Nicolaus Dumba, and are now preserved in the City Library, Vienna. (d) The concluding section, bars 176–201, was once in private possession in England, and is now owned by the Fitzwilliam Museum, Cambridge. The Fitzwilliam Museum also possesses the title-page with the censor's permit stamped upon it.

The history of the second manuscript pretty clearly indicates the course of events. It saw the light in the 1890's, found in the possession of Marie Riemerschmid of Munich, and was subsequently

R

owned first by Max Friedlaender and then by Mandyczewski. Marie Riemerschmid was a daughter of Schubert's friend Franz Lachner, from whom she inherited it. And so presumably Lachner was the unknown agent by whom the composition reached Diabelli.[1] What Schubert's reactions were we have no means of knowing. That he took no steps to repudiate the ascription of Fischer's work to him is astonishing, but in those days such an act, if it were brought to people's notice, merely invoked public derision; there was no legal offence. Evidently no one spotted the misattribution; and if Schubert made any protest, there is no surviving record of it.

But it would have been surprising if the truth had never come to light, even though it did so by the slenderest chance imaginable. Eder's first edition of Fischer's trio, published in 1805, has completely disappeared; no single copy is known. But at some later period, about 1815, a manuscript copy of it was made, and this sole relic survives today. A few years after Schubert's death the manuscript copy was owned by a Viennese financier, Bannereth, a music-lover, in whose home frequent musical evenings were held. At one of these a performance of 'Die Advokaten' was given. The bass was Wenzel Nejebsee, a friend of Schubert's, who had often sung in performances of the composer's choral works in the 1820's. After the performance Bannereth produced his manuscript copy of Fischer's work, and the singers were astounded to find that the trio, which they had always considered to be by Schubert, was, in fact, not his at all. Years later, Nejebsee told Kreissle of the incident, and it is recorded in his biography.[2] This actually established the truth, and the restoration of Fischer's name to 'Die Advokaten' was generally adopted; in 1874 Nottebohm added the information to the op. 74 entry of his *Thematic Catalogue*. But shortly afterwards the last two fragments of Schubert's manuscript were found (sections (c) and (d) above), with the date 1812. Now Bannereth's copy was known to be c. 1815, and since Schubert's manuscript pre-dated this by three years, there was a sudden change of opinion. Kreissle and

[1] See, in this connection, Kreissle, p. 267, footnote.
[2] p. 514.

Nejebsee were deemed to be wrong, the final truth to have been established. The further discovery of the second manuscript, dated 25–27 December 1812, seemed conclusive. Accordingly, when the trio appeared in the appropriate volume of the Leipzig *Gesamtausgabe* (Serie xix, 1892), the editor, in the *Revisions-bericht*, treats the work as authentic Schubert, and makes no mention of Fischer's part in it. Eder's publication was considered to be *c.* 1815, and any uncomfortable questionings as to why Fischer, an elderly conductor, should have appropriated a fifteen-year-old boy's composition and published it as his own were not aired. And then, finally, the actual date of Eder's edition — 1805 — was discovered and the true course of events was established beyond question. The facts were summarized by O. E. Deutsch in the *Zeitschrift für Musikwissenschaft*, Leipzig, November 1928. But the tantalizing questions still remain: why did Lachner undertake this venture? Was Schubert entirely unaware of what was going on? Why did he allow such a hope-lessly inferior work to appear under his name, which fact, apart from any moral questions, would have been damaging to his reputation? The questions are easy to ask, impossible to answer.

The first section of the supplement in Nottebohm's *Thematic Catalogue* of Schubert's works is devoted to three 'spurious and doubtful' compositions. Only the third is definitely spurious: it is the song 'Adieu', actually by A. H. von Weyrauch, but for years attributed to Schubert. Nottebohm's second composition is the 'Grosse Sonate' in C minor, for pianoforte duet, which we now know to be unquestionably Schubert's own work. The first of the trio of works is the Introduction and Variations in B flat, op. 82, no. 2, the only one that can be considered a 'doubtful' Schubert composition. In my own view it is an authentic work, and I have given my reasons for believing so elsewhere.[1] The problem to be considered here does not arise solely from its authorship, but from its publication. But in considering the second problem, some light may perhaps be cast on the first.

[1] *Schubert's Variations*, pp. 38–41.

The variations were published by Julius Schuberth & Co. of Hamburg in October 1860. The work was advertised in the *Neue Zeitschrift für Musik*, Leipzig, on 12 October 1860 as op. 82, no. 2. The manuscript has been lost, so that we have no means of knowing whether the source for Schuberth's publication was Schubert's original manuscript or a copy of it. No record at all of the composition appears in any of the lists devised by Ferdinand Schubert or by Schubert's friends. The work appeared out of the blue, as it were, thirty-two years after the composer's death. It bears all the marks of early Schubert, and not very inspired early Schubert at that: little wonder that Nottebohm, together with many other scholars of the day, considered the whole transaction very dubious and dubbed the work spurious. They never considered the pertinent question — if the work is not by Schubert, who else could possibly have written it?

But unless we are to look upon the publication of the variations as a deliberate hoax on the part of Schuberth & Co. — an idea not to be entertained — we must allow that they acted in good faith. In that case their opus-numbering of the variations is the obvious place to start any investigation. The firm called this set of variations on an original theme op. 82, no. 2; the companion piece, now known as op. 82, no. 1, is a set of variations, also for pianoforte duet, which Schubert composed in February 1827 on a theme from Hérold's operetta *Marie*. The two sets for the same medium seem an obvious coupling under the same opus number. Actually, however, the *Marie* Variations had been published in 1827 by Haslinger of Vienna as op. 82. In 1854 the copyright of the *Marie* Variations was sold by Haslinger's son Karl to Schuberth & Co. of Hamburg. On 6 October 1854 these variations appeared from the Hamburg firm with this information on the title page: 'We inform the public that we have obtained the copyright of this opus from the publisher Hasslinger [*sic*] of Vienna.' They used Haslinger's plates: no manuscript source was necessary. The manuscript of the *Marie* Variations has survived; it remained in Vienna and is now in the possession of the National Library.

If the other set of variations, in B flat, is authentic Schubert, it seems fairly clear that Schuberth & Co. must have bought it at the same time from Karl Haslinger, who, if this is the case, had Schubert's manuscript of the B flat Variations in his possession without any intention of publishing it. Have we any grounds for believing this to be so? I think we have; if Schuberth & Co.'s advertisement in the *Neue Zeitschrift* of 6 October 1854 is examined, it will be seen that the *Marie* Variations were announced as follows:

Schubert, Franz (von Wien). Op. 82. No. 1. Variations à 4 mains über Hérolds *Marie*.

The addition 'No. 1' is significant. There was no indication whatever in Tobias Haslinger's original publication that the *Marie* Variations were the first part of an opus: the work appeared simply as op. 82. Schuberth & Co. would hardly have advertised the work as op. 82, no. 1 unless there was a no. 2, at least, to follow it. And this implies that the B flat Variations were also in their possession in 1854, and that even then they had decided to publish them as a companion piece to the *Marie* Variations. The designation op. 82, no. 1 is also printed on the first page of the first edition of the *Marie* Variations. Why there was a delay of six years before the appearance of the second set of variations is beyond conjecture: but once it had appeared, the two numberings became inseparately attached to the works, and op. 82 for the *Marie* Variations gave place to op. 82, no. 1. Only Nottebohm, convinced of the spuriousness of the B flat Variations, restored the original numbering to the *Marie* Variations, calling it simply op. 82. Kreissle's remarks in the supplement to his biography of Schubert, p. 289, can be misread: he was alluding to the printed note above, about the purchase of the copyright from Haslinger, and had no private information about the other transaction.

If the above summary of the facts is a true one, then we may conclude that at some time in 1827 Schubert sold the manuscripts of the two sets of variations to Haslinger on the assumption that both would be published. This hope never materialized, and the manuscript of the B flat Variations remained with Haslinger. It passed to his widow and his son Karl, his successors in the business, and by them, in 1854, it was sold to Schuberth & Co. At what period Schubert composed these variations is not known. The style, and even some of the material, has strong affinities with the work of 1817–18, and the medium — pianoforte duet — leads to the supposition that they were composed at Zseliz in 1818. O. E. Deutsch includes them in this year in his *Thematic Catalogue* (D. 603) and one feels that this placing is as sound as any.

The Overture in C major, known as the *Rosamunde* Overture, is one of Schubert's most popular orchestral works, ranking next to the 'Unfinished' Symphony in frequency of performance. It has, actually, nothing to do with the incidental music that Schubert composed for the play *Rosamunde*, performed for the first time on 20 December 1823; he evidently had little time for the production of this music, and he composed no overture. For the first performance of the play, at the Theater an der Wien, the overture to his earlier opera *Alfonso und Estrella* was used. There is reason to believe that Schubert intended to transfer this earlier overture, in D minor/major, to the *Rosamunde* music, and to compose another overture for *Alfonso und Estrella*. This is what Schwind wrote about the matter to Schober just after the two performances of *Rosamunde*:

> Schubert has taken over the overture he wrote for *Estrella* as he thinks it too 'homespun' for *Estrella*, for which he wants to write a new one.   (22 December 1823)

Later on, in a letter to Seyfried, conductor at the Theater an der Wien, Schubert himself referred to the overture in D minor/major as his *Rosamunde* Overture (23 November 1826). But his reference was due to the fact that the *Alfonso* Overture had been used for the *Rosamunde* performance; by that time, as we shall have reason to mention later, the *Alfonso* Overture was beginning to lose its connection with the *Rosamunde* music, and the confused association should never have arisen again; it was due to the incomprehensible action of the editor of the *Gesamtausgabe* volumes of the operas, J. N. Fuchs. This man, in 1891, for some unknown reason, printed the *Alfonso und Estrella* Overture as the overture to the *Rosamunde* music. For many years at the beginning of this century, before the full documentation of the period was available, there was widespread misunderstanding of the situation where these two overtures were concerned; only since Deutsch has made available the letters, programmes, etc., connected with the three stage-works involved has the muddle been cleared up. Not that all the problems have been entirely clarified, but at least the action of Fuchs need no longer confuse the issues.

The other overture, in C major, also belongs to an earlier stage-work of Schubert's, the 'magic play' with music entitled *Die Zauberharfe* composed in the summer of 1820. To say that its connection with the *Rosamunde* music is even more tenuous than that of the previous overture is an over-statement: it has no connection whatever, and recent investigation of the matter has revealed a problem for which we shall probably never find a solution. Why, one might ask, has this *Zauberharfe* Overture become associated with the *Rosamunde* music at all? Until quite recently the answer seemed straightforward, and would have run on these lines. In March 1824 the publishers Sauer & Leidesdorf of Vienna announced the publication of the 'Romanza' ('Der Vollmond bracht') from the *Rosamunde* music as op. 26, and added to their advertisement that the overture and entr'actes, in an arrangement for pianoforte duet, would appear shortly.[1] The subsequent publication of the pianoforte-duet arrangement of the overture to *Rosamunde* as op. 26, no. 1 evidently took place *c.* 1827, since it was reported in Whistling's *Handbuch* for the year 1828. Early in the 1830's, probably in 1834, an arrangement of the *Zauberharfe* Overture for string quartet by J. von Blumenthal was published by Diabelli, and called the *Rosamunde* Overture, op. 26, no. 1. This was followed a few years later by further arrangements of the work, for pianoforte solo and pianoforte duet, from the same firm (Easter 1842). From that day to this it has naturally been assumed that the publication of a pianoforte-duet arrangement of the *Zauberharfe* Overture in 1827 was the forerunner of all the other subsequent arrangements. Accordingly the further conclusion was justifiably drawn: that Schubert himself in 1827

[1] *Schubert: Documentary Biography*, p. 335.

had authorized the retitling of the *Zauberharfe* Overture as the *Rosamunde* Overture. Had it not been for the doubts of Elizabeth Norman McKay, during her researches on the stage-works of Schubert, we should, in all probability, have gone on accepting this simple explanation. But directly one looks more closely into the matter of Sauer & Leidesdorf's publication of 1827, it becomes clear that the explanation will hardly suffice. To begin with, no single copy of this pianoforte-duet arrangement is extant in any library or collection of note in the world — and has never so existed. It is possible, but very unlikely, that the edition was such a small one that every copy printed has been destroyed, but it must be pointed out that this has not happened with a single other published work of Schubert's.[1] It is far more probable that Sauer & Leidesdorf projected the publication, but never carried it out (see p. 260). Whistling's *Handbuch* record, in that case, was based on an announcement of some kind, and not derived from an actual copy. Our doubts as to the existence of this pianoforte-duet overture are confirmed by a glance at an early catalogue of Schubert's works. This was printed in the summer of 1831 on extra pages in the fifth edition of Schubert's popular song 'Die Rose', op. 74; its publisher, Diabelli, printed there a list of all Schubert's published works, from other firms as well as from his own, set out in order of opus numbers. The entry for op. 26 gives only the vocal numbers from *Rosamunde* — the 'Romanza' and the three choruses. If there had been, four years previously, a pianoforte duet of the overture published called op. 26, no. 1 it would have been included in this entry. The fact that it is not so included seems to me to indicate almost conclusively that it never existed. The final point, and the most convincing, is that there is no advertisement in the *Wiener Zeitung* for the necessary period announcing the publication of the work. It was the invariable practice of the firm of Sauer & Leidesdorf, and later, of Leidesdorf,

---

[1] The only exception is the collection of dances published in 1825 and called *Terpsichore*; this contained fifty German dances, by as many composers, and one of them is by Schubert. No copy is known. But, even so, the dance is probably preserved in another collection, and we have no right to say that it is definitely lost.

when he managed the firm alone from 1827 onwards, to advertise each of their publications in this journal; the non-appearance of any such advertisement for op. 26, no. 1 clinches the matter.

The whole affair can now be seen to assume a somewhat more mysterious aspect. If the *Zauberharfe* Overture were never published in Schubert's lifetime as the *Rosamunde* Overture, and hence never officially retitled in this way by the composer himself, how did it come to be associated with *Rosamunde*, and who is responsible? One small difficulty can be disposed of at once; Sauer & Leidesdorf's announcement of March 1824 referred to the overture that had been played at the actual performance of *Rosamunde*; in February 1826 the firm did publish the pianoforte-duet arrangement of the *Alfonso und Estrella* Overture under its proper title. They called it op. 52 in error, and this was later corrected to op. 69. The arrangement was made for them by Schubert, and his manuscript is preserved. Their publication, incidentally, was included by Diabelli in his list, mentioned above, of 1831; any suggestion that the hypothetical *Rosamunde/Zauberharfe* Overture was excluded by Diabelli from op. 26 because it was a pianoforte-duet arrangement only is thus discounted. In a full-dress *Thematic Catalogue* of Schubert's works, published in 1851, Diabelli included the pianoforte arrangements of the *Zauberharfe* Overture, under op. 26, as the *Rosamunde* Overture.

The earliest traceable reference to the C major work as the *Rosamunde* Overture, with the appellation op. 26, no. 1, seems to be in the arrangement for string quartet by Blumenthal, mentioned above: this was published about 1834. By that time the other overture, written for *Alfonso und Estrella*, had ceased to be associated with *Rosamunde*. But the main question is not settled, and only tentative answers can be suggested. The score of the *Zauberharfe* Overture, separated from the main body of the opera score, is in the Paris Conservatoire. The only title on this manuscript definitely written by Schubert is the indication 'Andante. Overture'. Both titles, *Rosamunde*, and *Zauberharfe* (in pencil), have been added by other hands. The indication 'op. 26' is also written at the head of the first page and may be from the hand of Schubert; it suggests that this manuscript served as the source for the various arrangements that Diabelli published — he once owned this manuscript and it passed to his successors in the business, one of whom sold it to Charles Malherbe. From Malherbe it went to the Conservatoire. It is possible that this full-score manuscript was originally in the hands of Sauer & Leidesdorf, for their stocks were bought by Diabelli in 1834, on the eve of the first appearance in print of the overture, as the *Rosamunde* Overture.

The fact that no publication of the *Zauberharfe* Overture appeared under the title *Rosamunde* in Schubert's lifetime does not, however, exclude entirely the possibility that Schubert, unofficially so to say, intended the connection. He had no occasion to compose another overture, less 'homespun', to *Alfonso und Estrella*, since several efforts to obtain a performance of the opera were all unsuccessful; hence he may have decided to leave the D major/minor Overture as he had originally intended it. If such is the case, he would cast about for another overture, suitable for the *Rosamunde* music. Now the overture to *Zauberharfe* had been a great success at the performance of the 'magic play' in Vienna. A report in the Vienna *Conversationsblatt* of 29 August 1820, written the day after the first performance, has these words:

the overture begins with an uncommonly lovely *andante*, which is very delicately scored and merges into a quick *allegro*, whose theme is taken from the melodrama in Act I.... We think, too, that the overture has a greater merit as a composition pure and simple, than as a connection with this melodrama, *and might as well be played before an opera as before a fairy-tale* ... [my italics].

Even a harsh criticism of the music, which appeared in Leipzig, relents in discussing the overture itself. Schubert's friends evidently liked the overture well enough to get to know it well, for years later one of them, Leopold von Sonnleithner, wrote to Ferdinand Luib on 1 November 1857 these words:

The overture was the one published in the pianoforte arrangement of op. 26, and named as though belonging to the play *Rosamunde*. But I am convinced that this overture was composed for *Die Zauberharfe*; for I remember the theme exactly and this is also introduced in the piece itself, as a melodrama, where it illustrates very happily the flickering of the will-o'-the-wisp.

It is well known that in the *Zauberharfe* Overture, Schubert re-used material from his overture in D, one of the pair known as 'in the Italian style', composed in 1817. Is it possible that this music was very dear to him (as it well might be) and that when it came to deciding on an overture for the *Rosamunde* music, he selected the *Zauberharfe* Overture for the purpose, thinking perhaps that thereby he was saving it from oblivion? If this is our answer, then it is not outside the bounds of possibility that he himself made an arrangement of the *Zauberharfe* Overture for pianoforte duet; although this was not published by Sauer & Leidesdorf in 1827, his manuscript may have passed with their stocks to Diabelli in 1834 and have been used as the basis for the 1834–42 arrangements for string quartet and pianoforte duet and solo. And that is as far as it is possible to go; yet another mystery is added to those that surround various publications of Schubert's works.

The most baffling of these mysteries is in connection with the first of the two trios for pianoforte, violin, and cello, the one in B flat major, published as op. 99. Not only is it impossible to dispel the mystery, but it is difficult not to feel a certain exasperation that such a mystery exists; while there is plentiful, almost excessive, documentation in connection with the second trio, op. 100, all the contemporary records are completely silent over the first. There is not one single, decisive word from any source whatever about it. Even Deutsch, with all his useful and knowledgeable commentary, cannot give any lead in the matter. The original manuscripts, first drafts and fair copies, are all lost (in contrast with the E flat trio, whose manuscripts are all preserved). In fact, if it were not for the pre-eminently Schubertian character of this great and splendid work, on contemporary evidence alone one would be entitled to reject it as spurious, on grounds as plausible as those on which some scholars reject the variations of op. 82, no. 2.

To begin with we have no idea where, or exactly when, it was composed. Attributed dates, 1826 or 1827, are pure guess-work, derived from the fact that the second trio was composed in

November 1827, and therefore the first must have been earlier than that. There is a legend, not to be wholly discounted, that Schubert intended to use in the B flat Trio a folk-tune he had heard at Gmunden, in the summer of 1825.[1] The limits of the composition period are thus mid-1825 to late 1827. If one inclines to believe in a date nearer to the end of these two years, it is because the impulse for the composition of works for the three instruments came to Schubert from his acquaintance with the superb partnership of three musicians, Ignaz Schuppanzigh (violin), Josef Linke (cello), and Karl Maria von Bocklet (piano), and this association became established during 1827. We may assume that by the early autumn of 1827 the B flat Trio was completed. What became of it? Schubert's concern over the publication of the second trio, in E flat, can be seen in his numerous letters to the publishers, H. A. Probst of Leipzig and B. Schott's Sons of Mainz, which he wrote during 1828. Such correspondence to foreign publishers was, of course, necessary, and one would expect to find these documentary references. The lack of any concerning the B flat Trio suggests that it had already been sold in Vienna, for with a Viennese publisher Schubert could have had direct, personal contact and no written records need be expected. When he wrote his first letter to B. Schott's Sons, on 21 February 1828, he offered 'a trio for pianoforte, violin, and violoncello, which has been produced here with much success'; he refers here to the E flat Trio, and his words confirm the supposition that the other trio, in B flat, was no longer his to dispose of. His remarks lead us to examine two performances for which we have extant records. They are as follows:

1. 26 December 1827. Musikverein Concert Hall, Vienna. 'New Trio for pianoforte, violin, and violoncello, by Schubert.' (The players were Bocklet, Schuppanzigh, and Linke.)

2. 28 January 1828. From Franz Hartmann's diary. '... glorious music was made by Schuppanzigh, Bocklet, Linke, Schubert, and Gahy.'

The latter was a private performance at the house of Josef von

[1] *Schubert: A Critical Biography*, pp. 167–8.

Spaun. At first sight it seems fairly obvious that the same trio was played on both occasions, and that, in view of Schubert's own words, it was the second trio, in E flat, the one he was offering to Schott's. In his *Documentary Biography* Deutsch indicated that the first of the above two performances was of the E flat Trio (p. 698), but in his records of the second, private performance he contradicts himself. In his *Biography* (p. 725) he says the trio was probably the one in B flat major; but in the *Memoirs* (p. 279) he says it was probably the one in E flat major. At Schubert's concert, given on 26 March 1828, Bocklet and Linke, with Josef Böhm as violinist, performed the E flat Trio: of this fact there is no doubt. Like the trio in the first performance above, it was referred to as 'new'. The conclusion one draws from this survey is that all three of these performances were of the second trio, and there the matter might rest were it not for a further remark of Spaun's. In his very enthusiastic obituary-notice of Schubert, published in March and April 1829, Spaun has these words: '. . . two grand trios, for pianoforte, violin, and violoncello, both already performed in public by Bocklet, with the greatest success . . .'. Now those words were written many years before the first trio, in B flat, was published; Spaun must have known personally that it was a work independent of its fellow trio, which was much more famous and familiar to him. Since he says 'in public', that rules out the second of the above performances. We are compelled therefore to revise our views of these performances, and to conclude that the first trio was performed at the Musikverein on 26 December 1827, and, remembering Schubert's words to Schott's, that the private performance at Spaun's home was of the second trio, in E flat. No other conclusion, on the evidence available, seems possible.[1]

---

[1] Nottebohm (*Thematic Catalogue*, p. 117) and, following him, Grove (first edition of the *Dictionary*, p. 345) state that the first trio, op. 99, was performed publicly in the New Year of 1828 at a 'Quartet' Concert of Schuppanzigh's. This information derives from a letter written by Schubert to Anselm Hüttenbrenner on 18 January 1828. But the composer was referring to the concert given on 26 December 1827, the date of which was unknown to Nottebohm. Nevertheless, apart from the wrong date, it now appears that the trio was, in fact, performed at the 'Quartet' Concert referred to.

But this is not the sum total of the mysterious affair. If Schubert, at about the time of the performance of the B flat Trio, had sold the manuscript to a Viennese publisher, what became of it? Why was it not published then or very soon afterwards? Its opus number, 99, was given to it by the composer himself, so that he clearly expected an early publication. In view of the publication of the E flat Trio as op. 100 by a foreign publisher, a very successful venture, why was the Viennese publication of op. 99 not forthcoming? Seven years passed before it made its delayed appearance from Diabelli in April 1836. In the catalogue already quoted above, which appeared in 1831 in the pages of 'Die Rose', one reads with astonishment the entry 'Op. 99. Premier grand Trio pour le pianoforte, violin et violoncelle, in B'. No price is given, which indicates its non-publication, but evidently details of the work were fully known, its key, its opus number, and its relationship with the later trio, which had *not* been called on publication by Probst 'Second' Trio, but *is* so called in Diabelli's list of 1831.

In view of the 'Die Rose' catalogue one wonders whether the B flat Trio was sold by Schubert not to Diabelli, but perhaps to another publisher in Vienna. At the period concerned he was negotiating with three or four of these: with Artaria & Co., which had purchased from him instrumental works associated with the name of Bocklet (e.g., the Sonata in D, op. 53 and the Rondo in B minor, op. 70); with Pennauer, Haslinger, and T. Wiegl. If any of these firms had acquired the manuscript of the trio, intending to publish it as the 'Premier grand Trio', it would at least account for the entry in Diabelli's catalogue. It is significant that in 1833 and 1835 Diabelli bought up part of the stocks of the firms of Artaria and Pennauer and that the publication of the B flat Trio followed in 1836.

On the other hand, the records of his negotiations in 1830 with Ferdinand Schubert in connection with the unpublished works of Schubert do not bear out this possibility. If op. 99 had been the property of another firm at that time, it would have been included in the list of opus numbers not to be regarded as Diabelli's property, as op. 100, for instance, is specified. Eight or nine years elapsed between Schubert's disposal of the B flat Trio to a publisher and its actual publication. Why, in the face of everything to the contrary, there should have been this delay can be given no conclusive answer.

Another delayed publication is op. 160, the set of variations on the song 'Trock'ne Blumen' from the song-cycle *Die schöne Müllerin*. Schubert composed the variations in January 1824 for flute and pianoforte. This, for him, unusual combination was the result of his friendship with the flautist Ferdinand Bogner, for whom the variations were written. Nothing whatever is known about the work from contemporary documents; it was not recorded in Ferdinand Schubert's lists, and the manuscript was evidently not sold by him to Diabelli. Yet it was this man who eventually published the work as op. 160 in April 1850. Until recently there seemed to be no mystery here; one could only assume either that Diabelli had acquired the manuscript from a private source, possibly from the descendants of Bogner, or that it had been among the mass of manuscripts sold by Ferdinand to Diabelli, but unrecorded by him (this had happened with a few other works). But there is an entry in the Hofmeister-Whistling *Handbuch* for 1824 that seems to have escaped notice. It runs as follows:

Schubert (F). Grandes Variations sur un Thème original p. Pfte. et Flûte concertantes. Op. 28. Wien, Sauer & Leidesdorf. 1. Thl.

Obviously the publication of these variations was considered almost immediately after their composition, but for some reason, which can be examined now, the project was shelved. If it be objected that the variations in the above advertisement are said to be on a 'Thème original', instead of, more specifically, on the Müllerlieder theme, the objection can be met by two facts. The first is that the songs of the *Schöne Müllerin* cycle were being published in instalments during 1824, and the theme of 'Trock'ne Blumen', being one of the last, would not be known by the public either as a melody or even as a name; the second is that when the variations were published, in 1850, although by that time the song was extremely well known, they were still designated by the same title — they appeared as 'Introduction et variations sur un thème original pour Piano et Flûte'.

The probable reason for the scheme falling through is of some general interest in casting light on Schubert's dealings with his publishers — and on the publishers themselves — during the 1820's. Early in 1823 he quarrelled with the firm of Cappi & Diabelli, who, up to that year, had been exclusively his publishers. He suspected Diabelli of dishonesty in his dealings with him, particularly over the handling of op. 18, a collection of waltzes and écossaises. Matters came to a head in April 1823 when Schubert withdrew certain of his manuscripts from Diabelli and broke off all connections with the firm. Meanwhile, he had opened negotiations with the firm of Sauer & Leidesdorf, and for the next few years they were his publishers. The change was not for the better. The muddle and mishandling of the publication of his works date from this unfortunate step. It would be irrelevant to examine here all the strange sequences in the order of Schubert's opus numbers, all the misapplications of already allocated opus numbers and so on from now until his death. It is well known in the world of music that Schubert's opus numbers are no guide at all to the sequence of composition, but the reservation is usually made that up to op. 100, published just at the time of his death, the order is fairly trustworthy — the haphazard sequence of post-humous opus numbers is the field that must be distrusted; but it is equally true of the works published during his lifetime. Sauer & Liedesdorf, for example, commenced their association with Schubert by publishing his op. 20 in April 1823; six months later they published op. 24, and clearly by then the confusion over his manuscripts reached some sort of climax, for the next work to be published, the Pianoforte Duet Sonata in B flat, D. 617, was given the opus number 30 — to be on the safe side, as it were, and to give the firm a breathing-space to sort out the intermediate numbers. That this was a desperate move is proved when one considers that Schubert's op. 30 was thus published before his op. 29 — the String Quartet in A minor — was even composed! This is by no means exceptional in the story of muddle, but sufficient has been said to cover our particular investigation; to conclude the story, however, it might be mentioned that Sauer & Leidesdorf made another similar leap two years later, another move to cut a Gordian knot of confusion, by naming the Six Grandes Marches op. 40, with the result that the composer's op. 31 appeared three months after this and his op. 32 never appeared at all.[1] Evidently, in 1824, the scheme to publish the 'Trock'ne Blumen' Variations as op. 28 was abandoned, and instead the male-voice part-song 'Der Gondelfahrer', D. 809, was substituted. Schubert's manuscript of the variations passed from the possession of Leidesdorf in 1835, when Diabelli bought up the firm, and publication of the work was thus held up for twenty-six years. The variations were actually the last of Schubert's works to be published by Diabelli himself; in the following year he retired and the business was taken over by his partner C. A. Spina.

In January 1826 Schubert set the verses 'Mondenschein' by his friend Schober to music — for male-voice quintet (T.T.B.B.B.). The part-song was first performed in public two years later, 3 January 1828, at a concert given by the Gesellschaft der Musikfreunde. On that occasion the quintet was accompanied at the piano by Frau Schmiedel, wife of the conductor of the concert. A month later, in his letter to B. Schott's Sons of 21 February, quoted already in this essay, he offered the quintet, among other works, to the publisher. The firm accepted most of his offered works, eight in all, and invited him to send them. The intervention of his concert, and the fact that he was at the same time negotiating with Probst of Leipzig, distracted Schubert from his business with Schott's; after further letters he eventually sent them only two works, four impromptus (Nos. 5–8) and 'Mondenschein'. Six months elapsed with no reply from the firm, until at length Schubert wrote again, on 2 October 1828; he concluded his letter with the words: 'The opus number for the impromptus is 101, and that for the quintet 102.' The firm's reply, sent a month after that, dashed his hopes for the publication of the piano pieces,

[1] The number 32 was eventually used by Diabelli for a republication of 'Die Forelle' in 1828.

s

which they considered 'too difficult for trifles'; the manuscript was sent back. They accepted the part-song, but reduced Schubert's suggested fee for it from 60 to 30 florins. In a postscript they added: 'In order to save any delay we enclose a draft for 30 florins .... If you do not accept our proposal, return the draft to us.'

What was Schubert's reply to this? It has not been preserved, and the subsequent events are puzzling. Before considering a possible course of events, it is necessary to go to the end of the story and examine the publication of 'Mondenschein'. The first edition came from the firm of Diabelli early in 1829; the quintet was then published with pianoforte accompaniment and called op. 102. Nearly three years later it was published by Schott's, also as op. 102, in two versions; these were specified as 'with or without accompaniment for the pianoforte'. Schott's advertised the publication (as 'Der Mondenschein') in their journal, *Cäcilia*, of January 1832. The genuineness of Diabelli's pianoforte accompaniment has been doubted, and it is revealing to read the succession of commentary upon this question.

1874. Nottebohm: 'The pianoforte accompaniment has apparently been added by the publisher.'

1891. *Revisionsbericht* to the Leipzig *Gesamtausgabe*: 'The pianoforte accompaniment is a reduction of the voice-parts and surely does not derive from Schubert.'

1961. Deutsch: '. . . with a spurious PF. accompaniment *ad lib*'.

When one considers that in the first performance of the work (then unpublished, and so performed from manuscript copies deriving from Schubert himself) it was accompanied at the piano, one wonders whether such judgements are not a little hasty. Whether Schott's pianoforte part was identical with Diabelli's there is no means of knowing: in the archives of the present firm of Schott's there are no longer any copies extant of their 1831–2 publication of op. 102, nor have they any longer Schubert's manuscript or copy of the pianoforte part, which they once claimed to possess.[1]

[1] At the International Congress for Schubert Research, held in Vienna during November 1928, Georg Kinsky spoke on Schubert manuscripts in

The questions that arise are these: if Schott's still possessed Schubert's manuscript of 'Mondenschein' at the time of his death (1) how did Diabelli acquire a manuscript for his publication of a few months later, and (2) how did he know the opus number, which was supplied by Schubert in a private letter to Schott's, the contents of which were not made public until 1894? The answers to such questions seem obvious, namely, that Schubert demanded his manuscript back from Schott's and refused the trifling fee offered for it.

If this is the case, a possible course of events is as follows. On receipt of Schott's letter of 30 October he wrote asking for the return of his manuscript. The firm's dispatch of it may have been delayed, so that it reached Vienna after his death. If they ever possessed his autograph of a piano part this was not returned at the same time, although personally I doubt its existence as a separate manuscript — an extremely unlikely state of affairs. After its arrival in Vienna the quintet was sold to Diabelli, either by Schubert himself, or, if the manuscript arrived after his death, by Ferdinand Schubert. A few months later it was published.

If this summary be false, how can we account otherwise for the publication of the work by Diabelli, and not, as would certainly have been the case, by Schott's? For when the Mainz firm did, at length, publish 'Mondenschein', their edition was evidently inspired by Diabelli's of nearly three years earlier. If their business had been satisfactorily concluded with Schubert, by his acceptance of their draft for thirty florins, the part-song would have been published at least early in 1829. Only one small factor is embedded in this sequence of events that prevents my wholly accepting the above hypothesis as a true picture of events: it occurs in the catalogue, twice referred to already, printed in the pages of the fifth edition of 'Die Rose'; this, as we have seen, dates from the summer of 1831. The entry for op. 102 is given in detail:

private possession in Germany. In connection with 'Mondenschein' he said: 'Whether besides the still unpublished pianoforte part to the male-voice quintet "Mondenschein" of January 1826, the firm of B. Schott's Sons, in Mainz, possess any other Schubert manuscripts is unknown to me, since questions directed there have remained unanswered.' (*Report*, Augsburg, 1929, p. 163.)

'Mondenschein von Schober ("Des Mondes Zauberblume lacht").
Quintett für 5 Singstimen mit Begl. des Pianofortes' — but no
price is given. Now, as we have seen in the case of the B flat Trio,
when no price is quoted in this catalogue, it is because the publication is projected, but not yet carried through. If we could deduce
from this fact that in the summer of 1831 'Mondenschein' was still
unpublished, and that Schott's edition at the end of 1831 was
really the first edition, all the difficulties would vanish. But there
can be no doubt about the fact that even if 'Mondenschein' had
not actually been put on sale by Diabelli in the music shops of
Vienna — one interpretation of 'publication' — nevertheless he
had had the music engraved in the early months of 1829: his
'Publisher's Number' on the copy is 3181, and this unquestionably
belongs to that period.

No light is cast on the problem by existing manuscripts. The
alleged independent piano part, said to be once in the possession
of Schott's, is no longer there. The unaccompanied version,
preserved in the National Library, is written on pages that also
bear an unpublished trifle — a 'Canon a sei'; this manuscript is
evidently a first sketch of 'Mondenschein' and Schubert would
never have submitted such a manuscript, bearing other material,
to a publisher, particularly to a publisher in another country. The
fair copy he sent to Schott's, whether used by them, or returned
and used by Diabelli, is lost. And so one can only review the
whole problem and seek the solution in vain.

The final problem is concerned with an edifice of cataloguery
built upon what is probably a nonexistent work! It is included
here only to remove any doubts that might be raised in a reader's
mind if he encounters a reference to a 'Sonata in E flat minor for
Pianoforte Duet' by Schubert. The earliest reference to the work
occurs in the biographical essays on Schubert written by his
brother Ferdinand and published in Schumann's *Neue Zeitschrift
für Musik* of March–April 1839. In the works for the year 1828
Ferdinand includes 'A PF. Sonata in E flat minor for 4 hands (D)'.
The (D) indicates that the manuscript of the work was in the
hands of Diabelli, pending publication. Two years later, on 12

August 1841, Ferdinand sent a revised version of his biography to Anton Schindler; this version contained a corrected and amplified catalogue of Schubert's compositions, for the lists in the *Neue Zeitschrift* contained several misprints and errors. Ferdinand's revised notes are unfortunately lost, but Schindler used them as a basis for his 'Reminiscences of Franz Schubert', published in a Cologne newspaper during March 1857.[1] These reminiscences close with a very full list of the works of Schubert, clearly based upon Ferdinand's revised list and with many of the mistakes corrected. Schindler had also, in 1831, occupied himself with the Schubert manuscripts at Diabelli's in Vienna and incorporated some of his own observations in his Cologne articles. He gave, under the section devoted to the compositions of 1828, a 'Sonata in E flat minor' (but not, be it noted, for pianoforte duet).

Kreissle's biography of Schubert appeared in 1865; in the supplement he gave, among the list of unpublished piano duets, 'Sonata in E flat minor', the manuscript alleged (*angeblich*) to be with Diabelli (p. 613). He clearly derived this information from Ferdinand Schubert's essays and not from Schindler's list, since he gave the work as written for pianoforte duet. In Nottebohm's *Thematic Catalogue* of 1874, under 'Unpublished Compositions for Pianoforte Duet', p. 257, is the entry 'Sonata in E flat minor, composed 1828'. Finally, in 1876, Wurzbach, in his famous article on Schubert for the *Biographisches Lexikon des Kaisertum Oesterreich*, had a similar notification: 'Sonata in E flat minor. The autograph in the possession of Diabelli.'

Did the work ever exist, or was it due to an initial misunderstanding of Ferdinand's? The key is, for Schubert, extremely unusual, but there does happen to be a work for pianoforte solo in E flat minor, unquestionably composed in 1828 — in May 1828, to be exact: it is the first of the 'Drei Klavierstücke', D. 946. Deutsch, in his *Documentary Biography*, p. 924, surmises that Ferdinand's 'Sonata in E flat minor for 4 hands' is, in fact, this set of three pianoforte pieces, and repeats the explanation in his *Memoirs*, p. 323, to account for Schindler's similar entry in his

---

[1] 'Erinnerungen an Franz Schubert'. *Niederrheinische Musikzeitung*, March 1857.

1857 list. It is a very plausible explanation, and the fact that Schindler signified that the sonata was for pianoforte solo also suggests that Ferdinand, in the meantime, had corrected his original mistake.

But, as we have seen before, the problems exist because all these plausible explanations founder on one irreconcilable fact. In this case the above explanation fails to convince when we examine the background of the publication of the 'Drei Klavierstücke'. They were edited by Brahms (anonymously) and published by the firm of J. Rieter-Biedermann of Winterthur and Leipzig in February 1868. Brahms, in fact, was instrumental in getting them published, having persuaded Eduard Schneider, Schubert's nephew, to send the manuscripts to the Winterthur firm, and agreeing to edit them (see Brahms's letters to J. Rieter-Biedermann of 2 August and 10 November 1867). The manuscript of the three pianoforte pieces had evidently remained with Ferdinand, and was bequeathed by him, together with all other unpublished Schubert manuscripts in his possession, to his nephew Eduard; Ferdinand had died on 26 February 1859. Hence Diabelli had never owned the manuscript of the pianoforte pieces, and they cannot therefore be equated with the mysterious 'Sonata in E flat minor' — whether it was for pianoforte solo or duet.

The only other possible explanation — a very slight and unconvincing one — is that Ferdinand was confusing the two manuscripts of the Fugue in E minor for Pianoforte Duet, composed in June 1828; one of these is headed 'Vierstimmige Fuge' by the composer, the other, a first draft, contains no heading at all.[1] Diabelli certainly had the first, and possibly the second, of these two manuscripts. One small contributory factor in support of this tentative suggestion is found in yet another list of Schubert's works, the earliest of any discussed here. It is from the pen of Bauernfeld, published in June 1829. His list of works for 1828 contains the item 'Fugue in E flat minor for organ or pianoforte four hands'.

[1] The keys E flat minor and E minor could be more easily confused in German; they are *es moll* and *e moll* respectively.

THE POSTHUMOUS PUBLICATION
OF THE SONGS

Estimations of the number of songs composed by Schubert have been made at various times since his death. As early as December 1828 two obituary-notices hazard a guess at the number still unpublished: in one case a hundred, in the other two hundred. Leopold von Sonnleithner, Schubert's friend and patron, published a biographical sketch of the composer in February 1829; when he came to discuss his compositions he wrote these words: 'Some two hundred of his songs are already known in print, and almost as many again yet remain in manuscript.' Two years later Anton Schindler examined the many unpublished Schubert manuscripts with the publisher Diabelli and estimated that there were 570 songs and part-songs of all descriptions. The estimation closest to the truth is due to the enthusiasm of Karl Pinterics, the secretary of Prince Josef Pálffy of Vienna; he was a great music-lover and a good friend of Schubert's. Pinterics made copies of every Schubert song he came across; his catalogue gives the titles of 505 songs.

The fact that in all cases the number estimated is well below the true total is very understandable. Only in the last twenty years has it been possible to complete details of all the surviving song-manuscripts and only since O. E. Deutsch gathered the varied information together and tabulated it in his *Thematic Catalogue* has it been possible to assess the actual number of songs.

There is another factor, too, which might tend to produce differing totals — even today, when the facts are fully available. Schubert was the least selfconscious of composers, in the sense that he never took himself and his status so seriously as to consider his work worthy of cataloguing or recording. His shyness extended to this department of his life also, as we can see in his letters. The rare references in these documents to his compositions are typically modest or deprecatory, almost offhand, as if he had no wish to vaunt his achievements or to bore his friends. It is true that he had the excellent habit — excellent, that is to say, in the view of his bibliographers! — of dating his manuscripts, sometimes very precisely. But he made little effort to keep his song-manuscripts in order, to record them in notebooks, or to separate and discard the sketched song from the finished version, the rejected variant from the final one, with which, presumably, he was satisfied. What then constitutes a Schubert song? Which of the variants are to be classed as preliminary sketches only, and which as independent songs?

In offering the following totals the terms 'version' and 'variant' have been carefully distinguished as having two different and independent meanings. When Schubert returned at a later date to any particular poem and composed an entirely fresh setting of it, for example, Goethe's 'Am Flusse', the two settings are here considered versions; if he made alterations in an existing song, and the altered composition was written on a separate, fully executed manuscript, it is here considered a variant. There is, of course, no problem where versions are concerned; they are individual songs. But when should a variant be considered as a separate song? It has been decided to count any variant as a separate song, if it has been published as such; in nearly every case the publication of a variant has been deliberate; it has been deemed worthy of independent printing. Thus there are five variants of 'Die Forelle', each one published independently of the others. No doubt one of these five was held by Schubert to be the final, authoritative one, but which one we do not know. 'Die Forelle' is thus counted as five songs. Other songs with numerous variants, each published separately, are 'Geistes-Gruss' (five variants), 'Erlkönig' (four variants) and 'An Emma' (three variants). Versions are distinguished by roman figures, variants by small letters. Thus 'Am Flusse' (II) means Schubert's second setting of the Goethe poem, an entirely different song from 'Am Flusse' (I); but 'Erlkönig' (c) refers to the third variant of the only setting that Schubert made of this poem.

Using these facts as conditional, the number of songs composed by Schubert is 708. The following tabulation gives the manner of their publication.

(a)	Published in his lifetime - - - - -	172[1]
(b)	Published between his death and the appearance of the *Gesamtausgabe*, 1894–7 - - - - -	305
(c)	Published for the first time in the *Gesamtausgabe* -	200
(d)	Published since the *Gesamtausgabe* - - - -	12
(e)	Unpublished (mostly fragments) - - - -	14
(f)	Known to be lost - - - - - -	5
	TOTAL - -	708

No final claim can be made for these figures; they would have to be modified if fresh information came to light. For instance, Schubert wrote out a selection of his songs for a friend, Therese Grob; three of them are unpublished and are included in the fourteen of the table above. Other songs in this collection, however, differ from their published variants.[2] If they differ sufficiently to justify considering them as separate songs, the grand total above would be increased.

For two years after his death various firms in Vienna continued to publish his songs under opus numbers. In a few cases we know for certain that the collection of songs and its opus number had been devised by Schubert, i.e., op. 105, op. 89, Part II (the last twelve songs of *Winterreise*), op. 108 (which Schubert had intended to be his op. 93), op. 98, and op. 109. But in the other cases the song-manuscripts had been sold by Ferdinand Schubert to the publishers, who then allotted the opus numbers. One collection was published by a non-Viennese firm, H. A. Probst,

[1] The total given by Deutsch in the *Documentary Biography*, 187, includes fifteen songs that were, strictly speaking, published posthumously. They are the twelve songs of *Winterreise*, Part II (published December 1828), and the three songs of op. 108 (published January 1829).

[2] The collection is usually known, misleadingly, as the 'Therese Grob Album'. It is in private possession, and generally inaccessible, but all the manuscripts have been photographed.

Leipzig, only three weeks after Schubert's death. It consisted of four songs, 'Im Frühling', 'Der blinde Knabe', 'Trost im Liede', and 'Wandrers Nachtlied' (II), all of which had appeared previously as supplements to the *Wiener Zeitschrift für Kunst, Literatur, Theater und Mode* on various occasions during Schubert's lifetime. There appears to be no solid reason to doubt that Schubert himself was responsible for the publication; he was in close touch with Probst in the months just prior to his death, since that firm was engraving the Pianoforte Trio in E flat major for publication as op. 100. If the alternative view is taken, that the transaction of the Leipzig publisher was a shady one, a hurried attempt to profit by the death of a composer who was, thereby, no longer able to protest, a number of difficulties arise. The news of Schubert's death did not reach the larger German towns until at least the end of November; Probst could not possibly have obtained and engraved these four supplements in the space of little over a week. On what principle did he select the songs from the many that had appeared as supplements, and how was he to know that all four were available for republication?

A few months after Probst had published the four songs, that is on 16 March 1829, Diabelli also published the second of them, 'Der blinde Knabe', in a corrupt form, as no. 242 of his collection *Philomele*. He then called it op. 101. In the *Thematic Catalogue*, under the song 'Der blinde Knabe', D. 833, Deutsch has this comment: 'The first edition was republished by H. A. Probst, Leipzig, on 12 December 1828, as no. 2 of a spurious op. 101 . . . .' This is misleading. Probst called his collection simply '*Vier Lieder*' and gave it no opus number at all. The fact that 'Der blinde Knabe' was later called op. 101 by Diabelli meant that, by a process of association, the set of four songs has been called op. 101 *en bloc*; but Probst is not responsible for the numbering.[1]

The broad outlines of the publication of Schubert's songs in the nineteenth century are simple. The three or four years after his

[1] Diabelli's choice of '101' for 'Der blinde Knabe' might be better understood in view of the discussion of 'Mondenschein' in the previous essay: see p. 263.

death saw the publication of sixty-seven songs in Vienna from the firms of Leidesdorf, Czerny, Pennauer, Haslinger, Th. Weigl, or Diabelli. The opus numbers reached 131. Between 1830 and 1851 another 126 songs were published in Diabelli's great venture of a serial publication, which will be considered later in detail, usually called the *Nachlass*. For another twenty years after that a few song-collections appeared, at first under renewed opus numbers, in Vienna, up to the last of them, op. 173, and others in Berlin.

At some period shortly after 1870 a quantity of the unpublished songs, even then of the order of three hundred, were disposed of by the firm of Scheibler (successors to Diabelli) to a former manager of the firm, J. P. Gotthard, who was setting up independently in Vienna as a music-publisher. Two substantial collections drawn from the 300 or so songs were published during the next fifteen years; the first was a series of forty songs from Gotthard in 1872, the second was a series of twenty songs, edited by Max Friedlaender, from the firm of Peters, Leipzig, in 1885. A final eighteen songs appeared for the first time in the seventh volume of Peters's edition of the Schubert songs, called a *Schubert Album*, also edited by Friedlaender, which appeared in 1887.

In that very year Eusebius Mandyczewski was appointed archivist of the Gesellschaft der Musikfreunde. The Leipzig firm of Breitkopf & Härtel, having decided to start work on their *Gesamtausgabe* of Schubert's compositions, included him on the editorial board. Under his capable editorship the song-volumes assumed a masterly form, and in them the remaining two hundred unpublished Schubert songs were included; they appeared in the years 1894–7.

All of these large and easily classified collections were separated by and interspersed with numerous small collections and even the issues of single songs as supplements to periodicals or isolated ventures by more obscure publishers. The detailed setting out of each period, given below, contains little that is new, or that cannot be found somewhere in the pages either of Nottebohm's or Deutsch's thematic catalogues; but the complete facts have never

yet been concisely set out, and here and there an error is corrected
or a new fact incorporated. This is particularly the case in the
section devoted to Diabelli's *Nachlass* series; the information
given there has been based on a personal examination of the
whole series of songs and on reference to advertisements in
contemporary journals marking the first publication of each
number. Square brackets enclosing the title of a piece, indicate
that the item had been previously published, or that it is not a solo
song.

SECTION I

21 NOVEMBER 1828–26 JUNE 1832

21 November 1828

op. 105. *Widerspruch* (solo setting). *Wiegenlied* ('Wie sich die
Äuglein'). *Am Fenster. Sehnsucht* ('Die Scheibe friert').
Published by Czerny.

12 December 1828

[*Im Frühling. Der blinde Knabe* (b). *Trost im Liede. Wandrers
Nachtlied* (II).] Published by Probst (Leipzig), and known
later as op. 101.

30 December 1828

op. 89, part II. Nos. 13–24 of *Winterreise.* Published by Haslinger.

28 January 1829

op. 108. *Über Wildemann. Todesmusik.* [*Die Erscheinung.*] Schubert
intended this to be op. 93, but 93 had already been used.
Published by Leidesdorf.

31 January 1829

op. 110. *Der Kampf.*

op. 111. *An die Freude. Lebensmelodien. Die vier Weltalter.* Published
by Czerny.

13 April 1829

op. 116. *Die Erwartung.* Published by Leidesdorf.

Easter 1829

op. posth. *Schwanengesang:* fourteen songs. Published by Haslinger.

16 June 1829

op. 115. *Das Lied im Grünen. Wonne der Wehmuth. Sprache der Liebe.* Published by Leidesdorf.

19 June 1829

op. 117. *Der Sänger* (a).
op. 118. *Geist der Liebe. Der Abend* ('Der Abend blüht'). *Tischlied. Lob des Tokays. An die Sonne* ('Sinke, liebe Sonne'). *Die Spinnerin.* Published by Czerny.

23 June 1829

Supplement to the *Wiener Zeitschrift: Beim Winde.*

10 July 1829

op. 98. *An die Nachtigall* ('Er liegt und schläft'). *Wiegenlied* ('Schlafe, schlafe'). *Iphigenia.*
op. 109. *Am Bach im Frühling. Genügsamkeit. An eine Quelle.* Published by Diabelli.

27 October 1829

op. 119. *Auf dem Strome.* Published by Leidesdorf.

30 October 1829

op. 124. *Delphine. Florio.* Published by Pennauer.

5 January 1830

op. 126. *Ballade* ('Ein Fräulein schaut'). Published by Czerny.

January 1830

Supplement to the almanac *Gemeinnütziger und erheiternder Hauskalendaer für den österreichischen Kaiserstaat: Der Wallensteiner Lanzknecht beim Trunk.*

1 June 1830

op. 129. *Der Hirt auf dem Felsen.* Published by Haslinger.

12 July 1830

op. 130. *Das Echo.* Published by Th. Weigl.

25 September 1830

Supplement to the *Wiener Zeitschrift: Fülle der Liebe.*

9 November 1830

op. 131. *Der Mondabend*. [*Trinklied* (part-song).] *Klaglied*. Published by Czerny.

26 November 1830

op. 123. *Viola*. Published by Pennauer.

5 January 1832

Supplement to the *Wiener allgemeiner musikalischer Anzeiger: Der Kreuzzug*.

26 June 1832

Supplement to the *Wiener Zeitschrift: Die Liebende schreibt*.

In July 1830 Diabelli initiated his famous series of *Lieferungen* ('Parts') of an anthology of Schubert songs, and the periodical appearances of the parts extended over the next twenty years. In all, fifty parts were issued. It is a notable achievement of publication, and he could not have foreseen in the early days that public demand for the songs would have kept the series alive for so long. A publishing scheme such as this usually starts with a bang and ends with a whimper, but in this case the success of the series increased with the passing years until, towards the end, the final parts were being published simultaneously in Vienna and Paris; in the French capital the firm of Simon Richault was responsible for the publication.

The series was advertised in various periodicals in the summer of 1830 under Diabelli's name as *Franz Schuberts nachgelassene musikalischen Dichtungen für Gesang und Pianoforte: mit einer sehr schönen Titel-Vignette* ('Franz Schubert's posthumous musical poems for song and pianoforte: with a very beautiful title-vignette'). The following information was added: 'Since the above-mentioned publisher has acquired the complete posthumous works of Franz Schubert as his exclusive property, there will appear from now on, at fortnightly intervals, "Parts" containing his most splendid and superb songs, in a uniform and faultless "Edition de Luxe".' The opening words of this announcement refer to Diabelli's purchase, early in 1830, of a large number of manuscripts from Ferdinand Schubert, though these were far from being the   complete posthumous works. The fortnightly intervals, though maintained at the very start, was an over-optimistic promise. The long title was abbreviated by Diabelli himself, during the course of the series, to *Nachlass*, and this short title soon began to appear on the title-pages of the parts.

It is worth while looking into Diabelli's editing of the songs. One vexed question concerns the genuineness or otherwise of some of the preludes. Subsequent editors have too readily assumed that many of these preludes are spurious, added by Diabelli to Schubert's manuscripts prior to publication. It would be a forgivable interference, for unless a singer has a sense of absolute pitch — and few have — a song must *have* a prelude, if it be only a single note on the piano giving the key or the first note of the melody. Schubert was well aware of this, for all the songs of his maturity commence with a piano introduction. Now one manuscript of a Schubert song survives, on which Diabelli has jotted down a short prelude; it is the song 'An eine Quelle' of February 1817, and it was published with the spurious prelude in op. 109. The publisher based his prelude on Schubert's postlude, and made a very good job of it (Diabelli was a composer, of course). But the manuscript gives positive proof that he was not above making such additions. For many of the songs in the *Nachlass*, Schubert's manuscripts are still extant; in quite a number of cases the prelude printed in the *Nachlass* is not present in Schubert's manuscript. But before writing off these few introductory bars as spurious, the following consideration must be borne in mind: the manuscript in question was not necessarily Diabelli's source. Schubert frequently made several copies of his songs, and in them, particularly in the later ones, he sometimes added a prelude; two examples that occur to mind can be found in the various manuscripts surviving of 'Die Forelle' and 'In's stille Land'. The manuscript used for any particular song in the *Nachlass* may not be the one now preserved.

Using the same argument, we could largely clear Diabelli from the charge that he transposed some of the songs when preparing them for publication. There are plenty of examples to be found in the song-manuscripts where Schubert himself transposed his songs, either to accommodate a particular singer, or perhaps to modify an extravagant demand on the vocal range. If, to take an example, the three songs of *Lieferung 40* are all in different keys from those in Schubert's manuscript, it may be because Schubert had prepared a transposed version of the three songs and that that particular manuscript used by Diabelli is now lost. The second of these three songs is 'Berthas Lied in der Nacht', and this song, in the preserved copy, was composed in E flat minor; it could be argued that the printed version, which is in D minor, was an interference of Diabelli's, made with the pianist in mind. But against that we have the fact that the third song, 'An die Freunde', was composed in A minor, and in the *Nachlass* this is transposed to F minor — hardly facilitating matters for the pianist.

These considerations do not, of course, imply that Diabelli was entirely innocent where the matter of preludes to the songs and transposition of keys is concerned. They do suggest that we have no right automatically to assume that these interferences, whenever they seem to occur, are the publisher's, and consequently to dub the *Nachlass* version 'corrupt'.

Two glaring examples of unquestionable interference with Schubert's intentions are to be found in the first and third *Lieferungen*. The songs 'Die Nacht' and 'Lodas Gespenst' were each supplied with a rousing finale based on a male-voice chorus by Schubert; the first with a conclusion drawn from 'Jagdlied', D. 521, the second with one drawn from 'Punschlied', D. 277. The alteration of 'Lodas Gespenst' was due to Leopold von Sonnleithner, who frankly confessed his adaptation in a letter to the editor of the *Allgemeine musikalische Zeitung*, published on 30 January 1867; from his remarks, which may be read on p. 441 of Deutsch's *Memoirs*, it is pretty clear that he was also responsible for the addition to 'Die Nacht' as well. Where to lay the responsibility for these corruptions, on Diabelli or Sonnleithner, is debatable.

In other cases where the editorship of Diabelli has been criticized, we can clear him completely. He was not responsible for adding the second and third stanzas, written by Friedrich Reil, to the first edition of 'Hark! Hark! the Lark!'; Shakespeare's single verse is all that appears in the song (*Lieferung 7*). The addition of the words 'nach einem Ball' to the title of 'Der Morgenkuss', D. 264, was not made in the *Nachlass*, where the title appears as in Schubert's manuscript. The prelude to 'Augenlied' was not added by Diabelli; it appears on two completely independent copies of the song, made from Schubert's lost autograph. Nor did Diabelli supply a spurious ending to the song usually known as 'Gretchens Bitte' ('Ach, neige'); he gave Schubert's fragmentary song as far as the autograph extends, merely closing the work with a single chord of C major implied in the song.

Glancing through the fifty parts of the *Nachlass*, it is clear that some attempt was made to order the selection; a few of the *Lieferungen* do suggest a haphazard throwing together of a batch of songs, but most of them were thoughtfully assembled. Diabelli was a businessman, and his *Nachlass* venture was not motivated entirely by a pious devotion to Schubert's memory: he wanted to attract the public. Nevertheless, the arrangement of the songs is, in general, an artistic one, and was an invaluable and powerful factor in spreading Schubert's posthumous fame.

The first five parts are given the general title *Ossians Gesänge* and include all of Schubert's completed solo settings of poems by the legendary Ossian. It made an auspicious start to the series, for these specimens of pseudo-Gaelic balladry (actually by the poet James Macpherson) were immensely popular at the time, and Schubert's evocation of the Celtic twilight could hardly have been bettered. The five parts were widely reviewed in the various music journals of Europe, most notably by Ludwig Rellstab in the Berlin paper *Iris*. The 'very beautiful title-vignette' of the advertisement is found on these *Ossians Gesänge* parts; it shows a blind harper with his instrument, a young girl by his side, both seated, with a stormy sky and wild landscape as a background.

Six of Schubert's extended songs, ballads such as 'Einsamkeit' or 'Der Taucher', each has a 'part' to itself. In eight cases there is a small anthology of songs made from poems by the same author: Mayrhofer (twice), Schulze, Schlechta, Leitner, Matthisson, Goethe, and '5 Odes' by Klopstock. *Lieferung 21* contains two

T

flower-songs and *Lieferung 10*, the most carefully designed of all, is entitled *Acht geistliche Lieder* ('Eight Spiritual Songs') and was heralded by a specially written preface from the pen of Anton Schindler; it contained the celebrated 'Litanei auf das Fest aller Seelen'.

One problem raised by the *Nachlass* is likely to remain unsolved, unless Schubert's own manuscript is discovered. The first edition of the song 'Freiwilliges Versinken', D. 700, appeared in *Lieferung 11*. The first four syllables of the opening line 'Wohin, O Helios?' are given there to the notes F sharp, G, G, A. In the second edition of this *Lieferung* the notes were altered to A, B natural, D, C sharp. Why was the alteration made? The question has been side-stepped by editors. In the *Gesamtausgabe* Mandyczewski simply restored the notes of the first edition without comment. The alteration is too radical, on the one hand, to be a mere correction of a previous misprint, and too tentative, on the other hand, to make very much difference. It looks at first as if Diabelli might be attempting to correct consecutive octaves in the first pair of notes, were it not that they are introduced by the second pair! Is there a possibility that, in the meantime, he had encountered another manuscript of Schubert's, in which the composer himself had made the alteration?

The details of the *Nachlass* that follow continue the list of posthumous publications of the songs. Some of the songs in the *Nachlass* had already been published, and some of the items are part-songs of various kinds. As before, these titles are enclosed in square brackets.

SECTION 2

THE *Nachlass*: JULY 1830–AUGUST 1851

July–September 1830. The *Ossians Gesänge*: five parts.

1. *Die Nacht.*
2. *Cronnan. Kolmas Klage.*
3. *Lodas Gespenst.*
4. *Shulric und Vinvela. Ossians Lied nach dem Falle Nathos'* (b). *Das Mädchen von Inistore.*

5. *Der Tod Oscars.*
6. *Elysium.*

1831

7. *Des Sängers Habe. Hippolits Lied. Abendröthe. Ständchen* ('Hark! Hark! the Lark!').
8. *Die Bürgschaft.*
9. *Der zürnende Barde. Am See* (Bruchmann). *Abendbilder.*
10. *Acht geistliche Lieder:*
    Dem Unendlichen (b). *Die Gestirne. Das Marienbild. Vom mitleiden Maria. Litanei auf dem Festen aller Seelen. Pax vobiscum. Gebet während der Schlacht. Himmelsfunken.*
11. *Orest auf Tauris. Der entsühnte Orest. Philoktet. Freiwilliges Versinken.*
12. *Der Taucher.*

1832

13. *An mein Herz. Der liebliche Stern.*
14. *Grenzen der Menschheit. Fragment aus dem Aeschylus* (b).
15. *Widerschein* (b). *Liebeslauschen. Todtengräber-Weise.*
16. *Waldesnacht.*
17. *Lebensmuth. Der Vater mit dem Kind. [An den Tod.]* Verklärung.
18. *Pilgerweise. An den Mond in einer Herbstnacht. Fahrt zum Hades.*

June 1833

19. *Lied der Orpheus* (b). *Ritter Toggenburg.*
20. *Im Abendrot. Scene aus Faust* (b). *Mignons Gesang* ('Kennst du das Land?').
21. *Der Blumenbrief. Vergissmeinnicht.*
22. *Der Sieg. Atys. [Beim Winde.] Abendstern.*

September 1833

23. *Schwestergruss. Liedesend* (b).
24. *Schiffers Scheidelied. Todtengräbers Heimweh.*

Easter 1834

25. *[Fülle der Liebe.] [Im Frühling.] Trost in Thränen.*

Easter 1835

26. *Der Winterabend.*

Easter 1836

27. [*Der Wallensteiner Lanzknecht beim Trunk.*] [*Der Kreuzzug.*] *Des Fischers Liebesglück.*

Easter 1837

28. *Hermann und Thusnelda. Selma und Selmar* (b). *Das Rosenband. Edone. Die frühen Gräber.*

June 1838

29. *Stimme der Liebe* ('Meine Selinde'). *Die Mutter Erde. Gretchens Bitte. Abschied in das Stammbuch eines Freundes.*

Easter 1839

30. *Tiefes Lied. Clärchens Lied. Grablied für die Mutter.*

May 1840

31. *Die Betende. Der Geister Tanz* (III). *An Laura.*
32. *Der Einsame* (now known as *Einsamkeit*) ('Gib mir die Fülle der Einsamkeit').

Early 1842

33. *Der Schiffer. Die gefangenen Sänger.*
34. *Auflösung. Blondel zu Marien.*
35. *Die erste Liebe. Lied eines Kriegers.*
36. *Der Jüngling an der Quelle. Lambertine. Ihr Grab.*

Late 1842

37. *Heliopolis II* ('Fels auf Felsen'). *Sehnsucht* ('Was zieht mir das Herz so?').

Easter 1844

38. *Die Einsiedelei* (I). *Lebenslied. Versunken.*
39. *Als ich sie erröten sah. Das war ich. In's stille Land* (a).
40. *Das Mädchen. Berthas Lied in der Nacht. An die Freunde.*

1848

41. [*Licht und Liebe* (duet).][1] [*Das grosse Hallelujah* (terzett).]
42. *Die Götter Griechenlands* (b). *Das Finden. Cora an die Sonne. Grablied. Adelaide.*

---

[1] The first edition of 41 contained as no. 1 the song 'Lied eines Kriegers', D. 822, already published as *Nachlass*, 35/2. Subsequent editions of 41 substituted 'Licht und Liebe'.

June 1849

43. [*Im Gegenwärtigen Vergangenes* (quartet).]
44. *Trost. Die Nacht* ('Du verstörst uns nicht'). *Zum Punsche.* [*Das Leben* (terzett).]

1850

45. *Frohsinn.* [*Trinklied* ('Freunde, sammelt euch') (solo and quartet).] [*Klage am Aly Bey* (terzett).] *Der Morgenkuss.*
46. *Epistel von Collin: musikalischer Schwank.*
47. *Prometheus. Wer kaufte Liebesgötter? Der Rattenfänger. Nachtgesang* (Goethe). *An den Mond* (1) (Goethe).
48. *Die Sterne* ('Du staunest, o Mensch'). *Erntelied. Klage an den Mond. Trinklied* ('Bacchus, feister Fürst'). *Mignon* ('So lasst mich scheinen') (III). *Der Goldschmiedsgesell. Tischlerlied.*

August 1851

49. *Auf der Riesenkoppe. Auf einen Kirchhof.*
50. *An die Apfelbäume. Der Leidende* (1). *Augenlied.*

During the course of the *Nachlass* series, one other song, 'Wiedersehn', was published as a supplement to the symposium *Lebensbilder aus Oesterreich*, in 1843. This, together with the songs of the *Nachlass*, brings the total to 127 published in these years. By 1851 the grand total of posthumously published Schubert songs had thus reached 194. It was during these years that the critic of the London *Musical World* wrote the often-quoted words about a 'deep shade of suspicion' attending the continued appearance of new songs from a composer 'whose ashes, one would think, repose in peace in Vienna'. It is ironical to consider that in 1851 a further 340 songs were still unpublished.

Before the close of the *Nachlass*, Diabelli had begun a new series called *Immortellen*, subtitled 'A Selection of the most popular songs of Franz Schubert for Contralto or Bass with Piano'. Each part contained a single song, some from opus numbers published during Schubert's lifetime, others from the *Nachlass*. The only song that, at first glance, might appear new, is No. 12 — 'Naturgenuss'; but it is spurious, being the fitting of the poem to the melody of the popular 'Trauerwalzer'. The *Immortellen* continued well into the 1860's.

The engraving of unpublished songs continued without a break, even though the *Nachlass* had come to an end. In 1852 Diabelli retired from active participation in the business, and his successor, C. A. Spina, seems to have held back the few engraved songs for a number of years. Three songs, 'Die Liebende schreibt' (already published), 'Die Sternennächte', and 'Das Bild' were engraved in 1852, 'Die Täuschung' (already published) in 1858, and 'Eine altschottische Ballade' in 1863; the five were then published together as op. 165 on 15 August 1863. Two collections of six songs followed in 1866 and 1868 as opp. 172 and 173, and this closed the long sequence of publication of the Schubert works by Diabelli and his successor.

The newly established firm of J. P. Gotthard began publication of Schubert songs in 1870 and continued for a few more years. Details are given below, but the most sizeable collection was of forty songs in 1872. Three of these had previously appeared, the rest were new. An extremely odd venture of a Viennese firm, Kratochwill, in 1876, was the publication in two sets of eighteen Schubert songs arranged for pianoforte solo or pianoforte duet by Gotthard, and provided with the words of the songs. The first set of twelve, for pianoforte solo, contained four unpublished songs, 'Der Entfernten', 'Blanka' (under the title 'Das Mädchen'), 'Täglich zu singen', and 'Abschied: nach einer Wallfahrtsarie'. The second set of six, for pianoforte duet, contained a further two unpublished songs, 'An mein Klavier' and 'Trauer der Liebe'. All these can hardly rank as first editions of the songs concerned; with the exception of 'Täglich zu singen' they were first published in a collection, edited by Max Friedlaender, to be considered later; the omitted song had to wait for publication till the appearance of the *Gesamtausgabe*.

Meanwhile, the archivist of the Prussian State Library, Franz Espagne, had edited six songs from the manuscripts in that library, and these were published in 1868 by Wilhelm Müller of Berlin. Espagne also edited the facsimile publication of 'Erlkönig' (c) in the same library. The well-known biography of Schubert by August Reissmann, published in Berlin in 1873, contained four unpublished songs.

The period closes with the editorial work of Max Friedlaender (known in his circle as the 'Schubert' Friedlaender, to distinguish him from other, equally eminent, men of the same name). His first work was the production of an album of twenty songs for which the claim was made 'hitherto unpublished'. This was largely true, although one song, 'Die Wehmut', had already appeared and two of the items were not songs, but arrangements of arias from the operetta *Claudine von Villa Bella*. The volume also contained the first clean editions of five of the six songs mentioned above, which had been published in pianoforte arrangements. Friedlaender's album, *20 Posthumous Songs*, was published in 1885 by Peters of Leipzig.

Two years later he edited for the same firm the seven volumes of the *Schubert Album*. He wrote a full and useful editor's Report on the manuscripts and editions used for volume i, which contained the three song-cycles and a selection of the most famous songs; a second report did the same for the remaining six volumes. Volume vii contained fifty songs. The first twenty are reprinted from the 1885 volume just discussed. In the preface to volume vii, Friedlaender claimed that twenty-two of the remaining thirty songs were first editions, but, in fact, four of them had already been published. The reason for the inclusion of the two songs 'Die Wehmut' (Salis) and 'Abschied von der Harfe', as first editions is that their publication had been overlooked by Nottebohm, and hence also by Friedlaender.

In the same year, 1887, the Viennese firm of Weinberger & Hofbauer published a collection of new songs: of the three Schubert items, two were first editions — 'Der Gott und die Bajadere' and 'Bundeslied'. Together with the Friedlaender volume of the same year, these are the last posthumously published songs before the *Gesamtausgabe*. The details of this period follow, and, as before, the titles of songs already published are enclosed in square brackets.

SECTION 3

SONGS PUBLISHED BETWEEN THE
Nachlass (1851) AND THE *Gesamtausgabe* (1894)

1855

Supplement to *Zellners Blätter für Musik, Theater und Kunst*.
Die Täuschung. Published by Spina.

1860

Die Wehmut (Salis). *Abschied von der Harfe*. Published by
Spina.

August 1863

op. 165. *Liederkranz*. *Sammlung von Liedern aus dem Nachlasse*. [*Die
Liebende schreibt*.] *Die Sternennächte*. *Das Bild*. [*Die Täuschung*.] *Eine altschottische Ballade* (b). Published by Spina.

1866

op. 172. *Sechs Lieder*. *Der Traum*. *Die Laube*. *An die Nachtigall*
('Geuss nicht so laut'). *Das Sehnen*. *An den Frühling* (II). *Die
Vögel*. Published by Spina.

1868

op. 173. *Sechs Lieder*. *Amalia*. *Das Geheimnis* (II). *Vergebliche Liebe*.
[*Der Blumen Schmerz*.] *Die Blumensprache*. *Das Abendrot*.
Published by Spina.

1868

Sechs bisher ungedrückte Lieder. Published by Wilhelm
Müller (Berlin), ed. Franz Espagne.
Sehnsucht (I) (Schiller). *Thekla* (I). *An den Mond* (II)
(Goethe). *Das Fräulein im Turme: Romanze* (II). *Abendlied
der Fürstin*. *An die Entfernte*. (This is the correct order of the
songs in the collection.)

1868

Erlkönig (c) in facsimile. *Geistes-Gruss* (b).[1] Published by
Wilhelm Müller (Berlin).

[1] This publication is recorded by Reissmann (see 1873, below). It has been
questioned. If the song was not published then, it was not published until the
first edition of *Nachgelassene Lieder*, edited by Max Friedlaender (1885): see
below, p. 286.

April 1870

> *Mignonlieder*. Published by J. P. Gotthard.
> 1. 'Heiss mich nicht reden' (I).
> [2. 'So lasst mich scheinen' (III).]

February 1871

> *5 Canti per una sola voce con accompagnomento di Pianoforte.*
> Published by J. P. Gotthard. *Non t'accostar. Guarda, che
> bianca luna. Da quel sembiante. Mio ben ricordate. Pensa, che
> questo istante.*

1872

> *Neuste Folge nachgelassener mehrstimmige Gesänge.* Published
> by J. P. Gotthard.
> No. 5. *Das Grab* (II).

1872

> *Neuste Folge nachgelassener Lieder und Gesänge.* A series of
> forty songs, published by J. P. Gotthard. [*Wiedersehn.*]
> *Gondelfahrer. Am Flusse* (II). *Nachthymne. Nach einem
> Gewitter. Grablied auf einem Soldaten. Der gute Hirt. Das
> gestörte Glück. An die Sonne* ('Königliche Morgensonne').
> *Abends unter der Linde* (II). *Liebeständelei. Ammenlied. Lied
> der Mignon* ('Nur wer die Sehnsucht kennt') (II). *Hoffnung*
> (Goethe) (a). *Rückweg. Der Knabe in der Wiege* (a). *Lebens-
> mut* (Rellstab). *Der Jüngling an der Tod* (b). *La pastorella.
> Nachtviolen. Klage* ('Trauer umfliesst') (b). *Der Knabe.
> Hoffnung* (Schiller). *Herbstlied. Aus 'Diego Manzanares'. Die
> verfehlte Stunde. Der Fluss. Das Geheimniss* (I). *Liebesrauch*
> (II). *Die Sterne* ('Was funkelt ihr?'). *Die Perle. Leiden der
> Trennung.* [*Der Morgenkuss (nach einem Ball*).] [*Clärchens
> Lied.*] *Sängers Morgenlied* (II). *Der Flüchtling. Hymnen I–IV*
> (Novalis).

1873

> *Franz Schubert: sein Leben und seine Werke,* August Reiss-
> mann. Published by J. Guttentag (Berlin). *Schwertlied. Scene
> im Dome aus Faust* (a). *Des Mädchens Klage* (III). *Abschied*
> (von der Erde). [*Die Entzückung an Laura* (II): facsimile of
> first page only.]

Autumn 1876

> Supplement to *Blätter für Hausmusik*. Published by E. W.
> Fritzsch (Leipzig). *Der Strom*, ed. Brahms.

1885

> *Nachgelassene (bisher ungedruckte) Lieder für eine Singstimme
> mit Pianofortebegleitung.* Published by Peters (Leipzig). A
> series of twenty songs, edited by Max Friedlaender.
> *Die Gebüsche. Trost* ('Nimmer lange weil'ich hier'). *Minnelied.*
> *[Geistes-Gruss* (b).]¹ [*Liebe schwärmt auf allen Wegen* and *Hin
> und wieder fliegen die Pfeile*: from *Claudine von Villa Bella.*]
> *Abschied nach einer Wallfahrtsarie. Idas Nachtgesang. An
> mein Klavier. Furcht der Geliebten* (b). *Trauer der Liebe. Bei
> dem Grabe meines Vaters. Abendlied* (Claudius). *Lieb Minna.
> An den Frühling* (I, a). *Schweizerlied. Pflicht und Liebe. Der
> Entfernten. Am See* (Mayrhofer).² *Blanka.*

1887

> *Bisher unbekannte und unveröffentlichte Compositionen.* Pub-
> lished by Weinberger & Hofbauer (Vienna), ed. H. von
> Bocklet.
> Book 2. [*Sehnsucht* (Goethe).] *Der Gott und die Bajadere.
> Bundeslied.*

Autumn 1887

> *Schubert Album: Sammlung der Lieder für eine Singsstimme
> mit Pianofortebegleitung.* Published by Peters (Leipzig), ed.
> Max Friedlaender, volume vii. 21. *Geheimniss: An Franz
> Schubert.* 28. *Heimweh* (Hell). 30. *Trinklied* ('Ihr Freunde').
> 31. *Die Einsiedelei* (II). 35. *Freude der Kinderjahre.* 36. *Natur-
> genuss.* 37. *Daphne am Bach.* 38. *Nachtgesang* (Kosegarten).
> 39. *Frühlingslied* (Hölty). 40. *Der Jüngling am Bach* (I, b).
> 41. *Das Mädchen aus der Fremde* (II). 42. *Punschlied.* 43. *Gott
> im Frühlinge.* 44. *Liebhaber in allen Gestalten.* 45. *Die Liebes-
> götter.* 46. *Blumenlied.* 47. *Der Schatzgräber.* 49. *An die
> Geliebte.*

¹ This song was replaced in later editions by 'Die Wehmut' (Salis). See
below, p. 287.
² The version of 'Am See' was corrupt; it contained the first twenty bars
only. A second stanza was provided, written by Max Kalbeck. The surprising
thing is that in his editorial remarks Friedlaender makes light of this interference, adding that, in any case, the full version will shortly be published by
Mandyczewski in Breitkopf & Härtel's *Gesamtausgabe*.

The activities of Mandyczewski, collecting, correlating, and editing the song-manuscripts of Schubert, in preparation for the complete edition of Breitkopf & Härtel, were by then widely known. This accounts for the fact that between 1887 and 1894 no new Schubert songs made their appearance. When the completed song-volumes of Schubert were published, in 1894 and 1895, with a supplementary issue in 1897, the number of songs published there for the first time was two hundred. There are, altogether, ten volumes of songs, chronologically arranged, comprising Serie xx of the *Gesamtausgabe*. The songs published for the first time are given below as they occur in the ten volumes. As in previous lists, Schubert's versions are indicated by roman figures, his variants by small letters.

Volume 1

Hagars Klage. Des Mädchens Klage (i). *Eine Leichenphantasie. Der Vatermörder. Der Jüngling am Bach* (i, a). *Totengräberlied. Die Schatten. Der Taucher* (a). Three *Don Gayseros* songs: 1. *Don Gayseros*, 2. *Nächtensklang*, 3. *An dem jungen Morgenhimmel. Trost an Elisa. Erinnerungen. Andenken. Geisternähe. Erinnerung. Lied aus der Ferne. Der Abend* (Matthisson). *Lied der Liebe. An Emma* (a). *Das Mädchen aus der Fremde* (i). *Schäfers Klagelied* (b).

Volume 2

Der Sänger (b). *Minona. Am Flusse* (i). *An Mignon* (a). *Nähe des Geliebten* (a). *Sängers Morgenlied* (i). *Amphiaraos. Trinklied vor der Schlacht. Sehnsucht der Liebe* (b). *Die Sterbende. Stimme der Liebe* (Matthisson) (i). *Des Mädchens Klage* (ii, a). *Die Mainacht. Seufzer. Der Liebende. Die Nonne* (b). *Adelwold und Emma. Von Ida. Abends unter der Linde* (i). *Die Mondnacht. Huldigung. Alles um Liebe.*

Volume 3

An den Frühling (i, b). *Geistes-Gruss* (a) and (d) and possibly (b): see footnote on p. 286. *Die Fröhlichkeit. Abendständchen: An Laura. Morgenlied* (Stolberg). *Der Weiberfreund. Lilla an die Morgenröte. Totenkranz für ein Kind. Abendlied* (Stolberg). *Lied* ('Es ist so angenehm'). *Furcht der Geliebten* (a). *Selma und Selmar* (a). *Vaterlandslied* (a) and (b). *Die Sommernacht* (a) and (b). *Dem*

Unendlichen (a) and (c). *Hoffnung* (Goethe) (b). *Liane. Labetrank der Liebe. Wiegenlied* ('Schlumm're sanft'). *Mein Gruss an den Mai. Skolie* (Deinhardstein). *Die Sternenwelt. Die Macht der Liebe. Lied der Mignon* ('Nur wer die Sehnsucht kennt') (I, a and I, b). *Hektors Abschied* (a). *Die Sterne* ('Wie wohl ist mir'). *An Rosa I. An Rosa II* (a) and (b). *Idens Schwanenlied. Schwangesang. Luisens Antwort. Der Zufrieden. Klage der Ceres. Harfenspieler* ('Wer sich der Einsamkeit ergibt') (I). *Erlkönig* (a) and (b). *Das Grab* (I).

Volume 4

Klage ('Trauer umfliesst') (a). *Fischerlied* (I). *Lied* ('Ich bin ver-gnügt') (I). *An die Natur. Lied* ('Mutter geht'). *Morgenlied* ('Die frohe neugelebte Flur'). *Abendlied* ('Sanft glänzt'). *Laura am Klavier* (a) and (b). *Die Entzückung an Laura* (I). *Pflügerlied. Gesang an die Harmonie. Auf den Tod einer Nachtigall* (II). *Die Knabenzeit. Winterlied. In's stille Land* (b). *Der Herbstabend. Entzückung. Geist der Liebe. Klage* ('Die Sonne steigt'). *Stimme der Liebe* (Matthisson) (II). *Julius an Theone. Die frühe Liebe. Der Leidende* (II). *Seligkeit. Schlachtlied. An den Schlaf. Frag-ment aus dem Aeschylus* (a). *An Chloen* (Jacobi). *Hochzeitlied. In der Mitternacht. An den Mond* (Hölty). *Liedesend* (a). *Lied des Orpheus* (a). *Alte Liebe rostet nicht. Harfenspieler*: 1. 'Wer sich der Einsamkeit ergibt' (II, a). 2. 'An die Türen' (a). 3. 'Wer nie sein Brot' (I) and (II). *Lied der Mignon* ('Nur wer die Sehnsucht kennt') (III). *Der Sänger am Felsen. Lied* ('Ferne von der grossen Stadt'). *Der Hirt. Der Wanderer* (a). *Phidile. Lied* ('Ich bin vergnügt') (II). *Skolie* (Matthisson).

Volume 5

Jagdlied. Die Liebe. Der Alpenjäger (a, E major). *Das Lied vom Reifen. Täglich zu singen. Auf dem See* (a). *Der Jüngling und der Tod* (a). *An die Musik* (a). *Die Forelle* (a), (b), and (c). *Uraniens Flucht. Fischerlied* (II). *Das Grab* (III). *Thekla* (II, a). *Sonett I. Sonett II. Sonett III.*

Volume 6

Sehnsucht (Schiller) (a). *Der Jüngling am Bache* (II, a). *Marie. Die Götter Griechenlands* (a). *Frühlingsglaube* (c). *Der zürnenden Diana* (a). *Der Unglückliche* (a).

Volume 7

Die Rose (b). *Du liebst mich nicht* (a). *Schatzgräbers Begehr* (b). *Der Musensohn* (a). *Willkommen und Abschied* (a).

Volume 8

Der blinde Knabe (a). *Das Heimweh* (Pyrker) (a). *Fischerweise* (a).

Volume 9

Three variants from *Winterreise*: 1. *Rast* (a). 2. *Einsamkeit* (a). 3. *Der Leiermann* (a). *Heimliches Lieben* (a). *Eine altschottische Ballade* (a).

Volume 10

Misero pargoletto. Son fra l'onde. Didones Arie. Auf dem Sieg. Die Befreier Europas. Lied ('Brüder, schrecklich brennt die Thräne'). *Namenstaglied. Herbst.* Fragments: *Der Geistertanz* (I) and (II). *Die drei Sänger. Lorma* (II). *Gesang der Geister über den Wassern. Mahomets Gesang* (I) and (II). *Die Entzückung an Laura* (II). *Lied eines Kindes. Über allen Zauber Liebe. Johanna Sebus.*

Revisionsbericht to the ten volumes:

Romanze ('In der Väter Hallen ruhte'). *Die Nonne* (a). *Ossians Lied nach dem Falle Nathos'* (a). *Mignon* ('So lasst mich scheinen') (I and II). *Der Knabe in der Wiege* (b). *Der Alpenjäger* (Schiller) (a).

Supplementary volume (Serie xx)

Frühlingslied (Aaron Pollak).

The fine work achieved by Mandyczewski, under the generous provision of Breitkopf & Härtel, is patently clear, when it is realized that only twenty-six song-manuscripts, many of them fragments, have seen the light since 1897. Of these twenty-six songs, twelve have been published as follows:

1. *Das Fräulein im Turme. Romanze.* (I). *Die Musik* (Berlin, May 1902).
2. *Fröhliches Scheiden. Schubert*, Richard Heuberger (Berlin, 1902). (Facsimile.)
3. *Evangelium Johannes. Ibid.*
4. *Jägers Abendlied* (I). *Die Musik* (Berlin, 15 January 1907), ed. Mandyczewski.

5. *Lied der Abwesenheit. Moderne Welt* (Vienna, December 1925), ed. O. E. Deutsch.

6. *Liebesrauch* (1). *Musik aus aller Welt* (Vienna, January 1928), ed. O. E. Deutsch.

7. *Psalm XIII. Festblätter für das 10. Deutsche Sängerbundesfest* (Vienna, 1928), ed. O. E. Deutsch. (Facsimile.)

8. *Lied* (without title or text). *Radio Wien* (21 September 1934), ed. O. E. Deutsch.

9. *Meeresstille* (1). *Schweizerische Musikzeitung* (November 1952), ed. O. E. Deutsch.

10. *Frühlingsglaube* (b). E. Schreiber (Stuttgart, May 1958), ed. Hans Halm. (Facsimile.)

11. *Frühlingsglaube* (a). 'Zu Schuberts *Frühlingsglaube*', Andreas Holschneider, *Festschrift Otto Erich Deutsch* (1963). (Facsimile.)

12. *Greisengesang* (a). 'Schubertiade', Walter Gerstenberg. *Ibid.*

It is fitting that the last two of these songs should be in a *Festschrift* devoted to O. E. Deutsch, the man to whom so much is owed in the way of posthumous publication, as a glance at the above list indicates. The remaining fourteen songs will no doubt appear in print together, if the undertaking to publish a kind of second supplement to the *Gesamtausgabe* materializes; when this event occurs we shall have, at last, the entire mass of Schubert's extant compositions in print.

The word 'extant' recalls the astonishing fact, stated in the table given at the beginning of this essay, that out of the very large number of songs Schubert composed, a mere five (as far as we know) have been lost. And in view of the remarkable way in which, year by year, lost manuscripts of his see the light, it would not be at all surprising if the future restores to us some, or even all, of these lost five.

THE STORY OF THE 'TRAUERWALZER'

THE adventures of Schubert's most popular waltz among the publishing houses of Europe from 1820 until nearly the end of the century are incredibly involved. Various sections of its confused progress are touched upon in the biographies of the composer, but even if these sections are assembled into a whole they tell only half the story and do little to straighten out the tangle. In fact, by wrong conclusions and half-truths, they add to the confusion.

The reason why this short waltz — a matter of sixteen bars — has such a history of muddle and misattribution lies, ironically enough, in its very charm and attractiveness. Schubert's elevation of the short dance is comparable to his elevation of the Lied, save that the form is altogether more insignificant to begin with, and, in addition, quite incapable of the humanity and varied emotional appeal of the Lied. To turn the pages of the multitudinous collections of dances published in the early nineteenth century is to be appalled at the mediocrity and stultifying dullness of the music to which the Viennese so ardently danced. Even the most renowned collections are unbelievably commonplace. When one turns to Schubert's first Ländler and Walzer, with the abundance of harmonic and modulatory colour, the changing pattern of rhythm above the regular 3/4 metre, and, above all, the profusion of endearing melody, one can understand the impact of his dances on his friends and the quickly growing popularity of his dance-music. His 'Trauerwalzer' became immediately popular, and was soon widely known in Vienna under that odd nickname years before it was published in his op. 9, the thirty-six 'Original' Dances.

It is not known exactly when Schubert composed the waltz. There are four manuscript sources. The earliest consists merely of the first few bars of the treble part, jotted down with eight other similar waltz *incipits* on the last page of the song 'La pastorella al prato', D. 528; this song is dated January 1817.[1] The nine *incipits*, all in A major, were evidently intended by Schubert as a memorandum for a collection of dances, which he hoped would be published. The waltzes were already composed, and probably originated in 1816. This seems the most likely date for the 'Trauerwalzer'. In March 1818 he twice copied the dance for friends — an indication of its popularity. One copy was made for Anselm Hüttenbrenner (dated 14 March 1818), the other was for Ignaz Assmayer (dated, simply, March 1818); in both cases the dance is headed 'Deutscher' and each of the copies gives the dance in A flat major. The humorous inscriptions he added to these copies can be read in Deutsch's *Documentary Biography*, pp. 88–89. The two versions of the waltz are practically, but not completely, identical. The fourth manuscript contains a collection of six dances, five later published in op. 9 and one in the posthumous collection known as *Zwanzig Ländler* ('Twenty Ländler').[1] The second of the six dances is the 'Trauerwalzer', again in A flat major. A slight modification in the start of one of these dances shows that the fourth manuscript is, chronologically, the last of the four. But in all four manuscripts the anacrusis of the 'Trauerwalzer' is the same; it is quoted here since the fact will be found of some interest later:

Example 91

The widespread popularity of this dance in Vienna is something almost unbelievable; it was passed on from individual to individual, from group to group, sometimes by transcriptions, sometimes, evidently, purely by ear, until the whole city knew it,

[1] Details of the manuscripts can be found on pp. 228–31.

11. Copy of the 'Trauerwalzer', written by Schubert for
Anselm Hüttenbrenner (MS. 25)

12. Title-page of Johann Pensel's 'Trauerwalzer' variations

and began to call it the 'Trauerwalzer' — literally, the 'mourning' or 'mournful' waltz. Schubert himself, first learning of the nickname, said, 'What ass would compose a "mournful" waltz!' Only Schubert's immediate circle knew of his authorship of the dance; to the rest of Vienna its anonymity gave it the status of folk-music. Eventually the melody attracted the attention of a well-known Viennese dance composer, Johann Pensel, who wrote variations on it and published them as his op. 11. The existence of these variations was unknown until recently, and the date of publication is provided by an advertisement in the *Wiener Zeitung* of 21 December 1820:

Variationen für das Pianoforte, über den beliebten Trauerwalzer. Verfasst von Joh. Pensel, Op. 11.   Cappi & Diabelli.[1]

It seems obvious that Pensel had no idea who composed the waltz, or he would have acknowledged Schubert's authorship. His variations are delightfully written and thoroughly in keeping with the charm and wistfulness of the waltz-melody.

Ten months later a second set of variations on the waltz was published. These are the very famous variations by Carl Czerny. They were entitled

Variationen über einen beliebten Wiener-Walzer für das Pianoforte von Carl Czerny. Op. 12.

Czerny's work was published by Steiner & Co. of Vienna and advertised in the *Wiener Zeitung* of 15 October 1821. Again the waltz is anonymous, and it seems clear that neither Czerny nor his publishers knew that Schubert was the composer. Pensel's and Czerny's versions of the theme are of interest and will be considered in due course.

Just over a month later, on 29 November 1821, Cappi & Diabelli published Schubert's first set of dances, the thirty-six in op. 9. Above the second dance appeared the nickname 'Trauerwalzer'. A misunderstanding of the remark by Spaun, that Schubert's dances were given nicknames by the publishers, never

[1] Mr. Alan Tyson drew my attention to these variations, and Dr. Ignaz Weinmann of Vienna found the date of the advertisement. To both I owe my warmest thanks.

u

by Schubert himself, has led commentators, including Deutsch, to draw the conclusion that Cappi & Diabelli gave the dance its nickname when op. 9 was published. If one felt doubts about the plausibility of this assertion — why should one dance from thirty-six be singled out for the dubious honour of such a title?—there was no evidence to bring against it. Even Czerny's variations have always been assumed to follow the publication of op. 9, not to precede it. But the newly discovered variations of Pensel and the establishing of the dates of publication of both Pensel's variations and Czerny's prove beyond any doubt that the dance was extremely popular — and widely known under its nickname — some time before op. 9 was published. Finally, the waltz-theme in both Pensel and Czerny starts with the single-note anacrusis, or with a variant not by Schubert, showing that their knowledge of the melody derived from Schubert's first, unpublished conception; just prior to the publication of op. 9, the ornamentation of the up-beat, a small but inspired touch, was made by Schubert and repeated in the opening of the second phrase:

Example 92

Czerny's set of variations is decidedly inferior to Pensel's, but his name was better known, and in a very short time his work was internationally famous. It was imported to England by Wessel in the early part of 1823, and in October of that year was reviewed by the periodical *Harmonicon*. The review contains the earliest reference in English journalism to the work of Schubert, but naturally, since Czerny's waltz was anonymous, not to his name. The writer in the *Harmonicon*, commenting on various works by Czerny, added the words: 'Among these is the popular *Vienna Waltz*, with its variations. The Waltz is so graceful and expressive that we are induced to insert it in this place.' Entitled 'Vienna Waltz', the music is then quoted in full. In Paris, Czerny's variations were published by Maurice Schlesinger, *c.* 1825, as 'Variations sur une Valse Viennoise favorite', and various German firms also produced the work in this period, but in no case, of course, does Schubert's name appear as the author of the waltz itself.

In the spring of 1827 Robert Cocks & Co. published the work in London, entitling it 'Brilliant Variations on an Austrian Waltz for the Piano-Forte by C. Czerney' [*sic*]. The short-lived periodical *Quarterly Musical Magazine* reviewed the work in March and wrote: 'Mr. Czerney's variations are on a most beautiful subject of which they are well worthy. They contain a good deal of execution without extravagance, and are much in the style of Beethoven, without his originality, but at the same time free from his eccentricity.'

Cappi & Diabelli produced various arrangements of the 'Trauerwalzer'; in February 1822 it was published, together with other waltzes from op. 9, in an arrangement for flute or violin, accompanied by guitar, and in May 1826, arranged for guitar alone, the 'Trauerwalzer' formed volume v of Diabelli's serial publication called *Apollo an der Damen-Toiletten*. But these modest publications achieved merely a local renown, not to be compared with the popularity and widespread fame of Czerny's variations; the name of the composer of the waltz never 'caught up', so to say, with the progress of these variations. In consequence, it is not surprising to find that on occasion the waltz is attributed to Czerny himself, even extracted from his introduction and four variations and published separately under his name. What *is* surprising, however, is to find it very quickly associated with the name of another composer; by 1825, at the latest, the attribution of the waltz to Beethoven was well established, and for the next seventy years or so this false ascription persisted in spite of continual efforts to correct it. Exactly why this error arose is obscure, but its place of origin is certain. Early in 1826 the publishers Schott's Sons of Mainz were guilty of a piece of musical chicanery that is hard to reconcile with their standing as a reputable firm. They lengthened the 'Trauerwalzer' by incorporating with it a second short waltz, in the nature of a trio section, and published the whole as 'Le Désir: Walse favorit' by

Beethoven. An advertisement appeared in their house organ, *Cäcilia*, of April–June 1826. The attaching of Beethoven's name to the waltz thus took place during his lifetime, and he is said (by Anselm Hüttenbrenner) to have resented this misuse of his name and to have protested about it. Schubert's feelings about the ascription of his waltz to Beethoven are unrecorded.

Simultaneously with the publication of the 'Walse favorit' Schott's Sons also published an edition of it with words attached. The ill-fitting text was by Heinrich Schütz, a singer in the Court Opera at Karlsruhe, and this bastard Schubert song appeared as 'An die Geliebte'. The first verse runs:

> O süsse Himmelslust, bebt durch die trunkene Brust,
> Bin ich bey dir, lächelst du mir;
> Aber wer gleicht dem Schmerz, der mir durchzuckt das Herz?
> Bist du o schöner Stern, bist du mir fern.

The accompaniment was arranged for piano or guitar, and the composer, of course, given as Beethoven. The publication provoked an immediate and angry protest from Anton Schindler, which was actually published in Schott's periodical, *Cäcilia*, on 29 September 1827. He wrote:

> . . . but what is it? Two waltzes with verses fitted; the first is by J. [*sic*] Schubert and the second by Hummel, copied note for note.

For some reason, in quoting this passage, O. E. Deutsch corrects Schindler's 'Hummel' to 'Himmel' without giving any reason. It is true that Himmel is responsible for a well-known 'Favorit Walzer', but the name was a commonplace in those days; it certainly does not provide a sound enough reason, if there be no other, for altering Schindler. The astonishing thing is that unless another misattribution of authorship has been made, this added waltz is by neither Hummel nor Himmel: it is by Schubert himself! It was published eventually, in its original form, in the *Gesamtausgabe*, vol. xii, no. 15 (*b*), in 1888.[1] Schott's vocal version

---

[1] See D. 972 (2). Deutsch's information that the manuscript of the waltz is in the Vienna City Library is unfortunately not true; the manuscript is lost. There is thus no means of checking any possibility that Schubert had merely copied out this waltz from another composer's original.

of the 'Trauerwalzer' is the first of a feeble brood of such travesties spawned at intervals throughout the nineteenth century and in the early part of the twentieth century in all languages.

Schindler's protest was completely unavailing; Schott's persisted in their course of publishing this welcome money-spinner. A year later, in the autumn of 1828, they published a miscellany of pieces entitled *Souvenir à Louis van Beethoven: Six valses et une Marche funèbre.* None of the waltzes is, in fact, by Beethoven, and apart from the first one, which is Schubert's 'Trauerwalzer', the composers are unknown. The first three waltzes were given titles: 'Sehnsucht', 'Schmerzen', and 'Hoffnung' and that is why the name 'Sehnsuchtswalzer' rapidly displaced the original 'Trauerwalzer'. The German 'Sehnsucht' is roughly equivalent to the other title 'Le Désir'. The 'Sehnsuchtswalzer' went through numerous editions, both as a separate issue and included with the six other spurious Beethoven pieces. The name 'Le Désir' soon began to appear in Vienna, being given to the 'Trauerwalzer' only, not to the two-waltz travesty assembled by Schott's. Generally speaking, it will be found that in these years the title 'Le Désir' was given to the 'Trauerwalzer' alone, and the title 'Sehnsuchtswalzer' to the conjoined waltzes, but in every case Beethoven is given as the author.

Once again Schott's action came under fire, and once again the remonstrance was unheeded. When the Leipzig journal *Allgemeine musikalische Zeitung* reviewed the *Souvenir à Beethoven* in July 1829, the writer asked, with great surprise, why the 'Sehnsuchtswalzer' of Beethoven's was identical with the 'Trauerwalzer' of Schubert's? — although, he added, the latter dance has no trio. The title 'Sehnsucht' quickly established itself in Germany, ousting the other two, and when Schumann wrote about Schubert's op. 9, in the *Neue Zeitschrift für Musik* of February 1836, he referred to no. 2 as Schubert's 'Sehnsuchtswalzer'. He did not, however, succeed in establishing Schubert as the composer, even by such an authoritative statement. A later reviewer, for instance, praising the waltz in extravagant terms, finished his rhapsody with the words '. . . it is by that genius Beethoven, by the eternal, undying Beethoven'.

The story now returns to Vienna. The firm of Steiner & Co. passed in 1826 into the ownership of Tobias Haslinger. Three years later a third edition of Czerny's op. 12 was published. The title-page was now altered slightly. The variations were said to be on the 'beliebten Wiener Trauer-Walzer' and in brackets, obviously an engraved afterthought to the finished title, were the words 'von Fr. Schubert'. But by now, as we know, confusion over the authorship of the waltz had already begun, and numerous people were ready to step forward and dispute Schubert's claim. The third edition of Czerny's op. 12 was reviewed in the Vienna *Musikalischer Anzeiger* of 1829. The reviewer was anonymous, signing himself '18', and during the course of his review he asked: 'But is this so-called "Trauerwalzer" actually by Franz Schubert?' (Schubert, it will be recalled, had been dead only a few months when this review was printed.) He then went on to answer his own question by an implied negative; he said that it was as like an aria from the operetta *Liebe macht kurzen Prozess* as one drop of water is like another. The operetta, popular in Vienna some thirty years previously, was based on the farce *Der Jurist und der Bauer*, and the music consisted of an assembly of pieces drawn from the work of several composers. Schubert's waltz was supposed by '18' to have been plagiarized from Rosine's aria, a song by the almost forgotten composer Johann Henneberg. This accusation of plagiarism was well known to subsequent writers on Schubert; Kreissle, in his biography of Schubert (1865) deals fully with it.[1] The Viennese scholar, Dr. Alexander Weinmann, writing in the *Österreichische Musikzeitschrift* for January 1957, quoted Henneberg's aria, and shows on what absurd grounds the accusation was made. No defence of Schubert appeared in subsequent issues of the *Anzeiger*. In fact, there and elsewhere he was further attacked, and the sources of the 'Trauerwalzer' were found by his detractors to lie in works by half a dozen other composers. With one exception they are easily refuted, but that exception cannot be so lightly brushed aside: it was made by Bernard Kothe, who drew attention to a resemblance between the 'Trauerwalzer' and — ironically enough — a subsidiary theme in the first movement of Beet-

[1] p. 143. English ed., vol. i, p. 146.

hoven's Sonata in E flat major, op. 7; the theme appears in bars
67–71, and must have been familiar to Schubert in a way that the
rest of the examples, especially Henneberg's aria, are unlikely to
have been.

Example 93   Beethoven, Op. 7

By the time Schubert died the confusion and error associated
with his waltz, though widespread and complex enough, was
anything but complete. The composition was disseminated under
three distinct names and attributed to three different composers,
and titles and composers appear together in all possible permuta-
tions; numerous sets of variations on the waltz were added to
Pensel's and Czerny's, the melody being simply called 'den
beliebten Wiener-Walzer'. The variations are for all conceivable
instrumental combinations (including a military band). It was
known to many people as a song, and soon the many other vocal
versions begin to proliferate. In Vienna the melody was used by
Adolf Müller in his Singspiel *Fortunats Abentheuer*, with words
beginning 'Ich seh' nach dem Theueren mit thränenden Blick....'
Diabelli published a set of variations on this *vocal arrangement* in
November 1829, as well as publishing the arrangement itself in his
series *Philomele* (no. 267) the following month. The title 'Le
Désir' was even bestowed 'back', so to say, on Czerny's op. 12,

and Wessel, who obtained the copyright of the Steiner-Haslinger publication, brought out the work in London during 1829 as 'Le Désir de Beethoven: valse célèbre Viennoise, avec variations pour le pianoforte ... par Charles Czerny'. He chose to interpret the words in brackets 'von Fr. Schubert' as a dedication, and his title includes the phrase 'dediées à M. Franz Schubert'. A third English journal, the *Monthly Musical and Literary Magazine,* in its issue of February 1830 had this to say: 'The introduction to the beautiful air is by no means equal to the theme or the variations which follow, of which No. 4 is by far the most brilliant.'

In 1825 Wessel had begun to publish a periodical album of his own, inspired perhaps by the similar venture of Diabelli's mentioned above; he called it *La Salle d'Apollo: a collection of new and elegant German waltzes for the pianoforte.* The thirtieth issue, of February 1830, was devoted to Schubert's 'Trauerwalzer' under the title 'Beethoven's "Le Désir" '; it contains the waltz alone — without the variations. The music is of interest. It begins with the following anacrusis, which is found nowhere in Schubert's music and was evidently a fanciful variant of the composer's single-note anacrusis.

Example 94

Moreover, Czerny's theme is harmonized in chords that are like Schubert's, but differently disposed. Evidently Czerny was reproducing the theme and its harmonies from a recollection of it, as he had heard it played in the years 1818–20, before its publication. In spite of Wessel's direct, though false, attribution to Beethoven, the English public continued to ascribe the work now to Czerny, now to Beethoven. The first volume of William Gardiner's memoirs, *Music and Friends*, was published in 1838, and among the many pieces of music published in its pages he included the waltz with Czerny's name given as its composer.

WALTZ.

13. 'Trauerwalzer', attributed to Czerny

The music is transposed into G major, but is otherwise identical with Czerny's theme. Later in his book, p. 358, Gardiner quotes the longer, double-waltz version, this time giving Beethoven as the composer! In this version the anacrusis appears as in Schubert's final form.

14. 'Trauerwalzer', attributed to Beethoven

During the next fifty years, from publishing houses all over Europe and America, the 'Trauerwalzer' continued to appear in one or another of its many forms: alone, or in conjunction with the subsidiary waltz, or together with the other two waltzes mentioned earlier in the *Souvenir à Beethoven*; it appeared thus under any of the three established titles, but the ascription to Czerny gradually disappeared — except in one case. A publication by Robert Cocks & Co. of 1838 is entitled:

'Trauerwalzer', with variations, by Charles Czerny, Op. 12, very humbly dedicated to Her Most Gracious Majesty, Queen Victoria, by the Publishers . . .

and it is amusing to read on p. 3 of this piece a footnote to the effect that '. . . this waltz has been erroneously ascribed to Beethoven and entitled *Le Désir*'. Cocks & Co. evidently considered that it was their duty to restore the honour of composition to Czerny. But firms such as Bote & Bock of Berlin, and André of Offenbach am Main, making a start in 1840, continued to publish editions of the *Souvenir à Beethoven* waltzes up to as late as 1879; it was undoubtedly this continual republication of Schubert's waltz under Beethoven's name that led Grove to insert the entry under 'Trauerwalzer' in the first edition of his *Dictionary*, pointing out the mistake — an entry that has persisted through all five editions.

If we glance further into the periodical issues of Wessel's album *La Salle d'Apollo*, we shall find that a year after his publication of 'Le Désir' there was a Number devoted to a waltz called 'Le Nouveau Désir'. This is attributed to Schubert and Reissiger and was clearly designed to attract the public who loved (and bought) his earlier publication. The 'New Desire' turns out to be a hotch-potch of two more of Schubert's waltzes from op. 9 — nos. 13 and 14. One wonders if Wessel had his tongue in his cheek, and whether this amalgamation of two more of Schubert's waltzes under such a name shows that he was aware all the time of Schubert's true authorship of the 'Désir' waltz. But it may be that he had come across a peculiar new publication in Vienna of that period: this was a spurious 'op. 16' by Schubert, consisting of a combination of the 'Trauerwalzer' with the very dances that Wessel had used in his 'Nouveau Désir', provided, once more, with words. The verses were from Matthisson's poem 'Naturgenuss' and the pastiche was arranged for solo voice and pianoforte. Schubert's actual op. 16 is a setting of this poem for male-voice quartet.

Two years later another vocal version, called 'Die Sprache der Blumen', the words written by C. Schulz, was published in Berlin. It used the 'Sehnsuchtswalzer' combination, and again assigned the composition to Beethoven. When this song was reviewed in the *Allgemeine musikalische Zeitung* of 7 December 1831, the critic denied Beethoven's authorship and pointed out: 'It is by the late Schubert ladies, (your pet!), but is well worth buying and singing.' But the mild protest was unavailing to stop the flood of publication.

In nearly all the vocal arrangements the verses are either addressed by a lover to an absent mistress or by a lover who is unhappy or uncertain in his love. This is probably due to the underlying *tristesse* in the mood of Schubert's waltz, or possibly to imitation by one versifier of another. In the 1830's a popular vocal version was published by J. M. Dunst of Bonn, whose first lines run:

> Mädchen, du liebest mich; ich athme nur für dich,
> Madchen, mein einzig' Glück: kehre zurück!

But not in Germany and Austria only do we find these perversions of the waltz. The vogue for Schubert's songs in France produced several vocal versions of the 'Trauerwalzer' there too. The famous singer Adolphe Nourrit, who did much to popularize Schubert's songs in France, was not above including such a version in his recitals, and in 1840 the French publisher Simon Richault produced one that Nourrit had sung. It is called 'Amour et mystère' with words by M. Bélander:

> Que mon amour solitaire, ne soit qu'un mystère,
> Toujours dois me taire, moi seul dois souffrir . . .

It is a version of the 'Sehnsuchtswalzer' with the spurious trio, but at least it gives the correct composer. Finally, in recent times, the melody of the 'Trauerwalzer' was made the so-called theme-song of the popular *Das Drei-Mäderlhaus*, an operetta by Heinrich Berté based on fictitious events in Schubert's life and decked out with melodies butchered from the whole body of his work. In England and America a version of the operetta, under the title *Lilac Time*, had an enormously popular run. The popularity of this pastiche has done Schubert far more harm than good, and, in particular, it has, so to say, soiled the purity and delicacy of the most charming of all his waltzes. Instead of taking its place in the repertory of Schubert's pianoforte music, appearing as a contrasting and pleasurable item in a serious recital of his music, it is avoided because of its associations; and in thus losing the 'Trauerwalzer' we seem to have lost with it all Schubert's op. 9 dances. It is not suggested for one moment that the whole of op. 9 — containing thirty-six dances — is a desirable item in a pianoforte recital, but at least a selection from the opus would be so, and it is a pity that in passing over the 'Trauerwalzer' concert pianists also pass over its charming companions as well.

INDEX

(i) GENERAL

(ii) WORKS

(The sonatas, dances, and songs actually catalogued in the essays of Part
III are not indexed here.)

PRINTED IN GREAT BRITAIN
BY ROBERT MACLEHOSE AND CO. LTD
THE UNIVERSITY PRESS, GLASGOW